GESTAPO

The truth behind an evil legend

GESTAPO

Rupert Butler

ARROW BOOKS

Arrow Books Limited
62–65 Chandos Place, London WC2N 4NW

An imprint of Century Hutchinson Limited

London Melbourne Sydney Auckland
Johannesburg and agencies throughout
the world

First published in Great Britain
by Hamlyn Paperbacks 1981

Reprinted 1984 and 1985
Arrow edition 1986

Printed and bound in Great Britain by
Cox & Wyman Ltd, Reading

ISBN 0 09 938710 7

SELECTED BIBLIOGRAPHY

Bradley, John, *Lidice: Sacrificial Village*. (Ballantine 1972)

Brissaud, Andre, *The Nazi Secret Service*. (Bodley Head 1971)

Crankshaw, Edward, *Gestapo: Instrument of Tyranny*. (Putnam 1956)

Dank, Milton, *The French against the French*. (Cassell 1978)

Deacon, Richard, with West, Nigel, *Spy!* (BBC 1980)

Deighton, Len, *Blitzkrieg*. (Jonathan Cape 1979)

Delarue, Jacques, *History of the Gestapo*. (Macdonald 1964)

De Jong, L., and Stoppelman, Joseph W.F., *The Lion Rampant: The Story of Holland's Resistance to the Nazis*. (Querido 1943)

De Vomecourt, Philippe, *Who Lived to See the Day: France in Arms 1940-1945*. (Hutchinson 1961)

Dodd, Martha, *My Years in Germany*. (Gollancz 1938)*

Ehrich, Blake, *The French Resistance*. (Chapman & Hall 1966)

Gallo, Max, *The Night of the Long Knives*. (Souvenir Press 1972)

Gilbert, G.M., *Nuremberg Diary*. (Farrar, Straus 1947)

Gisevius, Hans Bernd, *To the Bitter End*. (Jonathan Cape 1948)*

Hoffman, Peter, *Hitler's Personal Security*. (Macmillan 1979)

Hoehne, Heinz, *The Order of the Death's Head*. (Secker & Warburg 1966)

Hoehne, Heinz, *Codeword: Direktor*. (Secker & Warburg 1970)

Hoehne, Heinz, *Canaris*. (Secker & Warburg 1979)

Howarth, Patrick (ed), *Special Operations*. (Routledge & Kegan Paul 1955)

Hutack, J.B., *With Blood and with Iron*. (Robert Hale 1957)

Kahn, David, *Hitler's Spies*. (Arrow Books 1978)

Karski, Jan, *Story of a Secret State*. (Houghton Mifflin 1944)

Koch, H.V., *The Hitler Youth*. (Macdonald & Janes 1975)

Koehler, Hansjurgen, *Inside the Gestapo*. (Pallas 1940)*

Korbonski, Stefan, *Fighting Warsaw*. (George Allen & Unwin 1956)*

Kranz, Joachim, *Stauffenberg: The Man Who Nearly Killed Hitler*. (Andre Deutsch 1977)

Kuby, Erich, *The Russians and Berlin 1945*. (Heinemann 1968)

Lampe, David, *The Savage Canary: The Story of Resistance in Denmark*. (Cassell 1957)

Lucas, James, and Cooper, Matthew, *Hitler's Elite: Leibstandarte SS*. (Macdonald & Janes 1975)

Manvell, Roger, and Fraenkel, Heinrich, *The July Plot*. (The Bodley Head 1964)

Manvell, Roger, *SS and Gestapo*. (Ballantine Books 1969)

Marshall, Bruce, *The White Rabbit*. (Evans 1952)*

Molloy Mason, Herbert, *To Kill Hitler*. (Michael Joseph 1979)

Mosley, Leonard, *The Reich Marshal*. (Weidenfeld & Nicolson 1974)

Payne Best, Captain S., *The Venlo Incident*. (Hutchinson 1950)

Peis, Gunther, *The Man Who Started the War*. (Odhams Press 1960)

Persico, Joseph, *Piercing the Reich*. (Michael Joseph 1979)

Petrow, Richard, *The Bitter Years: The Invasion and Occupation of Denmark and Norway*. (Hodder & Stoughton 1974)

Prittie, Terence, *Germans against Hitler*. (Hutchinson 1964)

Reilly, Robin, *The Sixth Floor*. (Leslie Frewin 1969)

Reitlinger, Gerald, *SS: Alibi of a Nation*. (Heinemann 1956)

Scholl, Inge, *Six against Tyranny*. (John Murray 1958)

Schellenberg, Walter, *The Schellenberg Memoirs*. (Andre Deutsch 1956)*

Shirer, William, *The Rise and Fall of the Third Reich*. (Secker & Warburg 1960)

Stern, J.P., *Hitler, the Fuehrer and the People*. (Fontana 1975)

Trepper, Leopold, *The Great Game*. (Sphere Books 1977)*
Van Duren, Theo, *Orange Above*. (Staples Press 1956)
Von Papen, *Memoirs*. (Andre Deutsch 1952)
Von Schlabrendorff, Fabian, *The Secret War against Hitler*. (Hodder & Stoughton 1966)*
Wheaton, Eliot B., *Prelude to Calamity*. (Gollancz 1968)
Wheeler-Bennett, John, *The Nemesis of Power*. (Macmillan 1961)
Wiener, Jan, *The Assassination of Heydrich*. (Grossman 1969)
Wighton, Charles, *Heydrich*. (Odhams Press 1962)*
Wykes, Alan, *Himmler*. (Pan/Ballantine 1972)

*The author would like to thank the publishers for permission to use quoted material.

ACKNOWLEDGEMENTS

In preparing this book I owe a particular debt to Mr George Clout and the staff of the Imperial War Museum, London, for their patience in supplying material and answering countless questions. I am in equal debt to the Institute of Contemporary History and Wiener Library, London, the Polish Institute of Catholic Action, the Hans Tasiemka Archive, the London Library and the Wandsworth Library. Special thanks are due to Mr Terry Charman and Mrs Vicky Clayton for research and editorial assistance. Invaluable additional advice has also been given by Mr Will Fowler. Finally, I would like to thank the *Guardian* for permission to quote the extracts on pages 58 and 59.

'In the SS one found the better type of people.'
SS Gruppenfuehrer Walter Schellenberg

1

It was the most beguiling summer anyone could remember in Berlin. Temperatures soared. Factory workers and their families sweltered by the lakes, glad to escape for a few hours from the cloying sweat of the city.

Couples strode beneath the leaf-shedding limes and chestnuts on the Unter den Linden, while the less energetic slaked their thirst in the numerous pavement cafés.

Nazi flags rippled lazily about public buildings, but inside there were no signs of weekend torpor. Blond lanky SS Brigadefuehrer Reinhard Heydrich would normally have spent a quiet few days playing chamber music with close friends. But now in the fetid atmosphere of Prinz Albrecht-strasse 8 it was just another working day.

Heydrich grabbed the urgently jangling phone, the reddening knuckles of his lily-white violinist's hands the only sign of stress.

He did not need to say anything – just listen to the vital whispered codeword: 'Colibri.' Now all the elaborate security machine of the Third Reich needed was the final push of a button.

In the streets no one paid much attention to the large mansion at the corner of the Tiergartenstrasse and the Standartenstrasse, headquarters of the Berlin-Brandenburg Sturm Abteilung (SA or Storm Troopers).

The SA consisted of the Nazi bully-boys, the strong-armed men at the Hitler rallies, the thuggish street fighters. There were four-and-a-half million of them in Germany, 600,000 in Berlin alone.

Now, alleged Hitler, many had turned against him. The hour of retribution had come.

Members of the SA in their brown uniforms emerged

with their hands raised in the air and were pushed and shoved into trucks by other troops touting carbines and sub-machine guns. It was all over very quickly; unlike those endless weekend exercises which the stiff-necked, rigidly traditionalist Prussian officers were so fond of inflicting on their men.

But there was one difference. The men who hustled along the Storm Troopers had not been dressed as conventional soldiers.

They were secret police. And one of their senior officers was that same snake-hipped violinist who had taken the succession of calls at Prinz Albrechtstrasse 8, headquarters of the Geheime Staatspolizei, otherwise the Gestapo.

It was going to be a tough time this weekend for Hitler's enemies.

The tentacles of the Gestapo had already stretched far beyond Berlin.

An unsuspecting housekeeper at nine in the morning let herself into the Munich apartment of Edgar Jung, a brilliant young right-wing journalist who was an avowed admirer of Hitler's current Vice-Chancellor, Franz von Papen.

Jung's bed was unmade. The furniture was overturned as if the room had been hit by a cyclone. Clothes had been ripped out of the wardrobe, the pockets turned inside out. In the study, the drawers of the heavy desk were upended, the papers cascading across the floor.

The housekeeper stood for a few minutes, taking in the brutal chaos of the apartment. Then she steeled herself to go into the bathroom. What she saw there sent her scurrying to Jung's telephone book. She clawed through, searching desperately for the journalist's closest friends.

In normal circumstances, she would have rung the police. But in Nazi Germany in 1934 that would have been foolhardy and dangerous.

Particularly as she had spotted the single word which Jung had been able to scrawl with shaving soap on the bathroom mirror. *Gestapo.*

*

For Adolf Hitler, the last fifteen months had proved highly satisfying. On 30 January 1933, the man once known as the Bohemian Corporal, the Vienna tramp and the apostle of violent revolution, had been summoned reluctantly by the ageing President Von Hindenburg to lead a coalition government of the right. In a Germany which had floundered in political chaos ever since the end of World War I Hitler became undisputed master.

Opposition had been crushed with all the brutality of a descending jackboot. There were no Communists, Socialists or Conservatives. Within months the trade unions had been dissolved; the press and radio had passed firmly under Nazi control. The universities, the civil service and the professions had been purged of 'leftists' and Jews – particularly Jews.

Unemployment had been stabilised. A new sense of national purpose coursed through a nation cowered and humiliated by defeat in the Kaiser's war. Hitler had proclaimed: 'The future belongs to us.' And indeed it seemed to be true.

And the Gestapo? It was only at the very start of its twelve years' reign of terror. Already it had achieved much.

On 13 October 1930, the man who was to be the creator of the world's most dreaded secret police marched with swinging step into the chamber of Germany's parliament, the Reichstag.

He was the burly Bavarian, Hermann Wilhelm Goering, who wore the Pour le Mérite around his neck, and across whose ample chest glistened the Lion of Zähringen with swords, the Karl Friedrich Order, the Hohenzollern Order Third Class with Swords and the Iron Cross (First Class).

An impossibly handsome fighter pilot from World War I, whose photograph had been peddled on the streets of Germany like a film star's, Goering, now coarsened and obese, had first entered the Reichstag two years earlier when Hitler's NSDAP (National Socialist German Workers' Party) had only been able to muster twelve seats.

11

Now there were 107 National Socialist deputies.

Goering, son of a senior consular official turned magistrate, first served with the Prinz Wilhelm Infantry Regiment, but had got himself a transfer to the Imperial German Army Air Service.

The glamour of being a fighter pilot with twenty-one victories to his credit and the highest German decoration round his neck was heady stuff. But it counted for little in postwar Germany, where jobs were hard to find. The man who had blasted one of the first British Handley Page bombers out of the skies and had been severely wounded in the process, was reduced to giving aerial displays and exhibition flights.

Resentment had burned deep in Hermann Goering – above all, against the provisions of the Versailles Treaty which had reduced Germany to armed and economic impotence following defeat in 1918.

There was bitterness too that he, a war hero, should be reduced to living on his wife's money and scraping a living.

Many believed that he had a future in politics, possibly a brilliant one. But they thought his rightful place was with the monarchists and conservatives, not with the tiny, brawling and raucous National Socialists led by a pinched-faced individual with a smudge of a moustache and a following restricted to Bavaria.

Yet within a week of meeting Adolf Hitler at a protest meeting in Munich in 1922, Goering had enrolled with the tiny NSDAP. By the following January, he was controller of the Sturm Abteilung, the group of rowdies who kept order at Hitler's meetings.

Hitler had told him: 'The Storm Troopers have got to be organised, disciplined and co-ordinated. That's your job.'

Possessed of abundant energy, Goering within months had hammered the promising but ill-organised rabble of the SA into something approaching the private army that Hitler wanted on the violent, brawling road to power.

By no means everyone welcomed the advent of the charismatic wartime hero. The roughnecks of the SA, many of them unemployed former private soldiers, saw Goering as rooted firmly in the past, associated with the bourgeois trappings of privilege, plutocracy and the Officer Corps. The SA, they felt, should be in the vanguard of genuine revolution; it should be sufficiently Socialist to sweep away the old order.

Soon Goering had singled out a potentially dangerous enemy: scar-faced, swaggering SA chief-of-staff Ernst Roehm, a homosexual who had gathered around him a stable of youths as a sort of praetorian guard.

Roehm was a power-seeker who had already had his quarrels with Hitler. He tossed down the gauntlet at Goering's feet. He was to proclaim: 'Anyone who thinks that the tasks of the SA have been accomplished will have to get used to the idea that we are here and intend to stay here. There are still men in official positions today who have not the least idea of the spirit of the revolution. We shall get rid of them if they dare to put their reactionary ideas into practice.'

As for Goering, Roehm confided to a friend contemptuously: 'He's just the sort of salon Nazi who will cut and run when the barricades go up.'

It was a fatally inaccurate judgement. Hermann Goering was more than prepared to fight, and his determination went hand-in-hand with a decidedly healthy sense of self-preservation.

Those who had served under him in the war soon realised that Goering was two people. Off-duty, he was the party man, ready to share games and girls, the hero around whom the women crowded and the champagne gushed. At war, he was a cold, ruthless martinet; in the air, a totally unfeeling technician with his killer instinct honed.

The social side of politics could now ensure that the salon invitations and the champagne flowed. But slaking the killer instinct? That could only be satisfied with power.

When Hitler became Chancellor on 30 January 1933, Goering, already President of the Reichstag, was to become Minister of State, Prussian Minister of the Interior and Commissioner for Aviation. It was far from being enough; blocking him was the severe figure of Franz von Papen, Prussia's Minister-President and Vice-Chancellor and a much respected representative of the old order.

How to neutralise von Papen?

Goering reasoned that he badly needed a cocoon of security – the sort Roehm enjoyed with his SA. His very own private army! The idea was immensely appealing. Goering set about prising the police away from the authority of von Papen. His was one office Goering desperately required for himself.

He needed an ally within the Prussian police, preferably right at the centre of power within Berlin itself. Goering didn't have far to look.

Among the right-wing, aggressively nationalist students of Marburg, Rudolf Diels was a legend. It was not so much for his academic achievements but because of his ability to drink beer in vast quantities. Furthermore, he had a disconcerting habit of chewing up the glass at the end of a drinking bout.

Eyebrows were undoubtedly raised in certain influential quarters at the excesses of Rudolf Diels. But in his drinking, glass-chewing and womanising Diels was always careful not to go too far. Besides, his vaunting ambition and utter lack of scruples disciplined him from offending too many of the wrong people.

A job in the police force made obvious sense to this main-chancer. Germany was an unstable place; politicians came and went. But there would always be the need for a bright lad in the police force, particularly in the political section, designated with deliberate vagueness Section 1A. In fact, 1A was concerned with the security of the state and there had been plenty for Diels and his colleagues to do.

Diels soon revealed his talents as a useful fixer.

When a leading Prussian politician wanted some evidence with which to muddy the SA, Diels was given the task of buying at an agreed price letters written by Roehm in which the chief-of-staff of the SA was very indiscreet in his terms of affection for young boys. The Prussian politician, with the letters in his hands, gleefully published them in an attempt to discredit the SA.

There had been other work. Von Papen, a previous Chancellor, had found some of the Socialist cabinet of

Prussia decidedly tiresome. Could Diels help? It had proved no problem. He cheerfully testified in a Federal Court that he had evidence of Socialist links with the Communists.

The mere hint was enough: leading left-wingers were ousted from office. Diels, Goering reasoned, was obviously a valuable sort of man to have. Of course, in the past he had readily given evidence against Nazis when the occasion arose, but now Hitler was in power he was prepared to see the grave error of his ways.

Diels had built up uncomfortably detailed dossiers on a variety of personalities. They would be excellent tools for weeding out anyone, particularly from the justice or police departments, even faintly suspected of being anti-Nazi.

Diels had files on leading Nazis as well. Goering's fat frame creased with laughter as he perused such delightful titbits as the blackmail by a woman of Joachim von Ribbentrop, the future Foreign Minister who had married a champagne heiress. And what was Alfred Rosenberg, the party's leading racial pundit, doing sleeping with a Jewish girl?

Another file caused Goering less amusement. It referred to a senior Nazi who (so claimed the dossier) 'exhibits many of the signs of a suppressed homosexual and is given to flamboyance in dress and the use of cosmetics.' Goering had found himself staring at his own dossier: Diels's collection of files was promptly reduced by one.

The merciless purges began.

Policemen from the days of the old Republic were thrust out of office and replaced by dyed-in-the-wool Nazis. Despite the rivalry with Roehm, Goering courted the SA, who added a much needed clout of terror to the activities of his own personal police.

But something more spectacular was called for. On 24 February 1933, just after the announcement of new elections, Goering's new police struck with a lightning raid on the Karl Liebknecht Haus, headquarters of the Communist Party in Berlin. Goering was able to announce triumphantly that incriminating documents had been discovered. They 'proved' that the Communists were on the brink of revolution. An official statement from the Prussian government alleged: 'Government buildings, museums, mansions and essential plants were to be burned down. Women and children were to be sent in front of the terrorist groups . . .' There were to be many terrorist acts against individual persons, against private property and against the life and limb of the peaceful population, and also the beginning of a general civil war.

The allegations were never substantiated. In this and other raids, the pattern of life under a dictatorship with a tireless secret police had become firmly established.

Suspects were rounded up in heavy, military-style trucks. In the early dawn, cars screeched through the streets to decant agents in front of private houses and apartment blocks.

It was the turn of the families of suspects: have them in custody, Goering argued, and valuable information could surely be gleaned in the cellars of the Columbia Haus in the General Pape Strasse, which had the grisly nickname among the Gestapo of the 'Columbia Bar'.

And at Oranienburg, near Berlin, hundreds were herded into the SA's concentration camp. Gestapo raiders were particularly keen to discover and destroy secret printing works of leftist publications. Frequently, the hoard was small: a duplicating machine in the apartment of a Communist worker. The pickings were richer where there were linotype machines in more affluent printing shops. These were systematically smashed and their owners beaten up.

All through the long nights, the trucks rumbled and the brakes screamed. Goering was just getting into his stride.

He had spelt out his intentions with brutal clarity, ranting at a speech in Dortmund: 'In the future there will be only one man who will wield power and responsibility in Prussia and that is myself. Whoever does his duty in the services of the State, who obeys my orders and ruthlessly makes use of his revolver when attacked, is assured of my protection. Whoever on the other hand plays the coward will have to reckon on being thrown out by me pronto. A bullet fired from the barrel of a police gun is my bullet.

'If you say that is murder then I am the murderer.'

Officially, the new secret police had no name beyond that non-commital 1A. In April, Goering approved of Geheime Staatspolizei, or Secret State Police. Originally, he had wanted GPA (Geheime Polizei Amt – State Police Office) but it was pointed out that this was uncomfortably like the GPU, the Soviet Political Police.

As it turned out, a weary bureaucrat in the Berlin Post Office solved the problem. Germany had always festered with initials; the only way to deal with them was to convert them to acronyms. The new department was filed away tersely as Gestapo.

2

At first, the Gestapo was limited to Berlin. Then a decree was passed creating a state police in every district throughout Prussia.

Goering was impatient to expand his empire still further. But, equally, there were those flexing their muscles to snatch it from him.

Roehm, the scar-faced leader of the Storm Troopers, stood fairly and squarely in contemptuous opposition to Goering. His band of bullies had grown with disturbing speed.

The official army, the Reichswehr, might throw up its hands in aristocratic disdain but the cold fact was that the SA was five times its size, with the nucleus of a general staff made up of former World War I officers.

The SA was organised and quartered in barracks. Three million SA could be mobilised at a moment's notice. Added to them, in June 1933, were a million members of the Stahlhelm (Steel Helmet), an organisation of ex-service-men of whom around 300,000 were ready for the call to arms.

It was an impressive record for an outfit which a few

years before had been merely a group of street rowdies. But the SA was getting increasingly like Frankenstein's monster: infinitely capable of turning on its creator.

There were certain fastidious souls who regarded the Storm Troopers as coming from the same highly questionable stable as the Austrian-born upstart who, for the moment at least, was the custodian of Germany's fortunes. Those who had knowledge of the night-time knock on the door or the street scuffle which heralded the sudden arrest were wise enough to keep quiet. But they could not fail to notice, nonetheless, that the influence of the Gestapo was creeping into every level of German life.

Gestapo tentacles extended with disconcerting speed and effectiveness. This was viewed with decidedly mixed feelings by the one man who, inaccurately, has gone down in history as the founder of the world's most notorious secret police.

The very name of Heinrich Himmler later stood for Gestapo fear and terror throughout Europe, but, in the very early days of Hitler's power, the nervous, stuttering crank with the pince-nez was in Munich, an out-of-town subordinate of Storm Trooper Ernst Roehm.

But as Himmler constantly reminded everyone, he was a subordinate with a difference – the commander no less of yet another intimidating private army in the Reich of his Fuehrer.

Members of Himmler's army had taken a personal loyalty oath to Adolf Hitler. They wore black uniforms. The silver death's head was their badge, their flash the double runic S of the pagan German. On the dull silver of their belts was engraved *Meine Ehre heisst Treue (My honour is loyalty)*.

These were men who regarded themselves as an élite, as virtual gods. This was Himmler's own unit, the Schutzstaffel (Protection Squad). Only those with a racial ancestry that was irreproachably Aryan over two centuries could even be considered for membership.

Just over ten years before Hitler came to power, Heinrich Himmler had been an unsuccessful fertiliser salesman who had been drummed out of his job for taking part in the notorious Munich putsch – the bid by a 600-strong group of SA led by Hitler to seize the nationalist and rigidly independent government of Bavaria. The moved had failed; Hitler had been sent to prison and the Nazi movement was written off as a spent force by the world.

On his release from Landsberg prison, Hitler had stated: 'I told myself that I needed a bodyguard, even a restricted one, but made up of men who would be enlisted unconditionally, ready even to march against their own brothers, only twenty men to a city (on condition that one could depend on them absolutely) rather than a dubious mass.' By mid-1925, that small tightly-knit group of fanatical Hitler loyalists had been named the Schutzstaffel; the SS had begun the twenty years of its life.

Member No. 168 was Heinrich Himmler. With his deprecating, apologetic manner and finicky unimaginative attention to detail worthy of a junior filing clerk, Himmler was not looked upon particularly as a threat to anyone.

But the brief, undistinguished World War I army career of this myopic pigeon-chested son of a Bavarian schoolmaster might well have provided some clue to Heinrich's future development.

As an orderly room corporal, he had enjoyed the reputation of being a blatant sneak, as a tireless collector of the weaknesses and indiscretions of his colleagues. These were not necessarily dangerous qualities: they are shared by conscientious policemen and officious public servants the world over.

But Himmler had something else – a deep and fanatical belief in the racial tenets of National Socialism, which absorbed the superman theories of Friedrich Nietzsche, with their glorification of brutalism, along with old Teutonic legends of a Germany of forests and hunters who lived by the sword and the dagger.

These fantasies were indulged in by an unremarkable bourgeois with sloping shoulders, close cropped hair, neatly trimmed moustache and those spectacles with the prissy earpieces. But the fantasies were also fuelled by a consuming ambition – to gain control of the black SS and wield it into a band of warriors whose impeccable pedigree would elevate it far above those unspeakable ruffians of the SA.

It was common knowledge throughout Germany that the SA stank. There was about it an odour of crime, blackmail, blind force, drunkenness and (here the puritanical Himmler shuddered) sexual perversion.

Such a bacillus could be removed for ever if only the SS had the power and the means. Time and again, the persistent Himmler, dazzled by his rag-bag of racial fantasies, drooled of his dreams to Hitler.

He announced wistfully: 'If I had the power to rule this superb handful of men, I could help to perpetuate the Nordic race forever. They would become the bulwark against the wave of Jewish influence which threatens to drown our beloved German people. They would become the symbols of the German race of which we are the guardians.'

These Nordic ravings undoubtedly struck a chord in Adolf Hitler, but the Fuehrer was sufficiently realistic to face the fact that his SS in 1930 numbered only 400 men. It was a sad and puny thing next to Ernst Roehm's SA.

Certainly, Himmler, created Reichsfuehrer (Reich Leader) of the SS, would be encouraged to build it up as a formidable force, but the time to strike down Roehm must be chosen with care. Hitler realised that in politics – even the politics of force – timing was everything. Fanaticism was all very well in its place but circumstances dictated a waiting game. Roehm must be encouraged to make himself a nice long rope.

And Goering? True, the original creation of the Gestapo had given him awesome power. But there was no reason for Himmler to suppose that he would hold on to it for ever.

For Hermann Goering, the master opportunist, the salons of the rich and influential in post-war Berlin had been fairly easy to penetrate.

For young Reinhard Heydrich, however, the doors of social acceptance had been slammed shut with humiliating force. The knowledge that this was largely his own fault scarcely consoled the arrogant blond with the eyes of ice-blue. He had been too young for war service – doubtless a considerable source of relief to his family, which was intensely musical but had few service traditions.

Heydrich's father, Bruno, had been director of the conservatoire in the Saxon town of Halle-on-the-Saale, while his maternal grandfather had held a similar position in Dresden.

The young Heydrich became a violinist of concert standard, a chamber music artist of considerable gifts and a useful pianist and singer.

But he grew up in the Germany of the Weimar Republic, constituted on 31 August 1919 after the Armistice. It had been based on democratic principles endorsed by a massive electoral majority. Liberalism was soon drowned however under the strident murmurings of nationalism working for the restoration of the Hohenzollern monarchy.

Heydrich was drawn to the movements of the right. In 1918-1919 he joined a pan-Germanic nationalist youth association, the Deutschnationaler Jugendbund Halle, and later threw in his lot with the Deutschvolkischer Schutz und Trutzbund. He then progressed to being a volunteer liaison agent with the Lucius division of the Halle Freikorps. After that he and a comrade forged their own organisation, the Deutschvolkische Jugendschar.

These were groups that were short-lived and soon forgotten: melting pots for extreme nationalism and militarism, crucibles of violence and terrorism. Such organisations lacked a cohesive policy and a firm leader. They were to get both. But not yet.

Originally, Heydrich had envisaged a career in music. But there was a less gentle world outside which had a greater pull. Soon his involvement with political groups led him to clashes with the Communists on the streets of German cities. His companions in violence were embryonic members of Roehm's SA.

His fringe political activities finally decided him on a choice of career: it would have to be in one of the armed services.

The army at the end of World War I was not a good

prospect for a young entrant: prospects were uncertain and promotion slow. The sea seemed a much better bet with, above all, a chance to travel.

In the late spring of 1922, Reinhard Heydrich left his home at Halle-on-the-Saale and reported to Kiel as a German naval cadet. He did not leave his early love entirely behind him, though. In his baggage, he carried a magnificent new violin, a present from a proud Bruno Heydrich.

The young man could have been at the start of a highly promising career; a fatal weakness was to bring it crashing down in ruins.

But all that lay in a future which seemed golden enough. Heydrich's quick, alert brain soon grasped the technical side of his navigational studies and handling small craft. Social life was vigorous and there was no shortage of girls for handsome young sailors.

Aboard *Berlin*, a former cruiser now rather ignominiously converted under the naval clauses of the Versailles Treaty into a training ship for cadets, Heydrich soon attracted attention. But to a certain Commander Wilhelm Canaris, the first officer, what made Heydrich interesting was not his future potential as a sailor. It was his talent as a violinist. Frau Canaris, herself an accomplished musician, was the centre of a thriving musical circle at her home in Kiel. It was the beginning of a pleasant interlude in the tempestous short life of Reinhard Heydrich. He would spend many Sundays at the Canaris home, relaxing completely in the quartets of Haydn.

The weekends were civilised interludes in the life of a naval cadet. Heydrich relished them – and the undoubted cachet of being taken up by a senior officer. He realised that if he played his cards right, the future could be bright indeed.

Heydrich served under Canaris for two years and his career blossomed accordingly. He also passed intelligence examinations in English, French and Russian.

Commander Canaris had fuelled Heydrich's imagination with stories of how in World War I he had once posed as a Chilean to avoid the British, and how in neutral Spain he had been a leading figure in a German espionage ring.

Heydrich had subtly dropped hints to Canaris. Somehow word got through to Berlin that young Heydrich wanted eventually to specialise in intelligence. He was sent to Wilhelmshaven on the North Sea where he eventually became chief signals and radio officer.

Life was busy. Heydrich played as hard as he worked. He seemed an industrious and tireless womaniser. The tall gangling youth with the rather too prominent nose and the flash of red in his striking blond hair had filled out into a superb Nordic specimen.

His speciality was blondes; he embarked on a series of rapid affairs. There was no reason to suppose that 19-year-old Lina Mathilde von Osten at first meant more to him than any of the others. Their meeting had been romantic – on a late night paddle steamer cruise soon after Heydrich's return to Kiel.

Lina rapidly made up her mind that she wanted this excitingly arrogant young officer not just as a lover but as a husband. Amid traditionally sentimental Christmas celebrations on Lina's native Fehmarn Island in the Baltic, Reinhard Heydrich and Lina von Osten became engaged.

Very soon, as he later wrote baldly in the account of his life for the SS files: 'At the end of April 1931, I was dismissed from the service on non-service grounds by a decision of the Reich President (Feldmarschall von Hindenburg), against the advice of my immediate superiors.'

The Furies had succeeded in bringing down Reinhard Heydrich with dramatic suddenness.

Certainly, the summons to an interview in Berlin had not been unexpected, even though it came from no less a person than the head of the German navy, Admiral Erich Raeder.

Heydrich knew what he was in for. He was already smarting from his encounter with one of Germany's foremost industrialists, a director of naval instruction of the IG Farben in Kiel who had dropped the bombshell: 'My daughter is expecting a baby. I demand that you marry her.'

The girl in question was a ravishing flaxen blonde with

whom Heydrich had been sleeping during his courtship of Lina von Osten. And now she was pregnant! Coolly, Heydrich assessed the situation. The only course was to take refuge in a sense of honour. He stated coldly: 'I must inform you that I am engaged to Fraulein Lina von Osten. It is inconsistent with the honour of a German officer to break an engagement, even in these circumstances. My fiancee is still willing to marry me.'

Heydrich's specious interpretation of the moral code of a German officer far from satisfied the injured industrialist. Within hours, the whole matter was laid before Raeder. Heydrich received the summons to Berlin.

He learnt that there was to be a naval court of honour. But Heydrich had few illusions. Raeder had already made the choice quite clear: either marry the girl or be kicked out of the navy.

To Heydrich's immediate superiors, the whole affair was a confounded nuisance. A highly promising career was now threatened because of a momentary carelessness. It was most regrettable, but quite clearly Heydrich would have to go.

One person, however, was not unduly perturbed. Lina von Osten had a will of iron and soon she was showing it. She made it absolutely clear that neither a prominent industrialist, her own horrified parents, Admiral Raeder or the entire German naval establishment were going to break the engagement. On the day after Christmas in 1931, the couple were married.

But before that a lot had happened to Reinhard Heydrich.

It had taken some time for Heydrich to grasp that the navy had turned its back on him. Reluctant to accept the truth, he hung around the ports of Hamburg, Lübeck and Kiel, acutely embarrassing old comrades. Then Lina took a hand. Her main mission was of course the rehabilitation of Reinhard, but by now there was a new preoccupation.

The potent appeal of Adolf Hitler's Nazism was increasing among the middle classes. Perhaps impressed with the manly virtues of Himmler's SS, Lina always carried an

NSDAP membership card with the swastika insignia and the number 1201380.

To her, the future was delightfully simple. 'You will join the party and get a job,' she announced. Heydrich was doubtful. To him, the Nazis spelt the SA, child of the old Freikorps, the brutal cadre of glorified boy scouts he had joined in adolescence. Besides, it would have been quite out of the question for a former naval officer to join a movement led by Adolf Hitler, ex-corporal.

Anyway, he was now far more interested in elementary survival; in his predicament, politics was a luxury he could scarcely afford.

Then one day he could stand Lina's proddings no longer. He took the train from Hamburg to Munich, making for an obscure chicken farm in the little village of Waldrudering.

It was Lina who had spotted a valuable half-forgotten link between Reinhard Heydrich and the SS. One of Heinrich Himmler's staff officers was a certain Freiherr von Eberstein, whose mother was Heydrich's godmother.

Whispers were dropped in the right places. Letters were sent and pleas forwarded. Which was why Heydrich made the long journey from the North Sea to the Alps and eventually found himself standing in Himmler's shabby farmhouse living-room.

The two men were an odd contrast. Heydrich, the former staff officer, was a tall impressive figure with a wide sensual mouth and ice-pick eyes. Himmler was still an unremarkable bourgeois. An outsider would have assumed that Heydrich was the one giving the orders and that Himmler would have obeyed them with totally unimaginative exactitude.

Conscious of being in the presence of a far stronger personality, the Reichsfuehrer-SS took refuge in deferential mildness.

He announced, using army terminology: 'I need an Ic man,' meaning an intelligence operative. 'If you think you could do the job, sit down and write how you would tackle it. You have twenty minutes.'

Heydrich's first reaction was one of incredulity. For all his ambitions, he had never had anything directly to do with intelligence; Himmler had misunderstood the term 'Nach-richtenoffizier', which meant signals officer, thinking it meant intelligence officer. But Heydrich kept the mocking look out of his eyes. At the same time, he dredged his memory for the slightest detail that might be useful.

Then he remembered how, night after night, he had listened entranced to the numerous experiences of Canaris. He sat down and began to write.

Himmler stared coldly at the result; his father had been a schoolmaster and it was an easy pose to assume. Heydrich was quick-witted enough to play his part. He stood to attention, the deferential disciple.

Himmler tapped the paper and made some suggestions. Heydrich was careful to reply: 'As the Reichsfuehrer wishes.' Himmler smiled slightly; the flattery had worked. Later, the able lieutenant was to joke to his wife and close friends about how easy it had been. Himmler had known as much about intelligence as Heydrich did about chickens.

Secretly, the Reichsfuehrer was delighted. Heydrich obviously had considerable executive abilities and was the man for the job. Even more important – and here the eyes must have glistened fanatically behind the glasses – the man was a superb Nordic specimen, offering magnificent proof of the innate superiority of German culture. Altogether, he would be an excellent choice!

When Himmler spoke he was again the brisk bureaucrat. He told Heydrich: 'You will be appointed to establish my new intelligence group with officer rank immediately.'

Thus, in the highly incongruous surroundings of a rundown smallholding was founded the SD (Sicherheitsdienst), eventually one of the controlling organisations of the most notorious machinery of terror in human history.

Himmler was moving one step further in his obsessive ambition – to gain control of the Gestapo and SA for himself.

3

Lina von Osten's parents grimly stitched smiles to their faces on the day their daughter married the libertine Heydrich.

But there was nothing remotely forced about the bridegroom's smile: it was one of pride as he stood before the altar resplendent in the black and silver Sturmbannfuehrer uniform of the SS.

Heydrich's rise under the patronage of Himmler had been breathtaking. First, there had been membership of the tiny Hamburg SS platoon whose members consisted largely of unemployed youths only too pleased to vent their grievances with fists in the city's red light district and beer cellars.

Then had come transfer to Munich with the promotion to Sturmbannfuehrer or platoon leader, the equivalent of major. Further promotions seemed in the offing.

But Heydrich was a realist. Smart uniforms were all very well. However, it had to be faced that the SS, which had been founded a full nine years before Heydrich joined them, still numbered less than 1000 officers and men. Furthermore, they were scarcely known outside Bavaria. There was a lot of hard work ahead.

The progress of the SD was proving annoyingly slow, too. The SS could not afford lavish offices; indeed, it could not afford an office at all. Heydrich operated from the cramped fourth floor of a house at Turkenstrasse 23 in Munich with Frau Heydrich as secretary and three helpers allocated by Himmler.

It was scarcely a promising beginning for what was envisaged as an eventual nationwide intelligence service.

The pay of around RM 180 a month was meagre in the

extreme. Neither of the newly-weds took kindly to the prospect of poverty, but the privations were thought more than worthwhile by the fanatically Nazi Lina.

Heydrich, totally cynical of all idealism, dreamt of future days of rich pickings. Meanwhile, he had the energy of three men, working day and night on his card index, the matrix of any dictatorship. He recorded the most intimate details of his fellow SS members and built up dossiers on anyone likely to be of interest later on.

There were frustrations. Both Himmler and Heydrich were made acutely conscious that increasingly all the big decisions were being taken by Hitler and Goering in Berlin.

Both the Fuehrer and the head of the Gestapo had no illusions whatever about Himmler. It was obvious that for all his tiresome racial fantasies and dreams of the SS as black gods, he was primarily interested in securing maximum power. Goering liked power too but did not waste time cloaking it with pseudo-philosophical speculations.

The chicken farmer with his mystic nonsenses was despised monumentally by the champagne-swilling veteran of the Richthofen Flying Circus.

When it came to gangster-style action against opponents nobody could touch Goering for sheer thuggery. But in the wheeling and dealing of power politics, Himmler more than came into his own.

The SS was ably represented in Berlin by Gruppen-fuehrer Kurt Daluege, who was the Reichsfuehrer's commander in the capital. Daluege, however, was no pale factotum and had very decided ambitions. He was known to be well in with Goering and it was rumoured he had his eyes on the SS leadership itself.

Himmler felt a clutch of fear. His infant empire, he felt sure, was gradually being chipped away from him. Well, Daluege must be put soundly in his place and told who was his master.

The rebuke, Himmler decided, must be administered by Heydrich, who forthwith set off for Berlin.

The result was a humiliating snub. Daluege declined even to receive Heydrich. Worse, the head of the SD was met by a posse of Goering police, acting under the orders of an anxious Rudolf Diels, who had scented trouble and saw in Himmler a potential threat to what had turned into a very comfortable life. Heydrich was told in no uncertain terms to mind his own business. He retreated to Munich. Himmler had lost the first round.

Heydrich boiled with intense fury, not lessened by the knowledge that in Diels he had an antagonist every bit as tough and ruthless as himself. Coldly, Heydrich began plotting the glass-chewer's downfall.

In September 1933, just seven months after Hitler had become Chancellor, Heydrich struck. A brief announcement was issued by Goering: 'Rudolf Diels has been relieved of his present post and will become Assistant Director to the Berlin Police.' Plainly it was a sideways transfer to get the former blue-eyed boy out of the way. What had happened?

Heydrich had adopted the role of Iago to Goering's Othello. He had let it be known that there was a Communist plot to eliminate Goering. The puny SS, with its tiny intelligence department, had come up with evidence of a 'Trotskyist plot'. Himmler was at last able to get the ear of Goering. SD agents had carried out interrogations of suspects; naturally, there had been confessions.

The Reichsfuehrer had been blunt: 'May I ask, minister, why your Gestapo people have failed to find this evidence? It is quite obvious that they are in total ignorance of it.'

Diels, as a handy scapegoat, was made to take the rap. In addition, Goering had his own severe problems.

On the evening of 27 February 1933, the Reichstag was engulfed by fire. The cause of the blaze remains inconclusive to this day. A half-crazed Communist Dutchman, Marinus van der Lubbe, had managed to make his way into the building and set off some small fires.

He and Ernst Torgler, parliamentary leader of the Communists, Georgei Dimitrov, General Secretary of the Comintern, and two other Bulgarians were tried for the crime before the Supreme Court at Leipzig. The trial, at which Goering appeared as a witness, turned into something of a fiasco for the Nazis.

All the accused, with the exception of van der Lubbe, who was sentenced to death and later beheaded, were found not guilty. Goering had lost his temper in court and been made to look a fool, even though the affair gave Hitler the excuse to step up his war with the Communists who, it was hinted, were in fact behind the fire.

Loss of face was not the only anxiety for the head of the Gestapo.

Ernst Roehm was speaking openly of starting a second revolution. There had even been talk of incorporating the SA with the army, against the express wishes of the Fuehrer. And now it seemed that there was a Red plot as well.

Himmler bided his time a little longer; he had no intention of overplaying his hand. Instead, he oiled his way slowly into Goering's confidence, eventually suggesting with studied casualness that the answer to the problem might be a unified police force and intelligence apparatus throughout the Reich. At the same time, Himmler assiduously courted those with the ear of Hitler.

In this Byzantine atmosphere of insinuation, intrigue, back-biting and power-grabbing, no one had more sleepless nights than Diels. If he wanted to escape with his life, let alone keep any sort of job, he would have to get out quickly and hope that Goering had not lost too heavily. He prudently resigned his offices.

Himmler, sensing victory, speedily moved some of his most trusted SS cronies to Berlin.

He grew bolder, even going so far as to announce his intentions openly: 'I want to reorganise the whole thing, create a simple Reich Police. Such a national police force is the State's guarantee.'

Himmler continued to report to Hitler. Meanwhile, Ernst Roehm was unwittingly digging his own grave and bolstering the case of the Reichsfuehrer. He had been heard proclaiming: 'Adolf is a prima donna. I've put up with a lot from him. If he thinks he can go on opposing me, he's mistaken. I've got a million men.'

The Fuehrer, surrounded by the toadies, place-seekers and back-stabbers spawned by any dictatorship, was eventually stung into action. Himmler might be a prosy bore but his loyalty was childlike and unquestioning. Hitler sent for Goering.

He proposed nothing less than the incorporation of Prussia with the rest of the Reich, policed by a single body. Goering had no alternative but to agree to a decree of his chief; the Gestapo (*Goering's* Gestapo) passed into the hands of Himmler and the SS – or, more to the point, into Heydrich's and the SD.

Goering assembled his Gestapo staff on 20 April 1933 before their new masters and pledged everyone's loyalty.

Himmler knew when magnanimity and sweet reasonableness were called for. Warmth was not in the Reichsfuehrer's character but he came as close to it as he could. He declared earnestly to Goering: 'I shall always remain faithful to you. You will never have anything to fear from me.'

Heydrich remained silent, his mind doubtless on his new Berlin filing system, which was developing most agreeably. After all, his staff in Munich had now grown to a hundred; he could afford to devote his time to a new challenge.

As for Goering, he was very conscious that, although nominally Himmler's superior, he was dangerously vulnerable. He harboured no illusions that Himmler and Heydrich would, if it came to the crunch, respect his person.

But Goering was, nonetheless, left with one dubious victory. The successor to Diels, Paul Hinkler, turned out to be an even more dedicated toper than his predecessor, but he lacked Diels's ability. After less than thirty days in office, Hinkler was dismissed and Diels returned.

He was to hold his job until April of the following year, when it became plain that he was no match for the intrigues of Himmler.

And with that Goering had to be content. Shorn of his old job, he began recruiting his very own personal secret police, the Landespolizeigruppe.

After all, he reflected, it was only sensible. Anything could happen in these uncertain times.

4

The powder keg which Ernst Roehm had straddled for so long and so arrogantly exploded under him during the weekend of 29 June 1934.

The swaggering SA chief had never attempted to conceal his disappointment at the way in which the National Socialist revolution was going. To his disgust, Roehm had come to the conclusion that Hitler was far more interested in nationalism than Socialism and had, as a major preoccupation, a lust for personal power. And to achieve that power Hitler had found it necessary to compromise.

Roehm had never ceased to nag Hitler about the need to place national defence solidly in the hands of the SA.

The Fuehrer was genuinely fond of Roehm; there were ties of loyalty stretching back to the street brawls of the previous decade. Hitler hesitated to cut down an old comrade.

Instead he had temporised. He had attempted to buy off Roehm in December 1933, by appointing him a member of the Reich cabinet, as minister without portfolio.

Roehm had not been impressed by the office at all. He continued to clamour for power for his SA, something that the stiff-necked Reichswehr abhorred and abominated.

The Fuehrer looked around for some formula that might satisfy both parties. It was a vain hope.

Generaloberst Werner von Blomberg, the Minister of National Defence, and Roehm, chief-of-staff of the SA, were obliged to sign a pact which proclaimed the Reichswehr as 'the only official armed organisation of the Third Reich'; while the SA, although it remained in existence, was designated a subordinate defence role.

Throughout the champagne reception which preceded the signing ceremony, Roehm maintained a façade of bon-

homie in front of the Reichswehr officers who both patron-
ised and despised him. But once the military men had
departed and the champagne started flowing anew, Roehm
let fly.

He stormed: 'This so-called Fuehrer doesn't cut any ice
with us. He thinks himself so clever because he's got the
support of the bankers and the military. He's betraying the
National Socialist revolution we started. Well, never mind,
we'll do without him . . .'

Roehm then proceeded to knock yet another nail into his
coffin by openly sneering at the racial and nationalist pre-
occupations of Hitler and Himmler.

He sneered: 'These Teutonic revelries are nonsense.
What I want is a Socialist and military republic with the
Brown Shirts wielding power. There's need for a second
revolution.'

This was tantamount to high treason and there were a
number of willing souls around to record it.

Viktor Lutze was SA leader in Hanover, a position he
reasoned he was unlikely to hold for very long. Indeed, he
reflected that the way things were going he could very well
end up a victim of SS wrath.

A man must look to his own. Lutze spent a lot of time
that day feverishly scribbling Roehm's more purple comments on to a bit of paper under the table and committing
the rest to memory.

But what was he to do with his evidence? The SS was
quite capable of branding him a troublemaker, benefiting
from his information and getting rid of him. Roehm would
not relish a traitor in his own camp. In some trepidation, he
took his information to one of Hitler's aides, Rudolf Hess,
who in turn referred Lutze directly to the Fuehrer, currently holed up in his Bavarian retreat of Obersalzburg near
Berchtesgarten.

The Reich Chancellor seemed distinctly embarrassed, as
if unwilling to attach much importance to Roehm's
drunken mumblings. He told Lutze: 'Let the matter ripen,
then we'll see.'

Plainly, Hitler was reluctant to move against old comrades, although in all conscience he had put up with

Roehm's disloyalties long enough.

Lutze was not prepared to leave things there. He sensed an impending clash and was determined to be on the winning side.

He turned next to Generalmajor Walther von Reichenau, a cold and calculating professional soldier who, although he had little time for the mystique of Hitler and the philosophical trappings of Nazism, was politically sensitive enough to realise that there could be certain advantages to the Reichswehr in co-operating with the new regime.

Like Lutze, von Reichenau had kept a foot in both camps. He was a confidant of von Hindenburg, but he had also made sure that he was well in with Reinhard Heydrich. The two men had talked many times in an effort to find a solution to the problem of Roehm. A stumbling block had been Himmler, who remembered with uncharacteristic sentimentality the early days when he and the SA chief had fought together for Hitler.

Heydrich, independently of Lutze, was also working on von Reichenau. He explained patiently that without Roehm the Reichswehr would have no rival. The army would become efficient without the embarrassment of a debauchee associated with it.

To Himmler, Heydrich stressed that the SS would be free of the very last ties that bound it to the Storm Troopers. Then, added Heydrich, it would be possible for the Reichsfuehrer-SS to bring his black guard to the very summit of efficiency.

Predictably, it was this last point which persuaded Heinrich Himmler. Now Roehm faced opposition which was to prove fatal. Goering, von Reichenau, Himmler and Heydrich formed the deadly quartet now poised for action against him.

Fresh events had pushed Hitler into final action against his enemies. The Nazis had other critics besides Ernst Roehm. The Vice-Chancellor, Franz von Papen, had created a sensation that summer by making a highly explosive speech to students in the little town of Marburg. Von Papen proclaimed that the political opposition to Hitler was

34

highly disturbed by the actions and threats of the Nazis – the persecutions, the arbitrary arrests and the outlawing of free elections.

It was a fresh manifestation of treason: worse, it was a blow at the very conception of the one-party state. But von Papen was a powerful figure in Germany: what was to be done about him? The Gestapo set to work.

Telephone tapping in the Third Reich was a comparatively new craft, but already Goering and Diels had proved expert at it.

Soon transcripts of conversations from von Papen's office began to pile up on Heydrich's desk. Most of the information was useless. But one nugget did emerge: a young writer of Conservative views named Edgar Jung, who had built up a small but potentially subversive following, had written the offending Marburg speech for von Papen.

It was Jung, alone in his flat that violent summer, who answered the door to Heydrich's men, just managing to scrawl *Gestapo* before he was taken away to the Munich torture cellars and eventual execution.

Heydrich and his lieutenants worked round the clock, sifting records for anything that might be construed even remotely as subversion by the SA.

Roehm had talked often enough about a revolutionary people's army of which he would be commander-in-chief.

The dossier was growing most agreeably fat. Then came an unexpected blow. Ironically enough, it was Hitler, still reluctant to move against Roehm, who nearly destroyed the value of Heydrich's carefully built up volume of evidence.

The Fuehrer himself later stated: 'At the beginning of June, I made a final effort with Roehm. I asked him to come to my office and we talked together for nearly five hours.'

The two men made a decision: the SA would go on leave during July. The whole matter would be thrashed out on its return.

Heydrich, Himmler, Goering and von Reichenau, who had given his approval to the proposed uprising against the

SA, were aghast. How on earth was Roehm to be despatched if the SA was allowed to go on leave? Who would believe now that he was plotting to overthrow the state? There was a new urgency. The Gestapo must strike immediately.

Early in June, Heydrich was able to breathe once again. Into the hands of the Gestapo came the advance text of a bulletin from the General Staff of the SA. It was due to be published within a few days in the newspaper, *National Zeitung*.

> 'I hope that on the first of August, a well-rested SA, filled with strength, will be ready to undertake the glorious mission it owes the people and the Fatherland. If the enemies of the SA think that it will not return from leave, or return only in part, let them enjoy their illusions as long as they can.
>
> When the day comes these people will receive an adequate reply, in whatever form necessity dictates.
>
> The Sturm Abteilung is and will remain the destiny of Germany . . .'

Heydrich read Roehm's text with astonishment and then grinned wolfishly: 'The man has no sense at all. He regrets nothing. It's as good as slapping the Fuehrer's face. We've got him.'

Eighteen days later, Hitler flew to Westphalia to attend the wedding of an old friend. It was scarcely a relaxed social occasion; hardly had the Fuehrer arrived than Himmler was on the telephone.

The normally bloodless bureaucrat was plainly agitated. He gasped: 'I've had alarming reports here in Berlin on an imminent SA uprising. You must return at once.'

Providentially, Goering was at Hitler's side and lost no opportunity in fuelling the Fuehrer's anger. A string of further reports followed; including an allegation that Karl Ernst, one of Roehm's closest aides, was even at that moment planning an armed insurrection in Berlin. Himmler was determined that Hitler was not to be given the time to think up further excuses for not moving against Roehm.

But Hitler's determination to scotch any proposed putsch was now absolute. He alerted his own bodyguard force in Berlin, the elite SS-Leibstandarte. There was going to be plenty for it to do.

Then he rang up Ernst Roehm, currently relaxing with some of his more personable SA youths at the Pension Hanselbauer in Bad Wiessee near Munich.

The Fuehrer ordered abruptly: 'You will have all your senior staff present at 11 a.m. tomorrow for a conference.'

Himmler kept up the pressure; his master must be made to act immediately before the white heat of his anger cooled off. Gestapo agents reported: 'Brownshirts are marching though Munich demonstrating against the Fuehrer and by Saturday afternoon all key government buildings in Berlin will be occupied by the traitors.'

Within hours, Hitler's private Junkers JU52 was carrying him, armed with pistol and riding whip, to Berlin to settle accounts.

Thirty-year-old Reinhard Heydrich, head of the SD and, under Himmler, virtually in command of the newly acquired Gestapo, was rapidly approaching the zenith of his power.

Yet to seventy-million Germans he remained almost unknown. This shadowy technician of dictatorship never courted personal publicity and frowned on his picture appearing in the paper. His ambition was to be the ultimate bureaucrat controlling legions of bureaucrats. The less subtle and often painful work of persuading suspects to see the error of their ways held little appeal. He wished no part in such crudities. The German navy's most notorious disgrace was happy enough to settle for simple power.

He handed agents at Gestapo headquarters a list of names, starting with the SA leaders, and told them: 'I wish you to complete new lists which will be based on the principal cities where these people are to be found at the moment. You will be supplemented with further information to keep these lists up to date.'

Security was absolute. Indeed, many Gestapo men were to recall later that Heydrich seemed almost neurotically ill-at-ease, as if sensing SA agents skulking behind the filing cabinets.

Senior men watched their fellows closely, both in the office and at home. Every telephone call was monitored; no agent was permitted to take any of the lists out of the office.

Heydrich had moved out of his own room to work in the general office. More than one operative sensed the hard blue eyes boring into his back.

While the filing and the indexing and the cross-referencing went on, the Gruppenfuehrers of the SS high command, previously summoned to Prinz Albrechtstrasse, were ordered to bring all units throughout the Reich to emergency strength. There was a link with opposite numbers in the Reichswehr: if needs be, the SS shock formations could depend on the support of regular army troops and weapons.

All that was needed was for Heydrich to receive the code word which would be passed to divisional commanders. Everyone was poised for Operation Colibri (hummingbird). The hands of SS leaders hovered over the sealed envelopes on their desks.

Heydrich had no scruples about using the occasion to work off some of his own grudges. He lost no time in adding the name of Rudolf Diels to those awaiting the SS firing squads, due to receive their instructions from the Gestapo.

Zero hour had been fixed provisionally for the dawn of 30 June. In the area of Munich, SD men were told that they would receive their orders at 2 a.m.

For Ernst Roehm, the night had followed a not unusual pattern. There had been brimming tankards of beer, countless marching songs and anthems. There was no snobbery among the SA: aides-de-camp, chauffeurs and bodyguards were all boisterous together. At 4 a.m., a happy Roehm, intoxicated by beer, back-slapping and general bonhomie, lurched amiably to bed, pausing only to don pyjama trousers.

As the scar-faced, bull-shouldered warrior snored in blissful ignorance, a convoy of cars snaked towards Bad

Wiessee. It carried Hitler, senior Nazi officials and SS armed detachments.

The cars coasted the last few minutes to the pension. The SS troops leapt from the vehicles, crouching low, their pistols cocked and ready. Progress over moss and grass was silent. As they reached the buildings, the men halted. Hitler was in absolute command. There was total obedience.

For a while, there was silence; the pension slumbered reassuringly. Hitler gave the signal. There was a short sharp crash as a jackboot sliced through the door.

SA Gruppenfuehrer Count Spreti of Munich was the first to be dragged from his bed and kicked into the corridor. Then the SS were dealing with Edmund Heines, thuggish veteran of many a street brawl, including the farcical Munich putsch of eleven years before.

Now Heines was naked, his arms entwined around his brawny young chauffeur. Too late, one hand darted towards the pistol on his night table. The SS opened fire and Heines slumped.

Then both victims were bound and dragged from the room. An SS firing squad was hastily assembled. The bullets slumped into the naked bodies. The corpses were left lying outside the pension like rotting vegetables.

While other members of Roehm's staff were meeting a similar fate, Hitler was knocking on the door of the SA chief-of-staff.

A drowsy, slightly irritated voice enquired: 'Who is it?'

'It's me, Adolf. Open at once.'

Roehm was puzzled. 'I didn't expect you so soon.' he mumbled, pulling open the door, his round fat face creased with the mark of pillows. Then he was recoiling with disbelief as Hitler, beside himself with rage, launched into a stream of invective, lashing the tails of his long leather coat with the hippopotamus hide whip. Roehm made various attempts to defend himself against a string of abuse. It was all too plain that Hitler now believed every word which had been fed him by Himmler and Heydrich.

The SS removed Roehm after Hitler had yelled at the guards: 'This swine is lacking in respect for me. Take him

39

away at once.' Roehm was to live for two more days. Once again, Hitler had shown scruples. 'Ernst will be reprieved because of his past services,' the Fuehrer announced.

Himmler and Heydrich returned to the attack, arguing that unless Roehm was disposed of, the threat of the SA would never be annihilated. Hitler gave way.

An SS officer in the Stadelheim prison handed Roehm a loaded revolver and a copy of the *Voelkischer Beobachter* newspaper, giving details of the 'purge of the SA'.

Roehm flatly refused to commit suicide. 'If Adolf wants me dead let him come and do the job himself,' he challenged.

The SS, the ground ably prepared for it by the Gestapo, was to act as Hitler's right hand. 'Aim slowly and calmly,' were Roehm's last words as he took the first of the three bullets full in the chest.

Colibri was now in full swing.

By no means all the victims lined up by Heydrich were SA men. Von Papen had been revealed as a traitor and an enemy of the state. But Hitler was adamant that to kill so eminent an elder statesman would be a serious blunder which would alienate Germany internationally. Things could be stage-managed to prove that the SA had been a security risk. There might even be some mileage to be gained in world approval, but the slaughter of an elderly man of distinguished reputation would achieve nothing.

Heydrich fumed; Goering brought his influence to bear to protect von Papen. The Vice-Chancellor later wrote in his memoirs: 'My home was surrounded by an SS detachment armed to the teeth. The telephone was cut off and in my reception room I found a police captain, who had orders that I was to have no contact with the outside world and that no one was allowed to see me. Later he told me that he was responsible for preventing any Brownshirts or Gestapo from attempting to abduct me, unless he received direct orders from Goering.'

Other members of the Vice-Chancellor's staff were not so lucky.

The two gentlemen who called at the office of the Vice-

Chancellor saying they were from von Papen himself were elaborately courteous but extremely firm. They told the servant: 'We have business with the Vice-Chancellor's secretary, Oberregierungsrat Bose. We don't mind waiting.'

When the unsuspecting Bose appeared, the Gestapo produced their revolvers as casually as if they had been commercial travellers with calling cards.

They left their victim to bleed on the carpet.

Other killings were scarcely less cowardly. Just after mid-day on 30 June, an open, reddish-brown car containing six men drove to the Berlin suburb of Neu Babalsberg. The men rang the bell on the garden gate of the villa of Generaloberst Kurt von Schleicher, Hitler's immediate predecessor as Chancellor and a one-time confidant of Ernst Roehm.

Unsuspectingly, the cook pressed the button and released the lock. As she went into the garden, two of the men brushed her aside and went straight to the study.

One man asked abruptly: 'Are you Generaloberst Kurt von Schleicher, the former Chancellor of Germany?'

The soldierly figure rose. Pistols were drawn. Von Schleicher slumped forward. But not before his wife, who had been arranging flowers in another room, hastened to the study, a basket of roses on her arms and carrying gardening gloves.

There were more shots: von Schleicher's wife, too, fell under a hail of bullets.

At the fashionable Hotel Adlon, Generaloberst Kurt von Bredow, a close friend of the von Schliechers, was having tea with friends. A grave-faced messenger brought him a note with the news of the Neu Babalsberg killing.

Von Bredow was silent for a moment. Then he turned to one of his guests, a French diplomat, and said in a deliberately loud, clear voice: 'I wonder why the pigs haven't killed me yet.' The diplomat, seeking to shield von Bredow from danger at least for the moment, invited the general to the sanctuary of his own home. Von Bredow declined with grave courtesy and left.

As he passed through the tea room of the Adlon, one of

41

the waiters promptly picked up a telephone.

A few hours later, von Bredow, still in the white tunic and field grey breeches he had worn all day, answered the ring at the door. He took a single shot in the chest.

Later, a young Oberst from the General Staff related how he had run into von Bredow outside the hotel. Von Bredow had told him unemotionally: 'They have assassinated Schleicher. *He* was my leader. There is nothing for me now.'

Heydrich's agents were everywhere; the Adlon was notorious as a listening post. If von Bredow had a death wish, the Gestapo had been only too happy to satisfy it.

At Prinz Albrechtstrasse 8, powerhouse of mass murder, orders were issued without pause. Heydrich's elaborately drawn up lists of intended victims had numbers by the names. Telegrams would flood in from all over the Reich stating: 'No. 8 has arrived. Nos. 17, 35, 37, 68 and 84 have been arrested. Nos. 32, 43, 47, and 59 have been shot.'

Heydrich was remarkably pleased at the tidy efficiency of it all. He had come a very long way from those two shabby rooms in Munich.

One arrest particularly delighted the head of the SD. Stocky Gregor Strasser, Bavarian by birth, who like his brother Otto had become an ardent Nazi as early as 1920, had always been an independent soul. He had made the fatal mistake of proclaiming sincere enthusiasm for the Socialism in National Socialism. Furthermore, like Roehm, Gregor Strasser had little time for the mystique of the Fuehrer, and had refused to use the title.

Far worse, back in 1924 he had actually organised a separate political movement which had contested state and national elections.

Strasser did not repent with the years. He had even advocated a coalition government consisting of Nazis and the followers of von Schleicher. Hitler had greeted this with a tirade and screams of 'Treason! Treason!'

That assiduous diarist, Dr Joseph Goebbels, Hitler's Propaganda Minister had long since summed up Strasser. 'A dead man,' he wrote tersely in his journal. And now it

42

was coming true.

Strasser had by now retired from politics, disgusted with the constant intrigues for power and much more interested in his wife and their twin children. The eight Gestapo men burst in at lunchtime, sent to Strasser's home post-haste by Heydrich. No explanation was given, not a word spoken.

It had been a dog-tired and impatient head of the SD who had granted an interview to Goering a short time before.

Goering announced: 'Strasser has given good service to the party in the past. He should be granted a death by firing-squad.'

Heydrich riposted: 'Nonsense, the swine is a plain traitor and will be given a straight bullet in the back of the head. The Leibstandarte firing squads are working overtime as it is.'

Goering allowed himself to be persuaded. An air of unreality gripped the prisoners of the Prinz Albrecht-strasse. Surely, they reasoned, the arrests were due to some extraordinary mistake. Loyal party members brushed shoulders with scared and demoralised SA men.

No one knew of the current wave of shooting going on both in Munich and at the Lichterfelde barracks in Berlin.

There was an air of humorous euphoria. Strasser was cheered as he was brought in to join the other prisoners: here was a new comrade in misery.

Suddenly, an SS man appeared with the announcement: 'Strasser, you are to be moved to your own cell.' Clearly, here was a special detainee. Respectfully, the prisoners moved aside as Gregor Strasser was led away.

Strasser walked down the corridor to the tiny cell with a single window. Peering through he could see the impassive figure of the SS guard.

Heydrich was beside himself with delight and immediately rang Himmler. He declared: 'We've got that swine Gregor Strasser.'

He listened with growing satisfaction to Himmler's remarks, announcing tersely: 'The swine will die. Let the pig bleed.'

Five hours later, a shadow fell across the window of

Strasser's cell. Instinctively, he recoiled. The bullet whistled past his ear and lodged in the cell wall. Then the guard was firing again. Strasser was hit in the shoulder and he slumped across the bed. Further shots were emptied into his body. Now the SS guards were in the cell, their boots crashing into Strasser's face and head.

But still Strasser did not die. Hans Bernd Gisevius, an official of the Prussian Ministry of the Interior and a Gestapo member at the time of Strasser's arrest who miraculously survived the war to become a prosecution witness at Nuremberg, wrote in his memoirs, *To The Bitter End*:

> 'A prisoner in the adjoining cell heard him thrashing about on the cot for nearly an hour. No one paid any attention to him. At last the prisoner heard loud foot-steps in the corridor and orders being shouted.
> 'The guards clicked their heels. And the prisoner heard Heydrich's voice saying: "Isn't he dead yet? Let the swine bleed to death."
> The bloodstain on the wall of the cell remained for weeks. It was the pride of the SS squadron, a kind of museum piece. These cut-throats showed it to all the terrified inmates and boasted that it was the blood of a famous man, Gregor Strasser. It was only after he had received numerous complaints that Heydrich ordered the bloodstains to be cleaned.'

Warden Koch of Stadelheim prison was a correct soul. Sentences of death, he reasoned, must be duly authorised by the court and accompanied by the appropriate papers. And here was a group of singularly unpleasant looking plain-clothes men touting a list of names, some of which were ticked off in red.

Koch was told: 'Those are our prisoners now. You will hand them over to us.'

Koch opened his mouth in timid protest at this casual administration of justice. Then he caught the steady gaze of the Gestapo and shut it again.

His visitors shoved him aside and seized their prisoners.

Heydrich's men did not do anything so crude as carry out the executions themselves: all must be done with complete rectitude. The firing squad was composed of the Leibstandarte, under the command of Hitler's former chauffeur, Joseph 'Sepp' Dietrich, whose beer-inflated bulk was now straining out of the uniform of an SS-Obergruppenfuehrer.

In the courtyard, SA leader and Munich Chief of Police August Schneidhuber stared in dawning horror at the line-up of Leibstandarte.

In his heart he had always known what was in store for him. Hitler, screaming and raging, had in person ripped off Schneidhuber's badges and stripes a short time before.

Sweating with fear in the mounting heat, he just caught the words of command before the bullets cut into his body and that of five other prisoners.

The black Gestapo car screamed along the streets of Berlin, making for Potsdam. In the back with five of Heydrich's men for company was wedged Paul Schulz, one of Strasser's aides. Schulz had been snatched at home just after 8.00 p.m. At first, he was thrown into a cell at Prinz Albrechtstrasse. Then the plain-clothes men took him on what was intended to be his last ride.

The death car skirted the park of the Grunewald Forest. It was Saturday night and traffic was heavy. This, it was intended, should be a quiet killing but there was a constant ribbon of headlamps.

At the wheel, the driver swore softly, then turned south and headed towards Leipzig. Eventually, he spotted a deserted strip of road.

The door of the car was flung open; Schulz was shoved out and told to walk. In sudden panic, he broke into a run. Then it was as if his back was on fire and he felt himself falling. He was soon on his feet again making for the welcome cover of the trees. Ahead of him he saw a stream. Oblivious to the fresh hail of bullets, he dived into the water, letting its coolness wash over his back in blessed relief.

All was silent. The Gestapo, looking for fresh sport, sped

off. Schulz dragged himself to the side of the road and hailed a passing car. The driver was sensible enough to take him out of Germany altogether and into Switzerland.

The shootings and the beatings went on for a total of four days before Hitler personally put a stop to them.

The last shots were fired on the morning of 2 July at seven o'clock. The following memo was circulated:

> 'From the Prussian Minister-President and the Chief of the Gestapo.
> To all subordinate police stations: All documents concerning the action of the last two days are to be burned, on orders from above.
> A report on the execution of this order is to be made at once.

Just how many victims fell during 'the night of the long knives' will probably never be known. But at the 1957 Munich trial of Sepp Dietrich, a figure of 'more than 1,000' was given.

There had never been any direct evidence of a proposed putsch. Not that it mattered. Himmler and Heydrich and the entire machinery of the Gestapo had succeeded in persuading the Fuehrer and the army that an insurrection was imminent. Heydrich's downright lies and half-truths had astounded arrested members of the SA, many of whom clearly knew nothing of any putsch at all.

Just before his death, August Schneidhuber had greeted Dietrich warmly and asked: 'Sepp, my friend, what on earth's happening?'

Schneidhuber, along with countless others, went to his grave without finding out.

The Gestapo had done its work well, building on the one indisputable fact that Roehm had been in touch with von Schleicher about his scheme to integrate the SA with the army. That had been construed as treason, and Roehm had paid the price.

The army stepped promptly into line. The master opportunist von Reichenau issued a communique stating that von Schleicher had been proved a traitor to the state in word and deed. It was, of course, tragic about his wife – but, after all, she had placed herself in the line of fire.

Defence Minister von Blomberg praised Hitler warmly. and the aged Paul von Hindenburg, the army's supreme commander and Reich President, weighed in with his congratulations.

Within Gestapo headquarters there was something like euphoria. The SD had at its disposal a team of experts who could produce evidence, real or false, to prove just about anything. The backroom boys of dictatorship had more than proved their worth.

And Hitler was showing his approval in most gratifying fashion. Not a week had passed since Roehm's death before the Fuehrer had announced that Heydrich's Sicherheitsdienst would now have power over all other Nazi party organisations. Heydrich himself was promoted to Gruppenfuehrer. The SS itself could go ahead and form armed units. It was all beyond Himmler's wildest dreams.

There were two lucky escapes from the Roehm purge. The name of the oleaginous Rudolf Diels was removed from Heydrich's death list at the intervention of Goering, who had the reputation of being loyal to certain old comrades. Diels was shunted into a succession of civil service jobs.

The other survivor was the arch sneak Viktor Lutze, now completely trapped in the tentacles of Himmler and Heydrich.

His reward was a dubious one: he ended up with Ernst Roehm's old job. It was indisputably the most unwanted post in Hitler's Germany.

5

Young Walter Schellenberg stared gloomily at yet another of the countless court judges he had faced over the last few months.

It was the early 1930s. Germany had slumped into super-recession. Schellenberg, the seventh son of a Saarbrücken piano manufacturer, had known constant poverty. The Allied occupation of the Saar at the end of World War I had driven his family to Luxembourg, and the depression had badly hit his father's business.

Now here he was making yet another application for state funds. Without them, he could say goodbye to further studies at the German bar. In addition, he had his young wife, Kathe, to keep.

The judge regarded the anxious boyish figure before him, then said with resigned cynicism: 'Your application would be greatly helped, Herr Schellenberg, if you joined the Nazi party and one of its offshoots. They have a way of looking after their own.'

Hitler had been in power since the previous January, pledged to slash the horrific unemployment figure of six million. At the moment he headed a coalition government; all the signs were of a feverishly mounting popularity, particularly among the young.

Anyone who joined the Nazi party was also required to be a member of one of its formations as well. Schellenberg simply wanted a job, but already his calculating qualities were showing themselves. He was to declare later: 'The beer hall rowdies of the SA were beyond the pale.'

The SS, on the other hand, had its potent glamour. There was the dashing and elegant black uniform. There was the feeling of belonging to an exclusive club of kindred spirits: quite a few of Schellenberg's fellow students had joined.

It was a romanticised view. The reality was rather different. Being a member of the SS required mandatory weekend cross-country marches, complete with full packs. Schellenberg did not care for Himmler's particular brand of carbolic puritanism but he admitted that it was useful in sorting out unsuitable disciples.

The SS, however, had its full share of indoctrination specialists as well. Their job was to peddle Hitler's highly individualistic view of history, coupled with virulent attacks on the twin hates of the Reichsfuehrer-SS: the Jews and the Catholics. This sort of work was far more to

Schellenberg's taste than trudging about the country like an overgrown boy-scout.

He was assigned to Bonn University to give indoctrination talks and lectures. At one of his earlier meetings, he noticed two men in their SS uniforms without insignia. After the lecture, they introduced themselves as professors. With studied casualness they eventually steered the conversation round to the real reason for the contact. One of them dropped the name Sicherheitsdienst, going on to explain that this was a highly secret institution whose job was to gather information 'to help the government evaluate policy'.

Schellenberg smiled and reflected that this was certainly one way of describing good old-fashioned spying. Then he listened intently as one of the professors asked him if he would like to join.

He would have accepted anyway but what really made up his mind for him was one man saying: 'You will of course be excused all other SS duties.'

Schellenberg's euphoria was such that he did not question the arbitrary way in which he had been recruited. Only later did he learn that there had been other agents at previous lectures. And they had not been wearing uniform.

For the next few months, Schellenberg was wafted through the various departments of the SD on a sort of introductory course, at first being given relatively simple assignments. Then came a very special summons.

Heinrich Mueller, who ran the Gestapo as Heydrich's deputy, was small squat man with a head like a football and the tough, rough hands of a professional bruiser.

Thirty-three years old at the time of Hitler's accession to power, Mueller had been a sergeant on the Western Front. His career as a professional policeman started in 1919 when he joined the Munich police. One of his first jobs had been to deal with the murders of hostages during the time when Bavaria was briefly in the hands of the Reds.

He claimed that the experience had made him a firm anti-Communist, a shrewd insistence which secured him a political position at police headquarters in Munich.

Mueller's unscrupulous ambition, however, made him useful to his new masters. A Munich-Upper Bavaria Nazi Party District report stated that he was an officer 'who at times would disregard legal rules and regulations'.

None of this was to say that the Nazis trusted him. The report went on: 'He would be bent on recognition from his superiors under any system.' Just how true this was the Nazis were to find to their cost.

On his first meeting with Mueller, Schellenberg was wary of the man's rather forced geniality, belied by the coarse Bavarian accent.

Mueller was one of those men who would quite cheerfully have seen all the works of art of the world burnt for firewood and all the intellectuals flung on the blaze. For the ideology and pseudo-philosophising of the Nazi creed he had nothing but complete contempt. Mueller recognised that Himmler was gradually building his SD into a sort of intellectual powerhouse; he wanted people with the sort of cerebral muscle evidently possessed by young Schellenberg. The SD was another organisation for which Mueller had little time, but he had to obey orders and he simply told Schellenberg 'Heydrich is very pleased with your reports. You're only here as a matter of routine.'

His next comments made Schellenberg's heart beat faster. He said: 'You're going to the main office of the SD which comes under the party rather than the government. A pity – I could make better use of you here.'

At this stage of the Nazi development, this was the nearest Mueller came to voicing his outright hatred of the leaders of the SD.

Schellenberg was not aware of it at the time, but he had just caught a glimpse of the miasma of intrigue and jealousy existing within the SD and Gestapo apparatus.

Everything was fitting into place. His progress through the minor offshoots of the SD had indeed been remarkably smooth and his reception decidedly cordial.

Now he knew why. All the strings were being pulled and manipulated by the as yet unseen presence of Reinhard Heydrich, puppet master of the Third Reich.

The head of the SD for some reason had singled him out

for some sort of special future. For anyone of just twenty-three, it was heady stuff indeed.

Schellenberg felt both excitement and fear. They were twin emotions he was to experience often during his colourful Gestapo career.

Over the years, Schellenberg was never to forget his first interview with Heydrich, his encounter with that tall impressive figure with the big sensual mouth and the broad high forehead.

Above all, he never forgot those musician's hands, which Carl J. Burckhardt, Swiss High Commissioner of Danzig, sitting next to Heydrich at a dinner party, had described as 'pre-Raphaelite, lily-white hands, formed for slow strangling'.

Heydrich's power was to grow rapidly in the years that followed the slaughter of Ernst Roehm. And the secret service network of Nazi Germany grew with him.

By February 1936 the Gestapo was given legal respectability. A Prussian statute decided to formalise what already existed in fact: the total unquestioned power of the Geheime Staatspolizei. Clause 7 of the law made it clear that there could be no appeal from any Gestapo decision. The judiciary had no power and would intervene only at its peril. An individual could be acquitted by the courts or released from prison at the end of a sentence and then rearrested by the Gestapo.

Hitler himself put it very succinctly: 'I forbid all the services of the party, its branches and affiliated associations to undertake enquiries or interrogations on matters which are the concern of the Gestapo. All incidents of a political police nature, irrespective of reports made through the party channels, have to be brought immediately to the knowledge of the competent services of the Gestapo now as before ... I particularly stress the fact that all attempts at conspiracy and high treason against the state which may come to the knowledge of the party have to be made known to the Secret State Police. It is not the business of the party to undertake on its own initiative searches and enquiries into these matters, whatever their nature.'

On 17 June 1936 Heinrich Himmler was formerly appointed Reichsfuehrer-SS und Chef der Deutschen Polizei (in stiff bureaucratic terms, RFSSuCHdDTPol). To many observers, it seemed a farcical formality: after all, Himmler had been assuming these powers for a long time, gradually eating away at the normal state apparatus and creating for himself a little kingdom responsible to no one.

All branches of the state administration were being swamped by the SS. The Prussian Gestapo became, in September, the headquarters of the political police throughout Germany. On 1 October, the term 'Gestapo' was extended to cover the unified political police of the Reich.

All this was but the first stage in Himmler's dream: he was thinking far ahead to the day when every single spy apparatus in Nazi Germany, including military intelligence, would come under his control.

The Gestapo would undergo many further organisational changes. A big start had been made. By the summer of 1936, the police in Germany was formally divided in two: the uniform and the plain clothes. The former consisted of the Order Police (ORPO). The latter was made up of Security Police (SIPO) which included the Gestapo, Criminal Investigation (KRIPO) and the SD, which was the party organisation.

The structure was abstruse – deliberately so. What it amounted to was a gigantic bureaucracy that transformed Germany into a police state.

No department worked in isolation, each interfered and intrigued in the business of the others. In overall charge of SIPO was Heydrich, determined to hold on to every vestige of power and increase his influence wherever possible.

Within three years, he was to merge the Gestapo and KRIPO and become undisputed master of a single organisation – an awesome assumption of power which was without parallel in the twentieth century, outside the machinery of terror of Soviet Russia.

Nothing, seemingly, could touch Reinhard Heydrich now. That little matter of disgrace from the navy had been put behind him. One of his old shipmates from those days had, at a naval cocktail party, imbibed too much gin and talked rather freely about Heydrich's amorous adventures. The man received a visit from the Gestapo and a sentence in a concentration camp. Heydrich reasoned quite rightly that one particular passage in his past life could safely be forgotten.

Even so, there was still one little matter to cloud his horizon.

Ancestral skeletons were being gleefully rattled by those who would be only too pleased to witness the humiliation and eclipse of the head of the SD. More precisely, there were strong rumours that Reinhard Tristan Eugen, that most professionally dedicated Nazi who was to become the scourge of Hitler's notorious enemies, the Jews, was *himself* possessed of Jewish blood and Jewish connections.

The same Gregor Strasser who perished in the Roehm purge had in 1932 received evidence from the Nazi Gauleiter of Halle Merseburg that Heydrich's paternal grandmother had, as a widow, married in 1877 an estate owner's son named Robert Suess. And this same Suess, furthermore, was Jewish.

Strasser was delighted. Here was a magnificent ingredient for a first-class scandal. A discreet enquiry was handled at the highest level. It was claimed that the offending Suess was not Jewish at all, but Lutheran. Heydrich was off the hook.

But not for long. An ancestral chart was drawn up by Nazi investigators. It showed that Reinhard Heydrich's mother was Elizabeth Maria Anna Amalie Krantz. daughter of Hofrat (Privy Councillor) Professor Krantz of Dresden. But No. 7 on the chart, which would have been an entry for Heydrich's maternal grandmother – was left blank. Neither were there any records of his mother's grandparents.

In his biography, *Heydrich: Hitler's most Evil Henchman*, author Charles Wighton writes:

'The implication of the missing grandmother is clear. The Nazi inquisitor into the Aryan blood of Reinhard

Heydrich found out all too much about this grandmother and her forebears – certainly too much to be inserted even in the confidential Party file of the Chief of the Sicherheitsdienst.'

There were other rumours – stories of a gravestone in a Leipzig cemetery bearing the name 'Sarah Heydrich'. This gravestone, it was alleged, eventually disappeared mysteriously to be replaced with another bearing the inscription 'S. Heydrich'. Just who this forebear was remains a mystery, but Heydrich's Jewish ancestry was firmly believed.

Felix Kersten, Finnish-Dutch masseur and confidant of Himmler, was to claim years later that after Heydrich's death in 1942, Himmler admitted that he had known about Heydrich's Jewish background right from the early days in the Munich police.

A horrified Hitler had been informed, but the Fuehrer had been astute enough to realise that in Heydrich he had an exceptional talent – 'highly gifted but dangerous', was Hitler's terse verdict.

Some Nazi fanatics believed that Heydrich should be disposed of. Hitler had retorted: 'On the contrary, the man is doubly valuable to us. He will always know we have the weapon of blackmail.'

This weapon, it might have been added, was also one possessed by Heydrich himself. It was encased in his invaluable and frequently used Panzers-crank, or armoured safe.

Here were filed away intimate – sometimes embarrassingly intimate – files on all the top Nazis. No one was excluded, not even the Fuehrer himself. There was an allegation that during World War I Gefreiter Adolf Hitler had been treated for syphilis: a disease the future Fuehrer had contracted in his early vagabond life in Vienna which even now could result in total paralysis.

Heydrich might perhaps have been forgiven for believing that his own position was reasonably safe.

Heydrich and his new subordinate, Schellenberg, were two

of a kind: young men on the make with a talent for organisation and a delight in power for its own sake that made conventional morality tiresome, irrelevant and, worse, potentially dangerous.

Neither trusted the other for a single instant. Heydrich played cat to Schellenberg's mouse for nine dangerous years. Only an assassin's bullet brought the game to an end.

Inside SD and Gestapo headquarters, Himmler, Heydrich and Schellenberg prepared to police Germany with a deliberately obfuscated machine: the more complicated it could be made, the less outsiders would understand or question it.

But, beyond the walls of Prinz Albrechtstrasse, Hitler's Germany knew the agents of KRIPO only as the Gestapo. It was a potentially sinister shadow in the life of everyone.

And few aspects of everyday life were to escape its tentacles.

The Sunday morning quiet of a Berlin church in the summer of 1936 was shattered rudely as a posse of uniformed SD and Gestapo edged their way to the front pews and dragged away eight members of the congregation who belonged to the Prussian Council of Brethren. Almost simultaneously at Saarbrücken, six women and a man of the Evangelical community were arrested at prayer for daring to circulate an election leaflet.

The church had previously been visited by Gestapo agents who posed as members of the congregation, even joining the long queues for Communion. Anything said from the pulpit that could be construed as remotely dissident was, of course, reported straight back to Heydrich and Mueller.

This form of Gestapo infiltration was denounced with consummate courage from the pulpit of his Church of Jesus Christ at Dahlem by the Rev. Martin Niemoeller, leader of the German Evangelical Church.

Niemoeller, a former submarine commander in World War I and initially an admirer of the Nazis, had been sadly disillusioned when Hitler came to power; he had urged his congregations to denounce National Socialism's encroachment on the freedom of worship.

In May of that same year, the Confessional Church addressed a courteous but firm memorandum to Hitler, protesting against mounting anti-semitism and increasing interference in the role of the churches.

Response was swift. The matter of the dissident Neimoeller and his tiresomely vociferous church was turned over to the Gestapo. Hundreds of pastors were arrested. One of the signatories of the memorandum, Dr Weissler, was murdered in Sachsenhausen concentration camp. The funds of the Confessional Church were confiscated and it was forbidden to make collections.

In July 1937 it was the turn of Dr Niemoeller. He was arrested and confined to Moabit prison in Berlin, was eventually hauled before a 'special court' and sent to Dachau, where he remained until liberated by the Allies at the end of the war.

Religious persecution bit even deeper. Chaplain Otto Graf, a teacher at Freiburg-im-Breisgau, had the temerity to tell his class: 'In fundamental characteristics, all men are alike, and there is a point of view which makes it possible to love and esteem all men. This is true even of Jews.'

The Roman Catholic chaplain's remarks publicised in the German Press brought forth a swift riposte from the Minister of Church Affairs, who accused Chaplain Graf of 'misusing' religious instruction to express political opinions.

The Minister added: 'His remarks were designed to raise doubts in the minds of his pupils as to the fundamental truth of the National Socialist world ideology in its racial theory, Fuehrer principle and doctrine of absolute obedience to the state.' Chaplain Graf also received a visit from the Gestapo, who administered a rebuke and told him he had lost his job.

Even the most trivial remark was construed as high treason. Another teacher, Vicar Knickenberg of Staufen, near Loerrach, lost the attention of his class when a platoon marched past the school. He shouted to his pupils: 'Stop looking at those miserable soldiers.' It was later announced that he had been 'deprived of the right to teach for lack of respect for the military'. He could only have been denounced to the Gestapo by one of his pupils.

Gestapo files were later to reveal that around 800 other pastors and leading lay followers of Niemoeller had been arrested that year.

The churches, of course, were not the only group to suffer. No one anywhere was immune.

Heinrich Mueller – soon to be dubbed Gestapo Mueller – may have professed anti-Communism. But this did not stop him being a keen disciple of Stalin's methods of forging a modern police state.

The technique, Mueller decided, was to isolate the individual so that personal trust became impossible. Mueller built up a cell system which had at its command a roster of citizens who were honorary part-time members of the Gestapo. The man in the street, anxious to shun politics and hang on to his job, had to contend with the spectre of the Blockwart, the concierge whose job was to report the activities of every tenant of his block of apartments. Every labour group had its vigilant Gestapo representative.

Mueller's activities extended even into the private lives of whole families.

Hansjurgen Koehler, who worked for several years close to Himmler and had a high position in the Berlin Gestapo, managed to escape from Germany at the outbreak of war. His memoirs, *Inside the Gestapo*, gave an insight into just how effective Mueller's technique could be:

'I used to know a Berlin family. The father was a retired naval officer, still connected with a large shipping firm. They were Aryans – not even the most painstaking research could find a single drop of Jewish blood in their veins. They had expected much from Nazism: a new national consciousness, sweeping economic reforms, a higher standard of living.

They were disappointed – at least, the father was. One night, in the privacy of their dining room, he voiced his opinions. Two days later, he was arrested and taken to a concentration camp, where he is still waiting for a release which may never come. His fair-haired little daughter, his pet and spoiled darling, had denounced him. She was twelve and had almost five years of undiluted Nazi training.'

Although it would still have been possible for the casual visitor to spend some days in Hitler's Reich and experience nothing unusual, the Gestapo was always there.

And it was at night, of course, that its agents walked abroad. At night that it came for those it had marked down, snatching victims, half-awake and terrified, from the arms of wife and children. Conversation, even in hotel lounges, was guarded and oblique.

Occasionally, something of the truth slipped out. The *Manchester Guardian* on 2 August 1934, as part of a series on the treatment of political prisoners in Germany, carried an account from one man who had previously been released from a concentration camp.

His ordeal had begun with the inevitable pick-up by the anonymous black car and the swift journey to Prinz Albrechtstrasse.

'I was taken to a room where I was searched, my notebook and some letters being taken from me. There was a table in the middle of the room and a writing desk in the background. Five officials sat down round the table. I was asked to sit down as well. I was closely questioned about persons whose names and addresses had been found in my possession (my rooms had been searched meanwhile, but nothing had been found save a few entirely harmless letters). Question followed question with extreme rapidity, hour by hour.

It was after midnight and the officials began to hit me as they questioned. My head ached. At about two or three in the morning, one of them read out a statement and told me to sign it. I was about to do so when I noticed that the sheet of paper had been skilfully folded, the edges of the folds being stuck together almost invisibly – when unfolded, they left a blank space which could be filled in with words which would not have been signed by me but would nevertheless appear over my signature.

Five pairs of eyes were fixed intently upon me. I put the pen down and said: "I'm sorry, I can't sign a statement of this kind."

"In that case, we're unlucky," said one of the officials in a dry, matter-of-fact voice.

I was taken down into the cellars and locked up in a cell. I was dead tired and fell asleep on some straw sacking . . .'

The next day the interrogation and accusations – that, among other things, the suspect had tried to get evidence to prove that the SS and SA were armed and organised in violation of the Treaty of Versailles – were resumed.

' . . . An official said to me: "So you know nothing do you?", and struck me across the head with such violence that the room seemed to spin round and I fell down. I was kicked about as I lay on the floor.

"Stand up!" one of them shouted. I had some difficulty in getting up. The same questions were again put to me, and I was again struck across the head until I collapsed, and again kicked about on the floor. This was done to me several times.

They then took me downstairs into the cellars. I sat down on a bench with other prisoners, men and women. Some had only just arrived, others had been cross-examined, and were bruised and bloodstained. I kept on coughing and spat blood; I was in great pain . . .'

From 1933, prisoners like this were to disappear into SS camps organised by Himmler, who had established his own model camp at Dachau, twenty kilometres from Munich. Himmler's brief order for protective custody ran:

'Based on Article 1 of the Decree of the Reich President for the Protection of People and State of February 28th 1933, you are taken into protective custody in the interest of public security and order. Reason: suspicion of activities inimical to the State.'

Telephone-tapping was another invaluable source of information. Here Heydrich and Mueller were able to take over highly organised surveillance techniques which had been perfected by Goering through his own organisation since 1933. With noticeably ponderous humour, Goering had dubbed it with a masterpiece of ambiguity: the Hermann Goering Research Institute.

Controlled by Rudolf Diels, it masterminded the telephonic and telegraphic networks and radio communications. Calls between Germany and abroad were monitored – and of course calls within the Reich itself.

Martha Dodd, the daughter of the American Ambassador to Berlin, wrote in *My Years In Germany*:

> 'Whenever a friend of mine connected with the Nazi party telephoned, he used another name and we had previously by word of mouth arranged a complicated language for meeting at a certain time and place without giving it away over the telephone. We both knew that all embassies were under suspicion, that particularly the American Embassy, after my father's long and consistent stand against dictatorship, would be under careful surveillance. Even though we were convinced that dictaphones had been installed in our house – perhaps before our lease or perhaps during our absences – we did occasionally talk in the rooms where there was no telephone. I had one friend, however, who refused even to talk in our sun porch which was made entirely of tiles and glass and would have been a difficult job of wiring.'

Gestapo agents in the home – almost a 'thought police' personally controlled by Mueller – were very useful, but Heydrich, forever restless and eternally keen to make a name for himself, came up with another device equally efficient. He proposed to Himmler that the SS should have its own weekly newspaper; as a propaganda organ it would have considerable value.

Himmler agreed readily enough, but he would have been as incapable of masterminding a newspaper as the most junior of his filing clerks. That job was turned over to Heydrich, who promptly appointed one of his bright young intellectuals, Gunther d'Alquen, to do the donkey work on the tabloid which was named, appropriately enough, *Das Schwarze Korps (The Black Corps)*.

D'Alquen may well have sub-edited copy and marked type sizes, but there was no doubt who was the real editor of *Das Schwarze Korps*. A technically brilliant piece of newspaper production, it was positively stuffed with Nazi propaganda. In it Heydrich unleashed all his pent-up bile against Jews and Roman Catholics.

Produced by d'Alquen with a staff of six operating from Zimmerstrasse 88, Berlin, it appeared on Thursdays, initially (in 1935) with sixteen pages. That was later raised to twenty. Within two years it was selling 189,317 copies. During the war, circulation figures topped 750,000.

The muscle of *Das Schwarze Korps* was not just its propaganda, not just signed photographs of Hitler as giveaways, not even articles by Heydrich on various aspects of Nazi policy. True, there were the gleefully reported scandals – obscene titbits such as alleged profiteering among bishops and rampant homosexuality in monasteries. But it was the letter column that proved to be of the greatest value to the SD and Gestapo.

Even correspondence critical of the Nazis was encouraged: after all, it gave some illusion of balance and open-mindedness. Naturally, the addresses of all correspondents were turned over to Mueller and appropriately vigorous action taken.

Sneaks had a field-day. On 7 June 1938, a Berliner named Paul Koch wrote to *Das Schwarze Korps* stating that a certain butcher, Gustav Schiewek, was in the habit of handing 'his customers their purchases wrapped in paper carrying an advertisement for a Jewish business'. The letter was obligingly forwarded by *Das Schwarze Korps* to the appropriate department of the SS.

Not everyone enjoyed reading Himmler's accomplished scandal sheet over their breakfast. One man who got decided indigestion was a certain Werner Grund of Zwichau who was ill-advised enough to write privately to England's Prime Minister Neville Chamberlain and thank him for his efforts to achieve peace in Europe. Grund received a courteous if somewhat sarcastic reply. But not from England.

His letter was acknowledged in the columns of *Das Schwarze Korps*.

For Schellenberg, learning his craft in the various offshoots of the Gestapo, there was a particular routine he came to dread above all others.

There would be no warning of the impending phone call from Mueller, just those flat Bavarian tones at the other end of the line saying: 'The chief would like an evening out – in mufti, of course.'

Schellenberg soon learnt that this was no cosy social invitation, but an order. A prowl round the restaurants of the Kurfuerstendamm and nightclubs was something that Heydrich could never resist. For his younger, rather priggish subordinate, these evenings were both exquisitely boring and embarrassing. More to the point, they could be dangerous, for a frequently drunken and lecherous Heydrich abandoned all caution and restraining the head of the Gestapo was not an enviable task.

Schellenberg, invariably dead tired and with a splitting headache from these nocturnal ramblings, could not help thinking how it all contrasted with Heydrich the homemaker, the bourgeois Canaris (now Admiral Canaris) and his wife.

The two families, with Schellenberg in tow, spent many pleasant weekends together – so pleasant that Schellenberg could scarcely believe in the existence of that other Heydrich, the lecherous, prowling nightclub king of pre-war Berlin.

It was during a particularly hectic evening that Heydrich concocted one of his more colourful schemes for extending the influence of the Gestapo still further. He proposed nothing less than the setting up of an SD brothel.

Of course, it would not be called anything so crude. It would all be managed with the utmost discretion. Heydrich envisaged a super night club, complete with exquisitely beautiful hostesses. Prices would be high; food and drink would be of a standard to attract diplomats, civil servants and foreign businessmen.

Under a cloak of strict anonymity, Gestapo agents were

instructed to look for a suitable location and a substantial four-storey villa in one of the best residential districts of Berlin was eventually earmarked. A madam was hired and told to recruit suitable girls. At no time was it suspected that the real owner of the establishment known as the Salon Kitty was the Gestapo.

The Salon Kitty became, of course, yet another listening post for the secret service. Monitoring equipment was installed and soon some most interesting comings-and-goings were recorded.

Ribbentrop, the German Foreign Minister, was a frequent guest. Mussolini's son-in-law, the pleasure-loving Count Ciano, had no love of the Germans, but all of a sudden he seemed to find that there was plenty of business which just had to be transacted in Berlin.

Heydrich, needless to say, made many tours of inspection and on one of these Schellenberg received a salutary lesson in just how treacherous his chief could be.

The next morning, Schellenberg received a peremptory summons to Heydrich's office.

All trace of geniality had vanished. Heydrich's Mongolian-slit eyes stared with a snake's menace. In a voice barely above a whisper he asked: 'Are you after my job, Schellenberg? I gave strict instructions that when I visited the Salon Kitty all the microphones were to be switched off. That didn't happen last night.'

Schellenberg felt a stab of fear. One of his subordinates had clearly blundered and the recording machines had done their job. Or was it a blunder? Heydrich was quite capable of setting the whole thing up in an attempt to trap Mueller's men, whom he distrusted along with everyone else.

Realising he would have to act fast or he was doomed, Schellenberg hastily secured sworn statements from the entire technical staff proving that the necessary orders had been given. Heydrich dropped the matter.

Schellenberg now knew that it was no good relaxing and expecting an automatically rosy future under Heydrich's wing.

There were rich pickings to be had, certainly, but the

guests at the feast were infinitely capable of devouring one another.

6

The shots which bespattered the brains of Gregor Strasser over a Gestapo cell had undeniably removed a very considerable annoyance for Adolf Hitler. But it had not erased the Strasser influence; Gregor's brother, Otto, was still very much alive. And, furthermore, was proving an even bigger nuisance.

An ardent revolutionary socialist, Otto had been accusing the Fuehrer of betraying party principles as far back as 1930. The wooing of big business interests and the attempt to recruit party members from the ruling classes had stung Strasser into seeking a meeting with his chief and voicing his disapproval.

Hitler had snapped: 'Either you and your brother toe the party line or get out.' Both had refused.

At that time, Hitler was gingerly edging his way to power. As allies, he needed pragmatists, not tiresome idealists. Only one course was possible. Otto Strasser was forthwith expelled.

But he had not done with Hitler yet and promptly formed Der Schwarze Front (the Black Front), a splinter group of disaffected SA men. Gregor, as has been seen, elected to stay with Hitler.

Der Schwarze Front lost no time in getting to work. Soon all parts of Germany were being flooded by a torrent of anti-Nazi propaganda.

Strasser agents crossed frontiers with copies of a newspaper called *Die Deutsche Revolution*. The papers would already be in envelopes carrying German stamps. When the agents reached Leipzig or Dresden and had visited the main post offices, they would buy enough stamps for the next consignment and return for more.

Strasser's boldness had more than a dash of impudence. On one occasion, he had an envelope of the German Medical Association sent to him in Prague and had fifty thousand facsimiles made there. He filled the facsimiles with the leaflets, left the flap unstuck and posted them in Germany as printed matter.

On doors, walls, windows, trains, trams, pavements and hoardings there also appeared a rash of stickers, carrying the legend: 'Schwarze Front will oust Hitler.'

The Fuehrer himself stormed at the blinking, stuttering Himmler: 'I demand that this propaganda be crushed forthwith and Strasser got rid of. It's an absolute priority. We're being made a laughing stock.'

One man who allowed himself to do a little laughing was Otto Strasser himself. He was perfectly aware that the entire Reich cabinet was buzzing like an upturned beehive and was out to get him. But, really, his Schwarze Front was having a lot of success.

Why, only a few days back he had received a visit from Frank, a wealthy Dutchman, who had all the signs of being a most useful ally.

Frank, who spoke somewhat halting German and was accompanied by a Jewish lawyer from Prague named Dr Soundso, came straight to the point.

He explained: 'Herr Strasser, I and my colleague want to buy five thousand copies of each number of your paper for the next three months and get them distributed all over Europe for you. I am authorised to pay you 60,000 Czech crowns on account.'

It sounded altogether too easy – just the sort of trap which Himmler and Heydrich would set up with fiendish glee. But all the signs were that the offer from Frank and Soundso was perfectly genuine. The Czech police confirmed that Frank had a bona fide passport. The Jewish lawyer appeared to be exactly what he claimed.

At the end of the three months, Frank reappeared in Prague. Strasser must come to Paris forthwith and meet Frank's chief. The head of Schwarze Front decided to make the journey. On arrival, he found his benefactor profuse with apologies.

Unfortunately, the chief had had to go to Saarbrücken to keep an appointment with a well-known anti-Nazi writer, Konrad Heiden. Would Strasser care to join them?

Frank had made a fatal mistake. A careful check would have led him to discover that Strasser and Heiden had previously known one another. As soon as he arrived in Saarbrücken, Strasser made immediate contact with the writer. Heiden knew nothing of Frank or his chief or of their alleged anti-Hitler organisation.

Now thoroughly alarmed, Strasser made his way swiftly back to his hotel. In his room, Frank was waiting for him.

The Dutchman's whole manner had changed sharply. Whereas before he had been suave and convincing, he was now noticeably ill at ease. Did he realise Strasser was suspicious?

After a few moments of casual conversation he left the room on the excuse of making a telephone call.

Now Strasser was sweating. Why should a man go out to telephone when there was a perfectly good instrument in the room already? Suddenly Strasser was remembering the knot of determined looking plain-clothes men he had seen outside the hotel. A swift abduction would not be particularly difficult.

When the man returned, Strasser said as casually as he could: 'I'll wait for your chief, but there's an appointment I must cancel.'

Disregarding his luggage, Strasser walked calmly through the hotel lobby and past the knot of Heydrich's men. Before they spotted him, he had hailed a taxi and sped away.

One man who had a lot of explaining to do was Dr Wenzel Heindl, a Gestapo operative detailed by Heydrich to track down Strasser. The mission had been a clumsy failure. Heindl's careful impersonation of Frank, plus his grooming of a Jewish Gestapo underling for the role of Soundso, had been for nothing. Heydrich would have to try again.

And Otto Strasser? He reckoned that 60,000 Czech crowns for his organisation was ample compensation for a few pieces of lost luggage. The time had clearly come to rub the Gestapo's nose in its own failure still further.

The SD and Gestapo, like security services everywhere, had their professional hitmen, impersonal technicians of terrorism who could be depended on for the really delicate missions.

Alfred Naujocks, a grocer's son from Kiel, was just fifteen years old when he first joined the National Socialist Party. It had all been due to his friend Gert Groethe. The two became inseparable, banging together many Communist heads in a succession of street brawls.

Then had come a blow for Naujocks. Groethe had been sent to Berlin to join the SD. Bereft, Naujocks longed to join him.

The idea of the SD had not appealed at first. There was a lot of unglamorous desk work attached to espionage, many of the trappings of police routine.

Eventually, Naujocks managed to get to Berlin, team up with his old friend and edge his way into the SD for a modest ninety marks a month.

Naturally ambitious, he came to the attention of Heydrich. The head of the SD tossed him a test assignment.

It was early in January 1935 that Naujocks first heard of the man he was instructed to kidnap on behalf of the Gestapo.

Naujocks was in Heydrich's office looking at a photograph carrying the caption 'Rudolf Formis'. It showed a tall, slim man with an attractive face, extremely striking eyes, a sensual mouth and dazzling teeth. Obviously one for the girls, Naujocks thought.

Heydrich filled in the background. Strasser had graduated from leaflets and stickers. Now he had set up a secret radio transmitter inside Czechoslovakia. Anti-Hitler broadcasts were being made twice a day and they were building up a disturbingly large audience in the Reich. Gestapo agents had discovered that the success of the broadcasts was due largely to a former Stuttgart radio engineer named Rudolf Formis, a recent recruit to Der Schwarze Front.

The Gestapo had previous knowledge of Formis. The

man was an idealist who had become disillusioned with National Socialism, but at first had been at a loss what to do about it.

Then during one of Hitler's speeches, the opportunity had presented itself. Formis had carefully arranged to be on duty. He waited until the Fuehrer was in full flood – and then cut the landline. Millions of German homes did not hear Hitler at all.

Formis had been one step ahead of Heydrich's agents. Now he was in Czechoslovakia – and with Otto Strasser.

Heydrich had a unique gift for assessing the strengths and weaknesses of subordinates. He thought to himself that unless Naujocks was closely briefed, the man might overreact with enthusiasm and kill Formis. Heydrich wanted the maximum glory out of this coup, and that would entail bringing the chief protagonist back alive. The Gestapo could deal with him then.

Heydrich explained this to Naujocks, adding: 'Above all, the illegal radio has got to be smashed. Let me have your proposals tomorrow morning,'

Naujocks promptly sought out the Reich engineers. They had placed the location of the radio between twelve and eighteen kilometres south-east of Prague.

'It's too nebulous to be accomplished in one trip,' he told Heydrich later. 'There must be a reconnaissance to pin-point the exact location. I propose to go with a girl on a supposed skiing trip by car. We'll just be an ordinary couple on holiday. That way I won't attract suspicion.

'When I've spotted the radio, I'll return here and make further plans.'

Heydrich was uneasy. The girl would be bound to take the agent's mind off his work. And, anyway, could she be trusted? Naujocks had proposed taking as cover a petite and pretty Berliner named Edith Karlebach who shared an apartment with his fiancée.

Heydrich laughed sarcastically: 'You seem to have worked it all out, my dear Naujocks. Obviously you are going to benefit enormously from this trip.' Then his tone became icy and Naujocks felt a tightening of the stomach muscles. 'Just remember that you have a job to do as well. I don't expect any slip-ups.'

For Rudolf Formis, the choice of *Der Freiheitssender* – the Freedom Sender or Liberty Radio – had been all important. Formis was the supreme professional. He held a diploma for the first radio apparatus ever used in Germany and had been a pioneer in the development of short-wave. He recognised that the site within Czechoslovakia had to be both technically suitable and secret: secret from the Czech Police and, above all, the Gestapo. His choice fell eventually on a lonely picturesque weekend inn, the Hotel Zahori. It was about thirty-two kilometres south of Prague in the valley of the Moldau.

Autumn was approaching and the valley was getting progressively colder. The proprietor was only too glad to have an out-of-season guest. He was a Czech patriot and disinclined to ask too many questions.

Formis had ample leisure to make his preparations. He installed the transmitter in the rafters of the loft. Only a thoroughly efficient search would have uncovered the cunningly concealed microphone which had been trailed down into Formis's bedroom.

Once a month Formis had dinner with Otto Strasser in the hotel, and his chief would hand over the latest batch of recorded anti-Nazi speeches which would be beamed into the Reich.

On 16 January 1935 the two men met for the last time. Strasser was acutely conscious of one serious weakness. Formis was utterly unprotected. A regular bodyguard would have been risky and would have attracted too much attention. Besides, bodyguards were expensive. There was always a risk, too, that a bodyguard would talk.

Strasser asked anxiously: 'Are there any other visitors? Have you noticed anything suspicious?'

Formis replied: 'There's a young couple here for the skiing. He's Alfred Gerber, a businessman from Kiel. Edith Karlebach, as far as I can gather, is a Berlin schoolteacher. They seem harmless enough.'

Alfred Naujocks thoroughly approved of the Mercedes

which the Gestapo had supplied. Paraphernalia for a skiing holiday had been particularly well chosen and didn't look suspiciously new. As well as the skis there were knapsacks, baskets, a couple of cameras, powerful binoculars and a set of clothes. These things were hardly likely to attract attention, any more than the well-thumbed maps which would obviously be needed by German holidaymakers touring the area as well as sampling the ski-slopes.

Heydrich had stressed Hitler's impatience to get the radio destroyed, but Naujocks refused to be hurried. He would take his time looking for the site. Haring around at top speed and asking too many questions would put paid to the whole mission.

Naujocks decided to make his headquarters in Prague and explore the area. For a time the search was fruitless then one morning he and Edith crossed the city, making for a trunk road which would take them to Pribram.

Signposts also offered Dubenee, which was one kilometre ahead, and Obory which was twelve.

Naujocks felt that if he had been in Formis's shoes he would have wanted to put as much distance as possible between himself and the Czech capital. He turned the Mercedes down the Obory road.

Further along, a sign indicated the Hotel Zahori. The couple were tired. Naujocks decided to stop for a while, get some food and nose around with some discreet questions.

At the hotel's entrance, Naujocks noticed a fresh set of tyre marks and a pair of skis leaning against a garage wall. So much the better if there was a holidaymaker there. It would make their own appearance seem perfectly natural.

The Zahori's interior was almost a tourist cliché: stags' heads, guns and sporting prints. But it was doubtful whether Naujocks even noticed the room or tasted his scalding coffee.

It was a little while before the other man in the lounge turned round and faced the newcomers. Naujocks took in a sensual mouth and dazzling teeth.

His mind raced back to the photograph he had seen in Heydrich's office. Yes, he was virtually certain that the other visitor to the Hotel Zahori was none other than

Rudolf Formis.

It proved easy enough to strike up a conversation and quite naturally the couple suggested getting together for a day's skiing. For Naujocks, it would be an opportunity to take holiday snaps of his suspect.

Naujocks was anxious to make one all-important check. He made the excuse of having to unpack now he and Edith had decided to stay.

He walked as casually as possible to the front of the hotel, noting thankfully that the evening was still light.

He climbed into the car, slammed it into reverse and moved away from the front windows of the Zahori.

When he had made sure that he could not be spotted from the hotel he whipped out powerful binoculars and trained them on the roof.

What he saw made him smile grimly. Over the roof top, a few centimetres from a dormer window, there protruded a short cylinder. Naujocks knew a telescopic antenna when he saw it. The Zeiss binoculars even picked out the white wire which connected it with – where?

Probably Formis's bedroom. If the man *was* Formis.

The priority was to get to Berlin with the photographs he would have next day and find out.

Of course, there was a chance that the man might make good his escape in the meantime, but the risk had to be taken. Anyway, he did not think it very likely. He had noticed the appreciative looks the stranger had cast at Edith.

The next day's skiing was pleasant enough and Naujocks got his photographs without difficulty. It was at breakfast that the blow came. The stranger suddenly said: 'I have a business lunch in Prague but I'll be back before the end of the day.'

Naujocks strove to appear normal. Was the man suspicious? Had he any intention of returning? He might well take the radio with him. Either way, Berlin must see those photographs.

With his quarry safely on his way, Naujocks went to his room to get ready for the drive to the airport. Outside the stranger's bedroom, a key protruded. Obviously the room was being cleaned. Naujocks quickly slid the key from the lock and pressed it into the lump of wax in his pocket.

Back in Berlin, Naujocks received no congratulations from Heydrich, who merely said: 'The photographs confirm the man is Formis. It was your job to track him down. Getting him here in one piece is going to prove a lot harder.

'You're going to need help. Take someone you can rely on.'

There could only be one man to share his mission: his old friend Groethe. They could actually have some fun together.

Otto Strasser was a survivor. He outwitted Gestapo agents in Berlin, Paris and Vienna. He prided himself that one of the reasons he was still alive was an inbuilt instinct for danger. The more he heard about the nice Alfred Gerber and the personable Miss Karlebach the more alarmed he became.

Strasser urged Formis: 'Keep in touch with the local police. They have no love for the Gestapo. And be on your guard.'

Naujocks and Groethe took the afternoon plane to Prague. It had been arranged that Groethe should stay at a nearby boarding house, while Naujocks returned to the hotel. He knew that if Formis stuck to his usual transmission schedule there would be a broadcast that night.

Naujocks planned to slip into Formis's bedroom. When Formis arrived, Naujocks would jump on him with a chloroform pad. Groethe would then climb into Formis's bedroom. Together they would lower the unconscious man to the car. They would drive at high speed to Prague and put Edith on a train for Berlin. After that, the Mercedes would streak for the border.

In the dining-room, there was no sign of Formis. Later, Naujocks found him in the bar huddled over a brandy. He looked frightened and seemed drunk. He barely acknowledged Naujocks's greeting and left hurriedly.

Naujocks reasoned that the man's suspicions had hardened, but because of the presence of the radio he could not leave.

His first instinct was to act at once, to seize Formis and get out of the hotel, damning the consequences. But that did not solve the problem of the radio.

If the hotel was in league with Strasser, the precious equipment could be smuggled out in a matter of minutes.

He sat in his room, hardly knowing how to interpret the almost total silence. What was Formis up to? Had he already left? Then just before eight he heard steps in the corridor. Was Formis going to his room? No, of course, to the attic. For fifteen minutes there was more silence. Then the sounds were repeated.

An hour later, Naujocks decided that the time had come to call on Groethe. The agreed signal was made. Naujocks opened the window and threw out a rope. He felt two short tugs then one long. Naujocks hauled in the rope. He attached two suitcases and dangled the load from the window. Groethe had his instructions to place the luggage in the back of the Mercedes. Finally, he was hauled into Naujocks's bedroom.

The two men went over their plans once again: Formis would be leapt upon with the chloroform pad when he next returned from the attic. A bottle of phosphorus would take care of the radio set.

It seemed like eternity until Formis was once again heard ascending to the attic. Naujocks stepped into the corridor. He thrust the skeleton key into the lock. He fought down mounting panic as he realised that it had jammed. The SD had supplied him with a copy from the wax impression but clearly the experts had blundered. Naujocks had taken the excellence of Heydrich's back-up services for granted. My God, they were amateurs back in Berlin.

There was no time to waste for now there was Formis's anxious voice saying: 'Who is there? What do you want?'

Naujocks said desperately: 'It's me, Alfred. Can you possibly lend me some soap?'

Formis opened the door a crack. Naujocks's hand streaked for his revolver. Then he was in the room and at Formis's throat. But Strasser's agent was lithe, athletic. He broke free, darted back and threw himself at the other man. Formis was looking for his own weapon now but he was wearing a dressing-gown and the weapon was tangled in the folds. Then a bullet from Formis's gun tore into Naujocks's hand. Where the hell was Groethe? There was a fresh shot. Formis bunched forward, then straightened before hurtling to the floor.

Naujocks barely took in the dead man. By now he had other wounds. Unspeakable pain was coursing through one leg. The wound in the hand was slight but that was smarting badly.

Even so, he did not forget to wrench open the case containing the transmitter. The phosphorus was poured in.

For a moment he thought the room had been torn apart. The phosphorus clutched at air already heavy with chloroform. It was eating into the cuts on Naujocks's hands, too. He staggered, gasping and choking, into his own room, barely able to throw open the window.

Groethe took charge. The hotel staff, who had flocked outside Formis's room, were menaced with a revolver. Groethe snarled: 'Anyone who tries to leave will be shot. Get down to the cellars.'

Naujocks managed to drag a dazed Edith to her feet, yelling for Groethe to wrench out the telephone wires. To leave by the front door was out of the question. God knows what burglar alarms were below and where they would be triggered off. Descent could only be by the window.

Somehow, the trio slithered down the rope and catapulted towards the Mercedes. Naujocks, despite the excruciating agony from his wounds, elected to drive. Pain shot through his left leg every time he pressed the clutch for a gear change.

It had been planned that the powerful Mercedes would eat up the kilometres first to the station where Edith would be decamped and then on to the frontiers of Germany. But Naujocks was simply too exhausted to keep up a consistently high speed.

Outside the station, the weary Naujocks ordered Edith: 'Take your ticket from my right hand pocket. You've got seven minutes till the train leaves. Good luck.'

The pain started up again as Naujocks forced himself into a pair of mittens to conceal his hands. Casually, he and

74

Groethe went to the gate reserved for pedestrians. Naujocks fought down fatigue and nausea as Groethe waved the passports. The customs officer handed them back without so much as a glance at their owners.

Naujocks and Groethe were back in Germany.

Hotel managers in the Reich had long since learnt that it did not do to ask too many questions from hotel guests who were either SD or Gestapo members. And that applied to guests who might turn up with wounds caused both by gunshot and phosphorus. Naujocks naturally raised no objection when a hastily summoned doctor tended the wounds and announced that he would have to inform the civil police. A quick word with Heydrich in the morning would take care of *that*.

The next day, Naujocks and Groethe recovered the car and sped to Berlin – and the office of Reinhard Heydrich.

Naujocks's story threw the Gestapo's supremo into a paroxysm of rage. A killing had specifically been forbidden. The mission had been to kidnap Formis and destroy the transmitter. The whole affair might have been written by a hack Hollywood screenwriter. God knows what the complications with the Czech authorities might be. Their Press would have a field day. As for the Fuehrer . . . Well, Heydrich dared not think of that.

Hitler's exasperation with Strasser was such, however, that he was more than delighted with Naujocks's success. An important section of opposition had been removed; the ensuing complications shrunk into insignificance. Heydrich was dumbfounded. As with all his subordinates, he longed to find a stick with which to beat Naujocks. He contented himself with a characteristic piece of spite: the Fuehrer's congratulations to Naujocks were not passed on.

A few days later, the heavily censored German newspapers were given a prepared statement:

'During the night of 23/24 January, a German emigrant in Czechoslovakia by the name of Rudolf Formis was found killed by a bullet from a revolver in a hotel near

Pribram. The Czech authorities say they suspect two men and a woman of German nationality of being the authors of the crime, but no further details have been supplied.'

Nazi diplomats, knowing that the Czechs were already fearful of Hitler, made tactful approaches and the matter was kept out of the Czech Press.

Heydrich may not have cared for the way that the Formis incident had been handled, but he had long relished a role outside Germany for the Gestapo. It had proved that it could work with some success on foreign soil. Other far stiffer tests were to follow.

But, before that, a particularly lurid domestic scandal was to occupy all the serpentine ingenuity of Reinhard Heydrich. Already he had shown himself no stranger to such phenomena.

7

Under an imposing oil portrait of Germany's Iron Chancellor, Otto von Bismarck, seven of the most powerful men in the Third Reich settled comfortably in big armchairs in Hitler's cabinet office. Outside, Berlin shivered in the sharp winter cold.

Something of that chill was to penetrate the Reich Chancellery in the Wilhelmstrasse on that fateful day in November 1937. But that particular fall in temperature had nothing to do with the climate. For on that day Germany took the fatal step towards world war – and the ultimate shame of total defeat.

At forty-eight, Adolf Hitler had carried out a ruthless domestic revolution, its success hastened by the awesome efficiency of the Gestapo.

It was all undeniably impressive, but for the Fuehrer it

was far from being enough. The time had come to implement the next stage of National Socialist policy – *Lebensraum*, living space for the German people.

Hitler spoke for close on four hours. He started with the flat statement: 'It is my intention, either by diplomacy or by war to annex my birthplace, Austria, and then Czechoslovakia and Poland. After that, it will be the turn of Soviet Russia.

'I wish to make clear that my decision is final. The Anglo-French powers fear the prospect of world war so much that they will do nothing.'

Then Hitler went into detail, stressing that the whole operation was to be comfortably concluded by the end of 1943.

If Hitler had expected elation from the heads of the various branches of the armed forces, he was disappointed. All those present listened first in open-mouthed disbelief and then in consternation. The first protests came from Generalfeldmarschall Werner von Blomberg, the War Minister, and from the commander-in-chief Generaloberst Werner Freiherr von Fritsch.

Desperately and with passion, they pointed out to Hitler that such proposals would inevitably mean war with England and France.

Von Fritsch stressed: 'I have to tell you, my Fuehrer, that it is a war which Germany is utterly unprepared to fight, let alone win.' There was a murmur of support from navy chief Admiral Erich Raeder.

Nervously, Constantin von Neurath, the Foreign Minister, reminded Hitler of his promise to von Hindenburg that never again would Germany be involved in a world war.

Hitler had one sole supporter – at least, outwardly. For all his bluster, Hermann Goering, head of the Luftwaffe, had never been able to stand up to his Fuehrer. Besides, Goering, realising that control of the Gestapo had slipped away from him for ever, was hungry for more power.

After all, Hitler had achieved much already without bloodshed. The previous year, Germany had denounced the Locarno Treaty and reoccupied the demilitarised zone of the Rhineland. That had taken just thirteen battalions of infantry and thirteen of artillery. What had the Western powers done? Precisely nothing! Obviously, reflected Goering, there were some rich pickings to be had in Europe at relatively little cost.

The meeting broke up. Hitler was left to his reflections. He had thought that he had dealt opposition a deadly blow at the time of the Roehm purge. Now it seemed that a new enemy presented itself. The army had always been a stumbling-block. It would plainly become necessary to clip the wings of the damned upper crust, *die Oberschicht*. But Hitler was determined to move slowly against the field-grey establishment. He needed their moral support and, above all, their muscle. The moment would have to be picked with care.

In the month following the secret get-together of service chiefs in Hitler's Chancellery, Germany bade farewell to one of its most illustrious sons.

Generaloberst Erich Ludendorff, von Hindenburg's chief-of-staff in World War I, was being buried. There came the thud of muffled drums and the crack of a nineteen-gun salute from the Hofgarten battery in Munich. The simple oak coffin, mounted on a gun carriage, began its solemn final journey.

If it had not been for the swastikas on the uniforms, observers could well have been forgiven for thinking that there had been no Great War, no end to the monarchy, no economic depression – and no Hitler. The coffin was draped with the colours of the Kaiser. Proud veterans wore the old imperial uniform. More than a man was being buried that day: it was the defiant death rattle of the old order.

Hitler had walked in front of the procession, flanked by Goering and von Blomberg, the latter resplendent in the uniform of the first Generalfeldmarschall Hitler had created.

After the ceremony was over, von Blomberg walked with Hitler towards the waiting cars. He said deferentially: 'Mein Fuehrer, can I speak to you in private?'

Hitler respected von Blomberg; the man was

less standoffish than some of the other generals who somehow always managed to convey to the Fuehrer that after all he was nothing but a former Gefreiter.

Unhesitatingly, Hitler took the Generalfeldmarschall back to the small apartment he kept in Munich.

Sixty-year-old von Blomberg came straight to the point. He said: 'Mein Fuehrer, I wish to seek permission to marry again.'

The news was hardly surprising. Von Blomberg was a good-looking man who had been a widower for some years. His children were grown up, one daughter married to the son of Generaloberst Keitel, one of Hitler's closest associates.

Von Blomberg was well known in Berlin café society and would be a good catch for any matron. It was common knowledge that he had a long-standing mistress.

Von Blomberg's next remark, however, slightly took Hitler aback. The other man said cautiously: 'My fiancée is of the people, Mein Fuehrer – a secretary with the Reich Egg Board. But surely that is what National Socialism is all about?'

Hitler hesitated, then agreed. Such a marriage would look good and democratic. The morals of some of the officers were, in Hitler's rather prim estimation, decidedly lurid. Von Blomberg's choice of wife was scarcely likely to cause trouble.

Goering, in whom von Blomberg also confided, was equally enthusiastic. In a mood of raucous bonhomie, the fat one slapped von Blomberg on the back in congratulation. It was then that the Generalfeldmarschall raised a somewhat delicate matter. Erna, the lady in question, had another lover who could prove difficult. Goering was breezily optimistic.

Erna's other entanglement was heard of no more. The story was that he had been presented with a sum of money and a one-way ticket to South America. It was doubtful whether Goering even needed to whisper the name of the Gestapo.

Nevertheless, Heydrich's bulging filing cabinets had

more than enough room for a potentially useful dossier on the Frau Generalfeldmarschall. But the time to act was not yet. Heydrich composed himself in patience.

On 12 January 1938, the German newspapers announced that Generalfeldmarschall Werner von Blomberg, Minister of War, had married Fräulein Erna Gruhn in Berlin. Witnesses at the wedding had been Adolf Hitler and Hermann Goering.

It had been a civil ceremony; well, that was understandable in the current climate in which churches were frowned on. There had been no pictures in the papers. Normally, the wedding of such a senior soldier would have attracted a great many column inches. On the other hand, it had to be remembered that von Blomberg was scarcely a young man. Berlin society agreed that a quiet wedding was more seemly.

There was a brief honeymoon and von Blomberg was soon back at work. Everything seemed normal enough – except to a certain Graf Wolf Heinrich von Helldorf, Berlin president of police.

A few days after the marriage, the press had carried an agency photograph of von Blomberg and his attractive young wife. It was what was known in the trade as a 'snatch photograph' – the couple had been caught unawares walking in the Leipzig zoo.

A flicker of memory stirred. Helldorf quickly sent for a print and instituted a few discreet enquiries. The dossier which arrived on the police chief's desk was nothing short of dynamite.

Erna's mother had been a registered masseuse and the girl, born in 1914 in Neukoelln, a working-class district of Berlin, had left home at eighteen to live with her Jewish lover, forty-one-year-old Heinrich Lowinger. He had persuaded Erna to pose for pornographic pictures as a way of making money. They had both been arrested.

As Helldorf thumbed through the dossier, a sheaf of glossy photographs cascaded on his desk. They were of a variety of sexual poses involving a man, a woman and a wax candle.

There could be no doubt that the file did belong to the

wife of the Generalfeldmarschall. A change of address had been registered: it was that of von Blomberg.

Von Helldorf was gripped with acute anxiety. He was a professional policeman, not a dealer in scandal. He had none of the power of the Gestapo and would be held personally responsible for any mistakes. Even more serious, the Fuehrer was implicated: he had been a witness at von Blomberg's wedding.

Who could be trusted? With considerable nervousness, von Helldorf forwarded the dossier to Goering, who scanned it with a mixture of incredulity and self-satisfaction.

The downfall of von Blomberg suited Goering. It left a vacancy for a top job. He moved fast. Hitler was away in Munich; Goering convened a council of war with Himmler and Heydrich.

Then Goering, shorn of his recent bonhomie, tackled von Blomberg head on and told him: 'You must get out. You must go into hiding abroad.'

Heydrich also had much cause for self-satisfaction. He had resisted the temptation to produce his own files on von Blomberg – an ace card which had been retained until the right time. Heydrich's file on Erna admirably supplemented those of von Helldorf.

She had been arrested in 1933 by Artur Nebe of the KRIPO, an old crony of Heydrich. Nebe's department had her fingerprints on record and much else besides. The Gestapo had received anonymous telephone calls from some of Erna's twilight friends anxious to work off old grudges.

The fact that the police dossier had turned up so conveniently *after* von Blomberg's wedding gave the bizarre affair just the right piquancy. Undoubtedly, reflected Heydrich, timing had been perfect. Not that fate had done with the upper crust just yet. The Gestapo's expertise in character assassination was very soon needed again.

The commander-in-chief of the German army was everyone's popular idea of the typical Prussian officer. Von Fritsch sported a monocle as if it were part of his uniform. He stood ramrod stiff and had the naive belief that everything he said would, since he was an officer and a gentleman, be automatically believed. Hitler focused concentrated hatred on this basically honourable member of the officer caste who, above all others, seemingly threatened to obstruct his future plans for Germany's destiny.

Even so, Hitler was staggered to have pressed into his hands so soon yet another dossier which brought potentially lethal discredit on the army.

It was a masterly compilation and a considerable tribute to the efficiency of Himmler and Heydrich and, through them, Heinrich Mueller.

Among all the files and folders with which he was surrounded, few were so useful to Mueller as those containing the list of regular informers. Any number of narks, anxious to avoid the more unpleasant excesses of the Gestapo, offered to trade titbits if only they would be left alone. Few had the intelligence to realise that the more valuable the information they supplied, the more vulnerable they became. Eventually, the Gestapo would pick up its informants and silence them, but not until they had been bled completely dry.

Mueller's cold thin lips twisted in distaste as he regarded the shifty wax-faced specimen who now sat opposite him.

At thirty-one, Hans Schmidt was a notorious male prostitute who undeniably would have rotted away in jail if the Gestapo had not bought him. He had proved invaluable, although Mueller would never have dreamed of telling him so.

Schmidt's speciality was spying on rich homosexuals and blackmailing them, preferably in the act. The fact that he frequently masqueraded as a policeman and demanded money with threats of prosecution by no means invalidated him in Mueller's eyes.

As it happened, Schmidt was currently serving a prison sentence. Mueller wanted information and sent for the blackmailer.

The interrogation was lengthy, but there was no need for physical violence. Schmidt was constitutionally incapable of heroics; he simply talked.

Out poured the list of homosexuals he had blackmailed –

high officials, doctors, lawyers, tradesmer   Blon
     Some of the names made even Muell   Th
brows, but when the name of von Fritsch w   even
managed to keep his eyes impassive beneath their heavy
lids.

Schmidt had talked to policemen so often that he had
begun to sound like them.

In a dreary monotone, this is what it was later claimed he
told Mueller:

'One evening in November 1933 I noticed at the Wannsee railway station a well-dressed gentleman who had
been picked up by a colleague, a male prostitute known to
the police. The person accosted had the appearance of a
former officer – fur jacket, green hat, silver-topped cane
and monocle. I followed the two men and after a short
interview on a building site behind the station accosted the
old gentleman. I told him I was Detective Inspector Kroger
and threatened to arrest him. The General produced an
army ID card and said, "I am Generaloberst von Fritsch."

'As the man had little money in his notecase, I accompanied him to his home in Lichterfelde. For several weeks I
blackmailed him, even forcing him to draw money from the
bank . . .'

Mueller could scarcely believe his luck. The upright von
Fritsch, ramrod-backed paragon of the army, a blatant
monarchist who had scarcely veiled his contempt for
National Socialism! If the testament of the creature
Schmidt could be found to be true, the moral blow to the
old order would be devastating.

A transcript of the Schmidt interrogation was forwarded
to Hitler. The Fuehrer flew into a blind rage. Homosexuality had been rampant among Roehm and his followers. It had been possible to deal with them. And now here
seemed to be fresh evidence of yet more perversion.

It was too much. Hitler stormed: 'I want this utter filth
destroyed.'

News of the order reached Himmler and Heydrich. They
realised that they must nail von Fritsch quickly or lose the
day. Even more disturbing, they learnt that Hitler doubted
von Fritsch's guilt and was even thinking of giving him von

...berg's job.

...ey lost no time in contacting the Fuehrer, who was ...tually won round. Soon he was snapping: 'Von Fritsch is not only a pervert, but a liar. I am relieving him of his command. But no one will say that I condemn a man without a hearing. I want him here this evening.'

It was a dramatic interview. Hitler, flanked by Goering, informed von Fritsch of the evidence against him. White-faced, the commander-in-chief indignantly denied the charge.

The Fuehrer's next action was straight out of cheap melodrama. He strode across his study to a side door and flung it open. There was the odious Schmidt, obligingly supplied by the Gestapo. The blackmailer pointed to the uniformed von Fritsch and shouted: 'That's him. That's the man.'

Without the slightest sense of the ridiculous, the accused man reddened at the sight of Schmidt, saying coldly: 'The gentleman must be mistaken.'

The wretched von Fritsch then proceeded to make matters a hundred times worse. He turned to Hitler and stumbled: 'Perhaps I am being accused of that affair over the Hitler Jugend?'

Hitler stared at von Fritsch in horror. What was this? Yet another scandal and one concerning an echelon within his very own pet organisation, the Hitler Youth.

Von Fritsch went on to explain haltingly that in 1933 he had befriended a needy member of the Hitler Youth named Fritz Wermelkirch and fixed him up with an apprentice's job at the Mercedes Benz factory at Marienfelde. Wermelkirch had repaid Fritsch's kindness by turning to theft and bragging to his underworld friends of his high connections within the army. Could it be, he suggested, that Wemelkirch had been a plant by the Gestapo? Von Fritsch had flung him out; was the whole thing a frame-up from the start?

Hitler by now was deaf to all reason. Whatever the truth of the matter, there was altogether too much scandal. Von Fritsch must resign at once.

But that the proud and stubborn commander-in-chief

refused to do. He demanded his entitlement: an official enquiry. Hitler temporised. The next day he telephoned von Fritsch and ordered him to visit Gestapo headquarters and, if he could, refute the charges which had been made against him.

To his closest confidants, the Fuehrer made it abundantly clear that he was no longer interested in the wrongs and rights of the matter. Both von Blomberg and von Fritsch had muddied the reputation of the army. That was bad enough, but the whole National Socialist state had been made to look decidedly grubby. The time had come to dispose of both these embarrassments quickly.

Heydrich saw possible disaster ahead. If a tribunal was held, the whole of Schmidt's testimony would come under the spotlight. It was full of holes and unlikely to stand up in court for very long. Schmidt had alleged that von Fritsch had an address at Lichterfelde, but there was no independent statement to confirm it. Not only were there no details of significant withdrawals from his bank account during the period it was alleged blackmail payments had been made, but there was no evidence that he even had an account in a bank at Lichterfelde.

An obvious question would occur to any tribunal: just how reliable – or how authentic – was the document that reached Hitler, following the original interrogation of the blackmailer? Had Mueller, prompted by Heydrich, coloured it more than somewhat to discredit von Fritsch?

Hitler had been fed the story of his commander-in-chief's homosexuality and had been persuaded to swallow it. In some ways he could not be blamed. History was, after all, full of precedents. There were still many who remembered the scandal surrounding the Kaiser's cabinet chief, Count Hulsen-Haeseler, who in 1906 had collapsed with a heart attack when dancing on a table. That would have been of little consequence if Hulsen-Haeseler had not been in the costume of a female ballet dancer at the time. Then there had been the matter of Prince Eulenberg, who had conducted a torrid affair with a cuirassier, Kuno von Moltke. Clearly fresh abscesses must be lanced quickly.

On Saturday, 3 February 1938 the blow fell. Hitler came on the Reich radio to announce an important reshuffle. The Foreign Minister, the Freiherr von Neurath, would be replaced by Joachim von Ribbentrop, recently Ambassador in London. Generalfeldmarschall von Blomberg, the Fuehrer announced, was retiring. At the same time, the commander-in-chief Generaloberst von Fritsch had asked to be relieved of his command because of ill-health.

Hitler went even further. Cocking a snook at the army was not enough, their faces must be rubbed in the dust. The Defence Ministry would be abolished. A new organisation, the Oberkommando der Werhrmacht (OKW) would take its place and would be the supreme command of the armed forces. Moreover, Hitler himself would lead it. The Fuehrer's personal representative would be General der Artillerie Wilhelm Keitel. Goering, more or less as a sop, was made Generalfeldmarschall.

Hitler was only too conscious of the army's smouldering resentment. But he was a shrewd enough tactician to make some concessions to the Establishment he despised. The von Blomberg affair could be quietly forgotten; the unfortunate Generalfeldmarschall had made a sorry error of judgement. But von Fritsch – that was altogether a different matter. It would be elementary justice to convene a tribunal. Anyway, the truth must come out.

For Heydrich, this was a decidedly tight corner. He enlisted the aid of Goering and Himmler. Everything must be done to persuade Hitler to drop the idea.

But the army's blood was up. Von Fritsch's fellow officers, backed by the examining magistrates, began to do some detective work of their own. It was to have some highly dramatic results

The investigators visited the Lichterfelde district, where Schmidt had alleged von Fritsch had gone to collect some money. There was no one named von Fritsch at the relevant address.

The investigators idly scanned the nameplates outside the block of apartments. One made them pull up short. It read: "Rittmeister von Frisch".

A housekeeper answered. No, they certainly could not

see the Rittmeister. He was bedridden and very ill. But the visitors scarcely heard her. In the front hall their attention was riveted by a green hat, a short coat with a fur collar and a walking stick with a silver knob.

They made to leave quickly, but were stopped in their tracks by the housekeeper. She asked curiously: 'What's wrong this time?' Soon the reason for the question became obvious: the Gestapo had been the day before. Anxious to conceal the real culprit at Wannsee station, Heydrich's agents had outstripped the army.

Even then, the full implications were not realised and the army made a bad mistake. A full twenty-four hours were allowed to elapse before anyone returned to question the sick Rittmeister. Furthermore, the magistrates discovered that Meisinger, a former Munich detective and protégé of Mueller, had checked von Fritsch's bank statements.

The wretched von Frisch, a dying man, then became the subject of a sordid tug-of-war between Goering and Himmler, the army high command and the Ministry of Justice. The army establishment won: an order was sent to the Gestapo to release the essential witness.

Hastily, von Frisch was removed from Prinz Albrecht-strasse to the federal penitentiary. The magistrates, only too conscious that he could not last long, remorselessly inter-rogated von Frisch. Just before he died, he readily con-fessed to being the Lichterfelde blackmail victim.

To von Fritsch's supporters, the implication was clear: von Fritsch had been the victim of a calculated smear campaign by the Gestapo. There was an immediate call for the libelled former commander-in-chief to be reinstated.

Heydrich assessed the situation. He realised that unless he came up with a convincing explanation, his whole meticulously constructed world of deceit, half-truths and terror would collapse around him. The army would de-mand his blood and Hitler would not be in a position to ignore it.

Heydrich began to plan for the tribunal that was con-vened on 11 March and would consist of the two presidents of the Leipzig Supreme Court and the heads of the three services – Generaloberst von Brauchitsch, Admiral Erich

Raeder and Hermann Goering, who in addition to being commander-in-chief of the Air Force, would preside.

Heydrich was adept at moving fast when his own skin was threatened. His tactics would be these: certainly there had been some confusion over von Fritsch and von Frisch. But *both* were homosexual and *both* being fleeced by Schmidt.

The blackmailer was hastily brought from the Gestapo cellars and coached by Heydrich with a new story. It is unlikely that Schmidt raised many objections. After all, there would be a fresh dossier conveniently on hand to reveal the real truth about the whole business. Heydrich reflected, not for the first time, that once you had power, life could become wonderfully simple.

But Hitler had other things on his mind besides the moral peccadilloes of certain members of the army. The tribunal had barely opened before it was adjourned hastily. Goering, von Brauchitsch and Raeder sped towards the Chancellery.

On 12 March, the troops of the Third Reich were pouring into Austria. Two days later, Hitler himself was in Vienna, the former imperial capital which he felt had spurned him in his youth but which was now throwing flowers in his path and greeting him as a liberator.

Himmler too had other things on his mind; the SS was beginning the round-up of political 'unreliables' – within a few weeks the numbers reached around 80,000 in Vienna alone. Needless to say, the SD was just as busy.

It was a whole week before the von Fritsch tribunal could be reconvened. By now there was a general feeling that the sordid business must be got out of the way as soon as possible. There were more important events in the air.

Goering, still resentful of losing control of the Gestapo, was in no mood to let Heydrich off the hook. Besides, the evidence in favour of von Fritsch was far too strong to be gainsaid.

In the witness box, Schmidt was asked: 'Did the Gestapo threaten you before you came into court this morning? What did they say would happen to you?'

Schmidt was a creature used to whispering threats in dark alleys, to heartless bullying when he knew he held all the cards. In the glare of open court he had the resilience of a punched paper-bag.

Nervously, he replied: 'Herr Meisinger told me that if I did not stick to my previous statements I would be in heaven by the morning.'

The court was not slow to seize on this picturesque phrase. It was not a style of speech that anyone would associate with Schmidt. His answer had the ring of truth. Meisinger was the next witness. Yes, he confessed uneasily, he had used the phrase but only to impress on Schmidt the need to tell the truth.

Goering rose to cross-examine the blackmailer. A skilled interrogator, he decided on a 'sweet and sour' technique.

At first, the newly created Generalfeldmarschall positively oozed bonhomie. He said reasonably: 'Schmidt, surely the time has come to tell the truth. There have been lies enough in this business.'

Truth was all very well, but Schmidt had seen the inside of the Prinz Albrechtstrasse. If he went against Heydrich's orders he doubted if he would see heaven quite as quickly as the morning; the Gestapo would play with him a little longer than that. He struck rigidly to his original story.

Goering changed. He did not make the mistake of losing his temper as he had during the Reichstag hearing, but he nevertheless threatened Schmidt, telling him that he could be as adept at dealing out punishment as the Gestapo.

For Schmidt, it was enough. He confessed that the man at Wannsee had been Rittmeister von Frisch. No one else had been blackmailed. Von Fritsch was acquitted.

Heydrich's immediate reaction was to order Schellenberg to his private office, adding: 'Bring a service pistol and plenty of ammunition with you.'

Schellenberg was greeted distantly and invited to stay to dinner with Heydrich and his adjutant. The meal was silent and the atmosphere tense. Heydrich suddenly said: 'I've heard you're an excellent shot.' Schellenberg was and said so. Heydrich seemed satisfied but was still ill at ease. After the meal, he took a considerable number of aspirins and without preamble stated: 'If they don't start marching from Potsdam in the next hour and a half the biggest danger will have passed.'

Heydrich's fear eventually led him to talk frankly. The SS was certainly at risk from an army putsch. Closely placed spies within the High Command had reported that a group of officers had been so enraged by the von Fritsch affair that they were planning violent action. The presence of a bodyguard was reassuring.

Schellenberg was not allowed to leave until one in the morning. As he slipped from the room, Heydrich's adjutant murmured: 'There hasn't been much evidence of outstanding bravery tonight.' Schellenberg could only agree.

The week following his acquittal, von Fritsch received a letter from Hitler congratulating him on recovering his health, but there was no hint of an apology from the Fuehrer for the way in which one of the army's most celebrated figures had been treated. Some time later von Fritsch was made honorary Oberst of his regiment. When war broke out in 1939, von Fritsch was with the victorious German armies before Warsaw. It is believed he contrived to get himself killed as soon as possible.

The Gestapo, however, remained inviolate. Meisinger, who knew altogether too much about the von Fritsch affair and had not shown up very well in court, was replaced by SS-Oberfuehrer Dr Werner Best, one of Heydrich's intellectuals who was regarded with unveiled contempt by the crudely laconic Mueller.

The proud officer corps of the German army had retired like so many whipped dogs, leaving the field undisputed to Hitler and, through him, Himmler and Heydrich with the SD and Gestapo.

In a speech on 20 February 1938, Hitler proclaimed:

'There now exists not a single institution of this State which is not National Socialist ... The party during the last five years has not only created a National Socialist state, but it has arranged for itself a perfect organisation which will maintain for ever its independence. The greatest guarantee of the National Socialist revolution is the control we now have of all the institutions of the Reich, at home and abroad. The nation is protected, so far as the rest of the world is concerned, by our National Socialist armed forces from now on.'

The cumbrous bureaucratic machinery of the terror in Nazi Germany had emerged unscathed from the one crisis that could have broken it. There were destined to be other plans for resistance against Hitler from within. None were to succeed. The Gestapo would only cease to exist when the entire structure of the Third Reich came crashing down in flames.

8

Events moved faster after the invasion of Austria. The military and political machinery geared for war moved on inexorably. Next it was to be the turn of Poland.

To Alfred Naujocks, it seemed that Heydrich never left his desk in the Prinz Albrechtstrasse, never managed to break away for more than a few hours from the mountains of buff folders that poured in from the network of agents.

His only relaxations were music and, incredibly enough, the reading of cheap thrillers – volumes by British writers in particular were devoured greedily. It was as if deception and deceit in the real world were not to be had in sufficient quantities.

Of course, there were still drink and women. Particularly women. But Heydrich's amorous pursuits could scarcely be described as a relaxation; the gropings in the half-darkness of the Salon Kitty and the other Berlin bars had become steadily more feverish.

And always he and his staff, afflicted by vicious hangovers, went back to the never ending tyranny of files and dossiers.

They threatened as usual to spill on to the floor that August morning when Naujocks was suddenly summoned to Heydrich's office.

Naujocks found his chief in a suspiciously sunny mood. Heydrich even greeted him by his first name – a sure sign that something singularly unpleasant was in the wind and that Heydrich was sweetening the pill in as subtle a manner as he was able.

Naujocks focused his attention on one particular file through which Heydrich was flicking. The head of the SD said: 'The title of this, my dear Alfred, is Operation Himmler. The Reichsfuehrer-SS did not conceive it, but he has given a personal order that it is to be activated as soon as possible. Personally, I think the scheme is crazy, but we're saddled with it.'

Naujocks's unease increased. This was typical Heydrich. He would be quite prepared to send an agent on a mission and then disown him if the whole thing proved disastrous. Now Heydrich was saying: 'The next move of the Reich is against Poland. We go to war next week. The trouble is that the German people are scarcely prepared for what is going to be a major military action.

'You, my dear Alfred, are personally going to provide the excuse for Poland.'

Naujocks steadfastly refused to provide Heydrich with the melodramatic reaction he clearly expected. The news, after all, was not exactly sensational. Rumours had been gripping Berlin since the middle of August. Hitler had been due to hold the annual Nuremberg Rally, which would have had the title 'Party Rally of Peace'. It had been secretly cancelled. And there had been rumours of large-scale troop movements. Plans were afoot to move army headquarters to Zossen, east of Berlin. On 15 August, the pocket battleships *Graf Spee* and *Deutschland* and twenty-one submarines were all set to sail for the Atlantic.

Despite himself, Naujocks felt excitement. Where did the SD and the Gestapo fit in?

Heydrich had moved across to a large wall map. 'Here,' he said dramatically, 'is a little place called Gleiwitz.'

Naujocks vaguely recalled a name which he had seen on

the dial of the radios. It was on the German-Polish border and not of particular importance. Then Naujocks remembered how radio had featured prominently in that untidy business of Otto Strasser and Rudolf Formis. He felt a quickening interest.

Heydrich went on: 'Consider it, Alfred. At Gleiwitz there is a small radio station some distance from the town but right on the border. Just *supposing* that the station was suddenly to change hands, if in one swift armed snatch it was to become Polish? You, Alfred Naujocks, will have the job of giving it to the enemy. We won't just be so crude as to hand it over, of course. Things will need to be stage-managed with a little artistry.'

Heydrich went on to say that he could foresee a situation where Polish troops would attack the station, seize the microphones and broadcast a message of defiance to the Reich. 'Well, it *could* happen,' he said to the now thoroughly mystified Naujocks. 'A more serious provocation against the Fuehrer could scarcely be imagined. Now supposing there was some handy evidence left behind – a few scattered bodies in Polish uniform for instance – and, most damning of all, that broadcast! It's just the sort of thing the Poles would do. We're going to give them a little push, that's all.'

By now bewilderment had given place to alarm. Naujocks's mind raced. Who on earth would think up such a lunatic scheme? Well, Heydrich had as good as said it was not Himmler. Naujocks believed him; the Reichsfuehrer-SS would be utterly incapable of such a flight of fancy. Heydrich himself? It was possible. Somehow Naujocks doubted it. There was a ruthlessness in the whole business that positively took the breath away. It was a bold stroke of impudence which could have only one conceivable outcome – it would unleash the world war that Hitler patently wanted. The whole affair had the stamp of the Fuehrer himself. Naujocks began to sweat.

At the Nuremberg trials after the war he was to swear an affidavit as to what actually happened over the Gleiwitz affair. Documents would survive proving Gestapo involvement. Naujocks was to remember the initial interview with

Heydrich only too well and to recall the story for a German journalist years later.

On that last August of peace he was listening to Heydrich saying: 'If you fail it will be your head on the chopping block and probably mine as well.' He added with a sour grin: 'I take it you have no ethical misgivings.'

Naujocks had none.

The date fixed for Operation Himmler was 5 August 1939. The Gestapo was poised to pull the trigger signalling World War II.

Admiral Wilhelm Canaris, now chief of the Abwehr (Military Intelligence) section of OKW, received a visit from SS Standartenfuehrer Heinz Jost, his opposite number in the SD.

Jost said: 'I bring a direct order from the Fuehrer for 150 Polish uniforms, the weapons and paybooks to go with them and 360 men who will be temporarily attached to the SD.'

Canaris, forever jealous of Heydrich's SD muscling in on what he regarded as his own territory, asked suspiciously: 'What are they needed for?'

Jost replied coldly: 'The matter is highly classified. I have no authority to discuss it.'

Canaris had long been opposed to Hitler's plans for war; Jost's secrecy seemed to suggest that there was something big in the offing. The request for Polish uniforms was bizarre but not unusual. Frequently agents violated international law by wearing uniforms as disguise and infiltrated Poland and other countries. Canaris himself had authorised such adventures. So what was the secrecy now?

In any case, such an operation should be an Abwehr matter and not one for the SD. Canaris was determined to scotch it. He went as near to the top as he could – to Keitel. But the Fuehrer's chief representative on OKW had no intention of sticking his neck out. He told Canaris blandly: 'Personally, I'm against such adventures, but the order has come from the Fuehrer. Nothing can be done about it.'

Canaris stifled his misgivings and duly supplied Heydrich with what he wanted.

For Alfred Naujocks, the next few days passed in a round of meetings. There was a long and detailed session with an engineer from Radio Berlin who forwarded to him one technical expert and one Polish-speaking announcer. There were endless conferences with a succession of top brass at OKW. Four men who were considered reliable among the staff officers were eventually picked out for the operation.

But above all there was the study of Gleiwitz - studies of maps and aerial photographs and plans of the station's interior.

Naujocks also inspected the uniforms. He had no love of the Abwehr, but he had to admit they had done a first-class job. And there were some superb touches, including packets of Polish cigarettes and matches and bills and letters, all to be distributed in the uniforms.

They were to be worn by Germans who were either of dual nationality or who spoke Polish fluently.

Operation Himmler was mushrooming. And that meant that an increasingly large number of people knew what was afoot. Naujocks was worried; it only needed one person to babble and the whole scheme could be ruined. If it had been a family affair within the Gestapo that would not be a major tragedy. But this was Hitler's own particular adventure and nothing must be allowed to jeopardise it.

Every person involved was sent for and made to swear an oath of secrecy; penalties for failure were spelt out with brutal clarity. Beyond making sure that everyone knew their own job but not too much about everybody else's, there was little more now that could be done about security.

The party of mining engineers who booked into the white stone Oberschlesischer Hof at Gleiwitz were charming. Their leader was disposed to be chatty to the young receptionist. He and his colleagues, he explained, were geologists carrying out a little advance reconnaissance. They filled in the registration form with names, occupations and birthplaces.

It was a busy hotel and nobody paid much attention to

the group, but some of its members were actually seen to collect rock samples and do a bit of digging.

The area chosen just happened to be near the radio station. A curious observer might perhaps have wondered what sort of geologists were so addicted to working late at night.

Back in Berlin, Alfred Naujocks went shopping for a corpse.

Heydrich had affected fastidious distaste at the suggestion that he should supply dead bodies for Operation Himmler. He did not concern himself with such crudities. He told Naujocks: 'One body will be enough. Get it from Mueller.'

Of course, Gestapo Mueller! Naujocks remembered the shaven head, the mountainous shoulders and the square jaw. Who better? Mueller was sticking his stubby fingers into the concentration camps, too. No doubt the body would come from one of them.

Mueller tersely outlined his plans. 'I'll give you an advance description of the black Opel I'll be driving. In the back, I'll have a freshly killed corpse in the uniform of the Polish army. I'll drape it very artistically on the steps of the radio station. And then I'll leave you to get on with the job.'

Despite himself, Naujocks could not rid himself of an obsessive curiosity about the corpse. Mueller looked surprised, snapping: 'What the hell does it matter who it is? Some Jew from a concentration camp.' Suddenly, he smiled wolfishly and added: 'This phase of the operation has been given its own title. We're calling it Operation Canned Goods.'

Europe buzzed like an upturned beehive during the dying days of August. In France reservists were summoned. Between Nijmegen and Maastricht in Holland mines were being laid. London and Paris prepared for war.

The coiled spring that was Hitler's army waited to plough east – 1,500,000 helmeted men consisting, in the north, of Generaloberst von Bock's forces and, in the south, the legions of Generaloberst von Rundstedt.

Alfred Naujocks rested in his room at the Oberschlesischer Hof, regretting the two drinks he had taken to bolster his courage. They had merely succeeded in making him sleepy and nervous.

The afternoon dragged agonisingly, but the time came when the entire team filed down the stairs and walked with deceptive casualness to the two cars. Naujocks took the first with Karl, the radio expert, and Heinrich, who would have the job of actually making the fake broadcast. The other car followed behind, both drivers exerting every ounce of self-discipline to keep their speed down until they were well out of sight of the hotel. But soon they were streaking down towards Ratibor Wood and the frontier, leaving the radio station to their left and slightly behind them. The cars were bumping now over a narrow track making for the clearing which had been earmarked. Naujocks pulled his car over to the side, killing the engine. He leapt out, quickly unlocked the boot and pulled out two trunks. The rest of the party stood around, expectantly.

Then within seconds the group was looking at seven shining Lugers, their black barrels faintly smeared with grease. Below them were the distinctive, clay-covered uniforms of the Polish Army.

The change was quick. The uniforms were not an exact fit, but this was no dress-parade. Karl was already crouched down over the radio set, waiting for the vital signal from Berlin.

Naujocks was nervous and had ripped the paper off a packet of Polish cigarettes. There was ample time, he told himself. There would be no possible benefit in the go-ahead coming too early.

At 7.27 the signal came and, still obeying the instruction to keep it casual, the men walked back to their cars with all the nonchalance of picnickers on the way home.

Naujocks had given an instruction for quiet gear-changes; no revving engines whose sound would carry. Nobody had made any provision for the radio; not that it mattered, it had served its purpose. Karl left it on the ground.

The cars bumped sickeningly over the track, but soon

they were on the smooth road and Naujocks was able to put his foot down.

All too soon, the radio station was looming up in front of them. Naujocks's car screamed to the entrance. The other vehicle, its tyres squealing, made for the side of the building.

Naujocks arrowed up the half-dozen wide shallow steps. In the gathering dusk he spotted a dark-blue uniformed figure. The man froze; then all at once Heinrich had leapt on him, thrusting him back to the wall and banging his head violently. A light flicked in a window, pinpointing the whereabouts of another enemy.

He seemed to be down a corridor. Naujocks ran as silently as a cat towards an office door.

The man was bending over a filing cabinet. He took the full force of the pistol barrel on his head. His body keeled over with a crash, sending a chair and hatstand straight into the metal cabinet.

The place was well and truly roused now. From elsewhere in the studio came nothing short of bedlam.

Naujocks backed out of the office – and straight into the arms of the man waiting for him. Then in the general confusion, he saw it was Karl. Both had only one thought – get to the studio, make the broadcast and leave the place as soon as possible.

Ahead of them was a green-painted door marked 'Silence'. But Heinrich was ahead of them and already installed in the small comfortably furnished room with the baize-covered desk and microphone positioned in the centre.

Heinrich seemed to be enjoying himself. He snatched up the microphone, fishing in his pocket for the prepared script. Karl made his way to the control room, impatiently studying the orderly rows of dials and switches.

Naujocks could smell trouble. He had joined Karl, who was staring in bemused panic at the row of switches.

He stuttered: 'I can't find the bloody landline switch. It links up with Breslau. Unless we can get through there we're done for.'

All at once, Naujocks recalled the trouble there had

been with the useless key during the Formis affair. The whole scheme was falling apart. Karl was turning out to be a disastrous choice. He forced himself to keep calm. He asked almost plaintively: 'Can't you put us on the air at all?'

Karl replied: 'Only locally. Without that landline, the signal will only travel a few kilometres.'

It would have to do. Panic was infectious. It was now spreading to Heinrich, who was standing, script in hand, in utter helplessness. Then he began to gabble, good strong stuff about Germany's leaders pushing Europe into war. Hitler was a bully, prepared to sacrifice a small country in his boundless quest for personal ambition. But who would hear it? All Heydrich's artistry would probably go for nothing.

At least the rest of the building seemed quiet. Maybe all the studio staff were dead. Anyway, it was time to get on with the rest of the pantomime. Naujocks pulled out his pistol and fired three times, shouting as loud as he could. Then he signalled Karl to kill the transmission.

All three men quit the smoke-laden chaos, teamed up with the rest of their comrades and, with guns at the ready, ran down the steps to the cars.

In front of them lay the body of a tall fair-haired man wearing Polish uniform. Blood trickled from a hole in the back of the neck. It crossed Naujocks's mind that he hadn't been dead very long; Mueller had probably shot him on the spot. Well, at least Operation Canned Goods had gone off according to plan. It would look convincing when the world's press was summoned next day. There was a Polish criminal who had made an unprovoked attack on a German radio station.

As he drove the big car away, Naujocks was attacked by sudden depression. He could imagine the scene at Breslau, where the engineers, duly primed, would have searched the airwaves desperately for the broadcast.

But that was nothing compared to Hitler's undoubted reaction. The Fuehrer's rage would have been terrible indeed. At this very minute he was probably screaming for blood. It would very likely be the gallows in the morning.

Well, he was so bloody tired now that he would probably not feel the noose. Ahead lay several hours' work on his report, then an appointment in Heydrich's office at 7 a.m.

Alfred Naujocks didn't go to bed that night and didn't bother to shave in the morning. It scarcely mattered how a man went to his death. And his head was knocking agonisingly. What's more, he realised that quite suddenly he no long cared particularly what happened to him.

Heydrich sat at his desk as insufferably aloof and as immaculate as ever.

He looked across at Naujocks and said: 'Congratulations.' What did this mean? With Heydrich you never knew. It could be a touch of irony, a mere preface to the tirade which would surely follow.

But here was the chief of the SD saying: 'It was a pity about the link up with Breslau, but it couldn't be helped. At least you went on the air and nobody seems to have tumbled to what actually happened.'

In a daze, Naujocks handed to Heydrich the report that had only been completed at three that morning. In the circumstances, it was a remarkably detailed document, describing how there had only been five men in the building because after six o'clock Gleiwitz, except for news bulletins and weather reports, only retransmitted broadcasts from elsewhere. There was a full account of how the men had been disabled before they could get to a telephone.

Naujocks added lamely, all the strength draining out of him: 'I was furious at not getting through to Breslau.'

He had under-estimated Heydrich, who now said: 'The possibility occurred to me that there might be some technical slip-up. Do you read the party newspaper, *Voelkischer Beobachter?* I recommend it. Now I suggest you go home and get some sleep.'

Naujocks picked up a copy of the newspaper on his way home. A front page story read:

AGGRESSORS ATTACK GLEIWITZ RADIO

'A group of Polish soldiers seized the Gleiwitz Radio building last night a little before eight. Only a few of the staff were on duty at that hour. It is obvious that the

Polish assailants knew the ground perfectly. They attacked the personnel and broke into the studio, knocking out those they encountered on the way.

The aggressors cut the relay line to Breslau and read out at the microphone a propaganda speech prepared in advance, in Polish and German. They stated that the town and the radio station were in the hands of the Poles and insulted Germany, alluding to "Polish Breslau" and "Polish Danzig".

The listeners, at first taken by surprise, notified the police, who arrived a few minutes later. The aggressors opened fire on the forces of order but at the end of a few minutes they were all taken prisoner. During the battle a Pole was killed.'

Naujocks felt justified in sleeping the clock round. He regretted it.

While he slept, Hitler spoke. The patience of the Fuehrer had run its course. The time had come to teach the Poles a lesson.

The attack on Poland came at 4.45 a.m. on 1 September 1939 with five German armies attacking from the north, west and south. Warsaw was flattened by bombing. After the annihilation of the Polish air force, there were attacks on railways and roads to hinder mobilisation. Close behind the German armies came the SS-Einsatzgruppen, the special task forces who carried out the extermination of the cream of the Polish professional classes.

OKW chief-of-staff General der Artillerie Franz Halder, following a message from Heydrich, entered in his diary cryptically: 'Housecleaning: Jews, intelligentsia, clergy, nobility.' Within just one week of the world going to war, Canaris reported that the SS commanders were boasting of 200 shootings a day.

Alfred Naujocks was not the only one to enjoy his sleep. Hitler was also reported to have untroubled dreams that night.

He could afford them. Heydrich had given him the excuse he needed. And now for the Geheime Staatspolizei there was a fresh and sinister role ahead.

9

It was two months since Gleiwitz. That particular episode had left Alfred Naujocks physically and mentally exhausted. He went on two weeks' leave, then he was sent to an espionage school near Hanover.

Meanwhile, events within the security service had been moving rapidly. The various offshoots of Heydrich's empire, the SD and Gestapo, he considered, had grown unwieldly and bureaucratic, overlapping and poaching blatantly on each other's territory. Heydrich had long dreamed of a single authority for German intelligence.

He eventually came up with plans for a Directorate General of Security for the Reich (the Reichssicherheitshauptamt or RSHA) with, naturally enough, himself at its head under the authority of Reichsfuehrer-SS Heinrich Himmler. The Gestapo, the original police organ of the Prussian state, became part of Section (or Amt) IV of the RSHA. The SD, originally an intelligence service of the Nazi party, evolved into the RSHA's Amt III and Amt VI.

Amt III performed an interior information service, now in the hands of an accomplished economist named Otto Ohlendorf, who had been clever enough – and lucky enough – to make the transition from the SA to the SS. Amt VI was set up to deal with security abroad. Its first director was Heinz Jost and, eventually, Walter Schellenberg.

Constipated by petty bureaucracy and riddled with intrigue, the various departments of the RSHA still stumbled over one another and interfered in each other's business, just as the Gestapo and the SD had done in their previous existence.

What was noticeably new was the addition to Amt IV of a fresh counter-espionage section. It was known as IV-E and was the province of Walter Schellenberg, now a recently created SS-Standartenfuehrer.

Schellenberg had soon built up a reputation as a trouble-shooter for Himmler and Heydrich on a number of bizarre missions abroad.

As for Naujocks, news that he was to work closely with Schellenberg on one particular assignment pleased him not at all. He intensely distrusted the other man's rather too calculated charm, his obvious desire to be liked. Above all, Naujocks was repelled by Schellenberg's blatant toadying to Heydrich.

But it could not be denied that it had paid off. Schellenberg in a short time had become one of the top ten most powerful men in the Reich, even though he was still to a certain extent under the thumb of Heinrich Mueller.

And when it came to explaining the latest assignment it was Schellenberg for whom Heydrich had first sent.

Heydrich had explained: 'For some time now we've had an agent in the Low Countries, a deserter from Czech intelligence. He has managed to build up some remarkably good contacts in British intelligence. He has worked in the usual way – tossed some perfectly genuine titbits along with a lot of rubbish. They appear to have fallen for it.

'He's in fact a former German policeman who was lucky to escape the Roehm purge. He is suspected of having worked for Otto Strasser.

'The reason he is alive is because he was approached by the Gestapo and, er, persuaded to work for them. The man would appear to love his wife and his freedom in equal measure. Provided he is co-operative we see no reason to deprive him of either, although naturally we mentioned the possibility.'

The agent registered in SD files as F479 had made two important contacts within rival British intelligence networks in the Netherlands, Major Richard Stevens and Captain Sigismund Payne Best. The two had become convinced of F479's desire to work against Germany.

However, Czech intelligence in London, with whom Best and Stevens were in contact, remained unconvinced. Its agents felt that the Czech alleged anti-Nazi was a little too good to be true.

London posed some pertinent questions. Could not the whole business be a subtle attempt by the Nazis to penetrate the British secret service network? Swift orders were issued that relations were to be severed.

Heydrich went on: 'That doesn't suit us at all. F479 was ordered to make further contact with this Best and Stevens. He told them that he was the bearer of important news. He was in touch with a certain captain Hauptmann Schaemmel, of the OKW Transport Service, one of a group of high officers in the Wehrmacht who were plotting to overthrow Hitler and take over the government of Germany. That group wanted to contact the English government.

'Best and Stevens fell for it. They will be meeting the leaders of this opposition movement shortly in the Netherlands.'

Schellenberg was steeped in the intrigue inseparable from all intelligence work, but this scheme to deal a serious blow to the British spy network impressed even him.

Heydrich was keeping his most sensational disclosure for a little while longer. He stared at Schellenberg in faint amusement: 'Don't you want to know more about this very special Hauptmann Schaemmel? His role will be crucial.'

Schellenberg, tired of playing games, snapped: 'I've never heard of him. Is he one of our men?'

Heydrich professed mock astonishment. 'I am surprised at you, Schellenberg. You know him very well. Captain Schaemmel of OKW is none other than SS-Standartenfuehrer Walter Schellenberg.'

Heydrich had made his little joke and had the satisfaction of seeing Schellenberg struck dumb.

He then went on to spell out the reasons for the exercise. The Nazi secret service should be able to penetrate the British intelligence network in the Netherlands and smash it just before Hitler's proposed invasion of the Low Countries. In addition 'Hauptmann Schaemmel' would be in a position to find out from Best and Stevens which *real* members of an anti-Nazi conspiracy had been in touch with the British.

Never in his wildest dreams had Schellenberg ever imagined being mixed up in such a bizarre scheme. The whole thing was something out of a Hollywood script – and not a very good script at that. Not for the first time, he suspected Heydrich of indulging in a childish gift for melodrama.

Schellenberg's own opinions, of course, could not have mattered less. In any case, what now lay ahead was the hard graft of homework and plenty of it. If it had not been for Heydrich he might even now be slaving away night after night on ill-paid lawyer's briefs, instead of enjoying Standartenfuehrer rank and all the power and kudos that went with it.

Thank God, it was not just a question of poring over endless documents. Soon Schellenberg was on the move – back with a vengeance into the murky milieu he had first embraced out of opportunism but which now held the potent appeal of a hopelessly addictive drug.

Schellenberg gathered together all the numerous dossiers on the Netherlands network. For two days he did nothing else but read. The conspiracy against Hitler had to sound convincing: there had to be names, times, dates. Equally, he had to know as much as possible about those key figures, Best and Stevens.

It was largely historical reasons that had led to the selection of Holland as a centre for espionage. The country had been neutral in World War I and as such was thought ideal as a directional centre for spying. Regional headquarters for Secret Intelligence Service (SIS) was in The Hague, masterminded by affable Major Richard Stevens, who controlled a formidable network of more than 100 agents in Europe.

But Stevens by no means had the field to himself. Captain Sigismund Payne Best might well have stepped from the pages of P.G. Wodehouse. It was known that he affected a monocle and wore spats. In fact, he was living confirmation of what many Germans fondly imagined a typical Englishman to be. But he was by no means a conventional silly ass; he had been an intelligence officer in World War I and had been awarded the OBE as well as the Belgian Croix de Guerre and the French Legion d'Honneur.

He was fond of the good life and he had a great deal of the arrogance which a man of his class and generation was traditionally supposed to exhibit to all foreigners. All this was useful background but what primarily concerned Schellenberg was that Best was the head of Z network, a second British spy set-up in The Hague, quite different from that controlled by Stevens, but also under the secret service in London.

Schellenberg doubtless reflected that Germany was not the only country to have a top-heavy bureaucracy of espionage. He knew – indeed, it was scarcely a secret from anyone – that the British espionage headquarters was at No. 57 Nieuwe Paarklaan and had the deliberately misleading address of the British Passport Control Office – a cover, incidentally, which had almost certainly been penetrated by every schoolboy in The Hague.

A strange lot, the British! Schellenberg next turned his attention to Hauptmann Schaemmel.

The Hauptmann had not entirely been an invention of Heydrich. It would have been much too risky to invent an OKW officer out of thin air.

In his memoirs, Schellenberg explained:

> 'I had found out that there really was such a Hauptmann in the Transport Department and I saw to it that he was sent on an extensive journey in the eastern areas ... I had also secured an exact and detailed report on Hauptmann Schaemmel – his background, his way of life, his behaviour and appearance – for instance, he always wore a monocle, so I had to wear one too, which was not difficult, as I am short-sighted in one eye. The more inside knowledge of the group I possessed, the more chance I had of gaining the confidence of the British for, of course, the smallest mistake would immediately arouse their suspicions.'

Schellenberg was beginning to enjoy himself.

On 19 October, accompanied by SS Obersturmbannfuehrer Bernhard Christensen, who now had the cover name of Grosch, Schellenberg made for Düsseldorf.

The house that awaited them was almost a shrine to modern espionage. Outwardly, it was an unremarkable pension, but concealed there were radios, tape recorders, photographic material, a small laboratory and powerful telecommunications links to the RSHA back in Berlin. A teleprinter was being installed.

On 20 October a long awaited message came to the pension: 'Meeting arranged for 21 October at Zuthpen, Holland. A black Buick will await you on the Issel bridge along the Emmerich-Zuthpen road.'

In the evening a telegram arrived from Heydrich in Berlin. It carried with Hitler's blessing complete authorisation of the mission. The message ended uncharacteristically: 'I advise you to be very prudent. It would be too stupid if anything happened to you. But in case of the business going wrong I have alerted all the frontier posts. Call me immediately on your return ...'

Schellenberg knew Heydrich too well to be deceived. The man was not anxious for his subordinate's welfare on humanitarian grounds. He was merely being practical.

Now was the time for last-minute checks. Schellenberg and Christensen looked at their passports and car papers again. The German frontier posts would not cause trouble; they had been ordered not to ask too many questions. The two men carried as little luggage as possible. Clothes and linen were scrupulously examined; tell-tale marks which could betray identity would be embarrassing.

The needle-sharp, driving rain was scarcely an encouragement in the early dawn. Schellenberg felt his spirits drop. The whole mission now seemed incredibly dangerous and foolhardy. There had not been time for sufficient homework. A briefing from F479, for example, would have proved invaluable.

Schellenberg's reception from the Dutch guards did nothing to raise his spirits. They were openly hostile, insisting on a thorough search which seemed to entail practically taking the car to pieces.

But eventually they were through to Zuthpen. The two Germans peered anxiously through the windscreen, making out the substantial bulk of a large Buick.

Captain Best remained at the wheel, extending a brisk welcome in excellent German. Schellenberg managed to suppress a smile when he spotted the other's monocle.

The Englishman seemed in no hurry to get to the point of the mission when Schellenberg clambered in beside him, leaving his companion to follow in the other car.

He merely said: 'We're going to Arnhem. Major Stevens and Lieutenant Coppens will join us there.'

Then Schellenberg had a slice of luck. During the journey, Best revealed an abundant enthusiasm for music, specifically the violin. Schellenberg reflected that it was his own enthusiasm for music which had forged some sort of bond between him and Heydrich and Canaris a few years ago. Here indeed was a common language!

Really, this Englishman seemed remarkably civilised and pleasant. At the same time, there was something uncanny about the way that Best managed so adroitly to dodge what was surely uppermost in both their minds. Schellenberg took a grip on himself. The sooner they got down to business the better.

At Arnhem, Schellenberg was introduced to Best's colleagues, Major Stevens and Lieutenant Coppens. The latter, unknown to Schellenberg, was in fact a Dutchman, Lieutenant Dirk Klop. He had lived in Canada for five years and his English was impeccable.

The Dutch army had insisted that their man should take part in the talks. In return, the Dutch would give full co-operation in allowing the German ring-leaders to cross the border unmolested.

Schellenberg was at his most bland. There was indeed, he assured his listeners, a powerful opposition group within the very highest circles of the German army. 'Its head,' he said impressively, 'is a German Generaloberst. Unfortunately, I am not at liberty to tell you who he is. That would be far too dangerous at this stage. Our aim is to overthrow Hitler by force and install a new regime.

'What I need to know is the attitude of the British government to an administration controlled by the German army. Would it be prepared to conclude a secret treaty which would eventually lead to peace overtures?'

The British group was clearly impressed. It was stressed that their government was interested in any move that would stop the spread of war. It was suggested that there should be another meeting when the attitude of Prime Minister Neville Chamberlain and his cabinet would be made clearer. Schellenberg was assured that Best and Stevens were in direct contact with the Foreign Office and the government.

Schellenberg reckoned he had made excellent progress. It was agreed that the two sides would resume their conversation on 30 October at the office of Allied Intelligence in The Hague.

The party split up on the best of terms. It might have been a semi-informal weekend business chat in a golf club. Schellenberg sped back to Heydrich to report.

The latter appeared satisfied and explained to his subordinate: 'Quite a lot of what you will be telling the English is perfectly true. The Fuehrer is certainly all in favour of our troops launching an attack across Holland, Belgium and Luxembourg on a wide front.

'Unfortunately, by no means all the generals are convinced. They are cowards and keep making excuses. They say the Wehrmacht is simply not up to confronting the British and French armies. There's an argument that an attack at this time of year would get bogged down in the mud. They would much rather the whole thing was forgotten. You can tell our British friends all this. It will give them the idea that there is serious opposition to the Fuehrer.'

Schellenberg's lonely, almost monastic life did not entirely preclude him from making friends. One of his closest confidants was an Austrian, Professor Max de Crinis, an Oberst in the medical corps of the Wehrmacht. Schellenberg stayed with the family whenever he wanted. De Crinis treated him with disinterested affection – a rare enough experience in Himmler's spy service.

Schellenberg found himself pouring out the story of the Dutch operation. The happy thought struck him. What he badly needed for Best and Stevens was an apparently reliable representative of the opposition group.

And now here he was, cantering elegantly beside him in the brisk morning air.

There was almost no need for words. De Crinis speedily read Schellenberg's mind. The two were soon eagerly discussing details. Schellenberg lost no time in securing the approval of the RSHA.

On 29 October, the two men, accompanied by Christensen, left Berlin for Düsseldorf. The name of de Crinis had, of course, disappeared, but the man who now had the cover name Martini bore a remarkable resemblance to Schellenberg's riding companion.

Schellenberg wrote in his memoirs:

'De Crinis and I agreed on a system of signs whereby we could communicate with each other during the discussion with the Englishmen. If I removed my monocle with my left hand, that meant that he would immediately stop talking and leave me to pursue the conversation. If with the right hand, that I needed his support. The sign of an immediate breaking off of the conversation would be my having a migraine.'

The crossing of the frontier presented no difficulties. But, unaccountably, Schellenberg felt uneasy. He told himself that there could be no possible reason for anxiety, but the nagging fear refused to go away.

The crossroads picked for the meeting-place were deserted. For three-quarters of an hour, the trio sat in silence. Schellenberg was up to the experience; much of espionage, after all, meant playing a waiting game. But de Crinis felt his nerves stretch taut and threaten to snap.

All at once, Schellenberg's eyes narrowed. He had seen the two Dutch policemen who were making their way slowly to the car. Schellenberg and Christensen hissed at their companion: 'We'll handle this.'

The policemen were scrupulously polite. One asked in Dutch what the three men were doing there. Christensen said as casually as he could muster: 'Waiting for friends.'

The officer looked like a man who had been told the same thing many times by errant motorists over the years.

110

He sighed, opened the side door of the car and got in, ordering: 'Drive to the police station.'

Schellenberg reflected bitterly that this was a nice end to everything. He had walked into a trap like a bumbling amateur. The only thing now was for everyone to keep their heads and see if this particular tight corner could be wriggled out of. He felt no worry for himself or Christensen. They were intelligence specialists, after all. But de Crinis was a different matter; he wouldn't stand up long to interrogation.

The charade of elaborate courtesy was rigidly maintained, but the search of each man at the police station was thorough. Well, the luggage wouldn't present any problems. It had been thoroughly checked for tell-tale markings back in Düsseldorf.

Schellenberg's stomach lurched as he suddenly spotted the open toilet case on top of de Crinis's luggage. It was in full view and sticking out was a fat tube of aspirin.

Nothing wrong with that. But the wrapper was a complete giveaway. It was stamped *SS Sanitas Hauptamt* (SS Medical Service). As casually as he could, Schellenberg edged his own luggage nearer to the toilet case, eventually covering it. Like lightning, he snatched the offending tube, at the same moment dropping a hairbrush under the table.

It was the matter of a moment to cram the aspirins down his throat. Thankfully he stood up, only to drop down smartly again as he realised that the tablets had stuck and he was in danger of vomiting. Desperately, he swallowed, praying fiendishly that he would not be noticed.

Fortunately, the searchers were too occupied.

Then began the interrogations. Who were they? Where did they come from? Who did they intend to meet? For Schellenberg it was a novel experience; he was used to being on the other end of incidents like this. Plainly, the best form of defence would be attack. In well simulated rage, he tore into his interrogators. The whole affair, he railed, was an insult. Here were perfectly innocent travellers being treated like common criminals. A lawyer would be consulted and there would be hell to pay.

The diatribe seemed to have its effect. The policemen began to look distinctly uncomfortable. Then came a welcome break with the sudden arrival of Klop, alias Coppens, flourishing some papers. At the sight of them, the police became positively abject. Profuse with apologies, they withdrew.

Outside were Best and Stevens in the familiar Buick. The monocled Best, dressed as always for a morning hike in his plus-fours, looked like an abashed schoolboy caught in an orchard. He actually blushed.

'My dear fellow,' he exclaimed to Schellenberg, 'I couldn't be more sorry. The fact is we waited at the wrong crossroads. Then we realised our mistake and went off to look for you. The whole thing is a most terrible misunderstanding.'

Schellenberg doubted it. The merest child could see that the affair was a put-up job. But it had been an undeniably effective way of checking up on them. Schellenberg vowed to be more on his guard in future.

The party sped to The Hague and the meeting took place in Stevens's office. The tone as always was studiously polite. Discussions were nevertheless detailed, with Best doing most of the talking for the British side.

But Schellenberg had done his work well. He had constantly rehearsed the bait that he was to dangle in front of British intelligence. He declared: 'Certainly, Hitler will be overthrown and Germany will enter into immediate peace talks with the Western Powers. Occupying forces would be withdrawn from Austria, Czechoslovakia and Poland. Those countries would return to their former status.

'But there remains the problem of Germany's surplus population. Colonies she possessed before the First World War must be returned. If Germany has no room to breathe, then inevitably there will be frustration. The seeds of nationalism will still be there and Germany will be a threat to the rest of Europe.'

At the end of the meeting, the proposals were set down in a memo. Stevens slipped out to telephone London and get the German offer placed before the Foreign Secretary, Lord Halifax, as speedily as possible. On his return, he announced: 'We should have an answer later this evening.'

The strain had told on Schellenberg. The bait of an end to the war which he dangled in front of Best and Stevens had been positively gobbled. The more that the British trusted the supposed anti-Nazis, the easier continued infiltration into British intelligence would prove.

But maintaining this elaborate cover was proving an exhausting business. After three and a half hours, Schellenberg developed a genuine migraine. Part of the trouble, he reflected, was over-smoking. Best, a heavy smoker, had never stopped thrusting infernally strong cigarettes on the Germans.

Schellenburg excused himself and made for the washroom. He ran the water over his wrists. Mercifully, he felt better and began to relax.

Then he heard Best's quiet voice say behind him: 'Tell me, do you always wear a monocle?'

It was an awkward moment, but Schellenberg had been well trained. He said casually: 'Odd, I was going to put the same question to you.'

The uneasiness passed. The next few hours were to seem even more unreal than anything which had happened so far. Best was in excellent humour. Plainly, reflected Schellenberg, he hoped to be the saviour of Europe. Probably he hoped to be decorated by King George VI at Buckingham Palace. The man was plainly in the mood for celebration.

The party piled into cars and made for Best's elegant home in the Lange Voorhout in The Hague. The dinner was lavish and the wine flowed. Speeches were made; endless toasts drunk to Britain and Germany. Later, Best and Stevens took their bosom friend 'Schaemmel' aside and, grinning like schoolboys, announced: 'We want to give you a present.'

They produced an English transmitting and receiving set, together with a special code with which it would be possible to maintain contact with the offices of the British

113

secret service in The Hague.

Schellenberg related: 'Lieutenant Coppens handed us credentials asking the Dutch authorities to facilitate any call from us to a secret telephone number at The Hague 556 331. After agreeing to set by radio the date and place of our next meeting, Captain Best accompanied us to the frontier, which we passed without difficulty.'

Schellenberg was in seventh heaven, positively babbling his enthusiasm to Heydrich. Before he left Holland, a message had come from London. Halifax had given his consent to negotiations. Schellenberg was able to relate that he had interested Best and Stevens in the idea of getting the bogus anti-Hitler general to London, to make the negotiations seem even more convincing. The British, Schellenberg was sure, were eating out of his hand.

Heydrich acted like a douche of cold water. He explained: 'The Fuehrer thinks perhaps you have gone far enough. He doesn't like all this talk about conspiracies, even bogus ones. He is about to leave for Munich for the anniversary of the 1923 putsch. On his return we'll discuss the matter again. Patience, my dear Schellenberg, patience!'

Schellenberg was not the only one to be worried about the delay in continuing the mission. Heydrich had an equal stake in its success and he had no intention of missing any kudos. He was also concerned at what he regarded as Schellenberg's impetuosity; the man was so hooked on his mission that he might do something stupid.

A brake clearly had to be applied. In charge would have to be an operative whose ruthlessness was every bit a match for Schellenberg.

Heydrich sent for Naujocks. He was perfectly aware that the two men disliked each other. So much the better: Naujocks would pursue his mission with more zeal.

Heydrich was blunt: 'Frankly, I don't like this business about going to London. Supposing Schellenberg was arrested. If that happened, we might just as well give up. And you can have too much of an agent hobnobbing with the enemy.

'I feel that things are likely to come to the boil, despite the Fuehrer's wish to play the mission down. I want you to act as protection for Schellenberg. Take a dozen of your best men and stand by for trouble.'

It was the sort of mission which Naujocks relished, an absolute gift after all the inactivity following Gleiwitz.

Twelve trusted SS were ordered to report in civilian clothes forthwith. The party then left for the SS listening post in Düsseldorf to await developments.

Naujocks was delighted that his arrival so clearly annoyed Schellenberg, who exploded: 'It's taken a lot of meetings and smooth talking to get the confidence of the British. Why do you have to butt in? The sudden appearance of more people is bound to create suspicion.'

Naujocks realised that he would have to be diplomatic. He explained to Schellenberg: 'This latest order comes direct from Himmler. If you were kidnapped or arrested it would be a marvellous coup for the British secret service. Somebody of your rank and importance has got to be protected. It's only common sense.'

An appeal to his vanity always worked with Schellenberg. His dislike of Naujocks was as profound as ever, but plainly there was no point in squabbling among themselves. The two men began discussing what to do if the Dutch pulled any surprises at the next meeting, due on 9 November at Venlo on the German-Dutch border.

To Schellenberg intrigue was a narcotic; now the supply had suddenly been cut off. But it was not the fascination of the job alone which attracted him. His prestige was at stake. He would be blamed if the attempt to penetrate the Netherlands' spy network fell apart. And that was precisely the danger that faced him now. How could he make convincing new excuses to his English contacts?

A breathing space was given to Schellenberg by the announcement that the King of the Belgians and the Queen of Holland had both offered their help in getting the belligerents to negotiate. It would now be possible to tell the English that the opposition to Hitler was hanging fire, waiting for the Fuehrer's reaction to the royal proposals. It was not an ideal excuse, but it was a lot better than nothing.

The time arrived for the next meeting with Best and Stevens. There was a wait of three quarters of an hour. During it, Schellenberg noticed several civilians desperately trying to look casual.

It all made Schellenberg uneasy. Plainly, Best and Stevens were once again suspicious. However, he was later to tell Heydrich that this eventual brief meeting with Best and Stevens had been cordial enough. His reasons for delay had been accepted; he had been lavish in his regrets that the still anonymous Generaloberst was indisposed and unable to meet them.

But it was a mission that would take a turn that neither Schellenberg nor any of his lieutenants in Section IV-E of the RSHA could possibly have foreseen.

10

The Mercedes 770-K with its bullet-proof glass was just one part of the vast mobile fortress knifing its way through the streets of Munich on a cold November night.

Some thirty SS and SD bodyguards hugged Hitler's car with its front, back and side armour plating.

Each man was armed with two 9-mm pistols and fifty rounds of ammunition. Escort cars could boast another six pistols in reserve, half-a-dozen sub-machine guns, a light machine gun with 4,500 rounds. In all there was enough armour to stave off a platoon attack. Hitler himself wore a specially designed officer's cap reinforced with a steel band weighing three-and-a-half pounds.

On this particular evening, 8 November 1939, Hitler's destination was the Bürgerbraukeller, packed with loyal Nazis waiting to commemorate the anniversary of the Munich putsch of 1923 at which the future Fuehrer had been arrested and where National Socialism had gained its first martyrs.

In the hall, all was noise and sociable confusion. Waitresses staggered under the weight of foaming steins of beer which they slapped down on wooden benches. It was an evening out that had been looked forward to for months.

But it was also something else. The beer hall was shortly to be transformed into a place of worship where respectful tribute would be paid to the one-time Vienna vagabond now hailed triumphantly as the saviour of his adopted country.

At eight o'clock the mood changed. Silence was total. Chairs were scraped back, hands raised in the Nazi salute. From the band came the jaunty strains of the Horst Wessel song.

Ten minutes later, Hitler was at the lectern, his back directly in front of a column draped with the black and red swastika banner.

He began: 'Comrades of the Party! My comrades of the German people! I have come to you in order to relive with you the memory of the day which was for us, for the movement and for the German peoples a day of the greatest importance.'

The low-key mood of reminiscence switched to a diatribe against England, a country which, he stormed, had dared to speak of liberty after subjugating millions within its own empire.

As always, the audience was spellbound. Then, to the puzzlement of many, Hitler showed signs of winding-up rather abruptly: 'Comrades of the Party! Long live our National Socialist movement, long live our German people and now, especially, long live our victorious army!' He strode off the platform.

It was explained that the Fuehrer had an urgent appointment at ten o'clock the next morning in Berlin and was anxious to catch the scheduled train from Munich to which a special coach had been attached.

A speech intended to last ninety minutes had been cut to fifty. Almost absently, the Fuehrer said his formal goodbyes, pumped a few hands and left the hall.

At 9.20 precisely, eight minutes later, the gigantic bomb which had been placed inside the swastika-shrouded pillar

117

tore the beer hall apart. The air was split with the screams of the injured and dying, many of them crushed under falling beams. The remains of the speaker's rostrum was buried under six feet of broken timber and rubble.

At Nuremberg, the train halted for a few minutes so that important messages could be received and sent. A white-faced Joseph Goebbels dashed to Hitler's side with the sensational news of the explosion at the Munich beerhouse. The news galvanised the Fuehrer. He proclaimed: 'This is indisputably the work of the British secret service. Only divine providence has saved me. If I had stayed behind there, my enemies would have succeeded in doing away with me.'

Hitler demanded action and the Reichsfuehrer-SS was summoned forthwith. Himmler found his master inflexible in his belief that the British infiltrated their agents into Munich and planted the bomb.

Plainly something had to be done to satisfy the Fuehrer. And fast. Himmler thought he knew what it was.

The jingle of the telephone sliced into Walter Schellenberg's sleep at dawn on the morning of 9 November. In fuddled irritation he growled: 'Hullo.'

For a moment, he failed to recognise the voice at the other end. It was surprisingly meek, as if its owner was unused to being spoken to roughly: 'What's that you say?'

Schellenberg was only too conscious that he had taken a sleeping pill a few hours before. 'Nothing for the moment,' he riposted frostily. 'Who's speaking?'

The voice had now lost all its subservience. It cut into Schellenberg's weariness with: 'This is Reichsfuehrer SS Heinrich Himmler. It that you at last?'

Schellenberg jerked into full consciousness, stammering: 'Yes, sir.'

Himmler continued crisply: 'I want you to listen. This evening, just after the Fuehrer's speech in the beer hall, an attempt was made to kill him. A bomb exploded. Luckily, he had just left. Several old party comrades were killed and there is a lot of damage. The Fuehrer was already on his train when the news arrived. He's absolutely in no doubt that the British secret service is behind this.

'Anyway, Schellenberg, this is an order. Tomorrow, when you meet the British agents you are to arrest them immediately and bring them back to Germany. That may mean a violation of the Dutch frontier. That doesn't matter one jot. The SS detachment appointed for your protection – which, by the way, you certainly don't deserve after the arbitrary and obstinate way you've been behaving – will help you with your mission. Any questions?'

Schellenberg was awake now, his heart pumping wildly. He could only stammer: 'But, my Reichsfuehrer . . .'

Himmler snapped: 'No buts. You have an order from the Fuehrer. Now do you understand?'

To protest any further would be futile. And dangerous. Schellenberg said humbly: 'Yes, my Reichsfuehrer.'

But the line had already gone dead.

Schellenberg reviewed the situation. It was, from every angle, extremely ugly. Himmler had talked of orders to arrest, but this was blatant kidnapping in a neutral country, no matter what plans Hitler might have for it in the future. The risks would be hair-raising: particularly as the Dutch were becoming increasingly suspicious of German intentions and stiffening their borders.

Schellenberg had been awakened from heavy sleep with a nasty shock. Well. he would dish out the same medicine to someone else just for the hell of it.

And so it was Alfred Naujocks's turn to have his night ruined. He picked up the receiver, dropped it, swore and grunted hullo.

Schellenberg rasped: Naujocks, get down here instantly. I've had Himmler on the line. There's work to do.'

And, reflected Naujocks, almost certainly very dirty work. Schellenberg, the rather pasty-faced intellectual, was not a man who liked getting his feet wet. He would leave that sort of thing to Naujocks, whom he tended to regard rather sneeringly as an SD artisan.

Blearily, Naujocks flung on some clothes and groped his way to Schellenberg's room.

The very sight of Schellenberg in scarlet silk pyjamas

sitting up in bed smoking rasped on Naujocks's nerves.

Schellenberg tossed a cigarette from a gold case across, then outlined what had happened in the beer hall. He said: 'Finding who's directly responsible is a job for Mueller. What we have to do is work out how to nab Best and Stevens.

'Frankly, I think it is one of the craziest and most dangerous ideas I've ever encountered. I don't believe they had anything to do with the bomb, but it doesn't matter. We must act fast, not just because Himmler says so but because the English are constantly blowing hot and cold.

'If they call the whole thing off, we've had it. The cold truth is that Best and Stevens have got to be in Berlin later today.'

Suddenly, both men felt as exhilarated and as fresh as if they had enjoyed an untroubled night's sleep. They began hastily to rough out a plan, bearing in mind that the Dutch had doubled the number of frontier guards.

Naujocks pointed out: 'We'll have at least a dozen to deal with, to say nothing of any strays who get in the way. And we'll be working in a pretty confined space. The café at Venlo is single-storeyed with a car park at the back. It'll be a lot like wrenching a stuck cork from a bottle. It's just as well Himmler says we can shoot our way out. There's unlikely to be an alternative.'

Naujocks was speaking now like some hack Hollywood movie director. 'The best thing would be for the British car to crash through the frontier and keep on driving all the way to Berlin. That's only possible if there's a nice big steel barrel sticking in the driver's back. And how do we arrange that?'

Naujocks began working on the answer to his own question.

The next morning's weather was unspeakably foul. Grey rods of icy rain beat against the car windscreen as Naujocks drew off the road some distance behind the German frontier post. Crouched uncomfortably inside the vehicle were the SS bodyguards. More were in another car behind. There was nothing to do now but wait and stare into Holland.

120

Naujocks could just make out the café with a lone figure on the veranda. The scene looked remarkably peaceful. A shopkeeper contentedly puffed a pipe in a doorway. Naujocks felt a moment of anxiety at the approach of a French Renault which pulled up at the raised barrier, but it was soon waved on. There was also a young man on a bicycle who came up from the Dutch side, while a little girl with a black Labrador was loitering by the side of the road.

On the Venlo side, the scene was very different. The Dutch frontier post was being reinforced with tank traps and the sentries touted their sub-machine guns. In addition, there was a sprinkling of civilians trying desperately to look casual. Schellenberg sat in the café, nervously twisting his aperitif glass. He had brought agent F479 and the bogus Generaloberst. The latter had been left in the German customs house; no one was quite sure if he would be needed.

The rain was a cursed nuisance and just might ruin the whole enterprise because soon it was going to be necessary for Naujocks to take down the hood of his car which, in the circumstances, would look decidedly odd.

But suddenly the skies began to look brighter at the precise moment when Naujocks and one of the SS clambered out and started folding down the canvas. The other occupants did not allow themselves to be distracted; their cold eyes were glued to the café and the ribbon of road.

Naujocks leant inside; the silence was broken by the rasp of the engine. Then he walked around and spoke to the driver of the car behind.

What happened might have been pure Humphrey Bogart or George Raft on the back lot at Warner Brothers, but the hit men were strong-armed Nazis in deadly earnest.

Six men clambered out and bunched round the first car, three to each side and with one foot each on the running board. The guards and the onlookers darted some apprehensive stares. Naujocks hoped the whole thing was not going to take too long.

What on earth would happen if no one turned up? Either way, there would probably be a shooting match. There was plenty of ammunition in the open suitcases which lay on the floors of the cars.

Providing the Englishmen obligingly turned up for their own kidnap, there was no real reason for anxiety. After all, they were on the right side of the frontier and had Schellenberg in full view. Best and Stevens would be approaching around a curve; they wouldn't even get a sight of their reception committee until they were almost at the café. They would be looking at Schellenberg, who would provide the necessary distraction. After that, it was all down to speed and muscle.

At precisely 3.20, Schellenberg gave the pre-arranged signal by getting to his feet.

Sigismund Payne Best, looking in briefly at his office before making the journey to Venlo, absently turned over the morning paper and scanned the report of the attempt on Hitler's life. He found it oddly reassuring. Plainly the conspirators were at work, which seemed to lend some credence to Schaemmel, the still mysterious Generaloberst and the rest of them.

Over the last few weeks he had become oddly uneasy, hating the periodic trips to the frontier to meet the Germans. He and Stevens were so vulnerable. There were huge windows in the café where they talked. What would be easier than for a group of SS to cross the border at the back of the café, creep up and pick them off at leisure? It was all nonsense of course. There was no earthly reason why the mission should not be successful, provided the elusive Generaloberst actually showed up.

The shilly-shallying had gone on long enough. Best vowed that if this Schaemmel failed to produce the goods, then the mission would have to be called off.

Now he and Stevens were each pocketing a Browning automatic and Klop-Coppens was to act as chauffeur. Jan Lemmens, driver to Best, also joined the party so that he could bring the car back if the party decided to return by train.

All the way from The Hague, they noticed that military precautions were intensified. There were hold-ups at every road block and tank barrier. As they entered the straight bit of road which gave them a view of the frontier, they noticed that the German barrier across the road, which had always been closed, was now lifted. There was nothing between them and the enemy.

The long low car drifted along slowly to the front of the café, then reversed into the building farthest from the frontier.

At that point, Alfred Naujocks banged in the clutch of his own Mercedes. The jerk sent the men on the running board clutching at the side for support. For some anxious seconds, the vehicle seemed to be sluggish, then the full power of eight cylinders catapulted it forward past the astonished guards.

A weapon appeared like lightning in the hand of every man and now the car was streaking towards the other vehicle, the acrid smell of hot rubber welling up from tyres that screeched like a tortured animal.

The SS men leapt off, running and shouting towards their quarry. Naujocks was brought up short for a moment as a bullet whipped past him and shattered the windscreen.

A man was crouching and running towards the road, firing every inch of the way. Then a burst of machine-gun fire broke above Naujocks's head. The man crumpled. It was Klop, now collapsed in a dark heap of clothes on the grass.

Best was now standing next to Stevens and the latter commented ruefully: 'Our number is up.' Then the two were seized and handcuffs slipped quickly over their wrists.

The whole contingent, with the captors in the centre, moved off at the double, but not before Naujocks had pointed to Best's car and ordered: 'Take it to the frontier.' Later Best was to recall that his main emotion was of anger that the Germans, who had duped him so successfully, should take his car too.

Naujocks clambered into his own car and reversed out. As he drove away he caught a glimpse of a little girl, her arms around a black Labrador, cowering in terror in a garden.

The raid was over. On the whole, it had gone like clock-

123

work, but Naujocks was taken aback to learn that the so-called Lieutenant Coppens was in fact the Dutchman Dirk Klop, now seriously wounded. Taking on the British was fair game, but wounding a soldier from a country with which Germany was not officially at war could turn out to be awkward.

On the other hand, Himmler had plainly not been bothered by such scruples. In the German customs house, where the prisoners were lined up, Naujocks decided that the sooner they all reached Düsseldorf the better. He snapped to his men: 'Get them out of there into the cars. We're off.'

The barriers closed behind the party. The two surviving Allied Intelligence operatives, together with the wretched Lemmens, were soon in Nazi Germany. The Dutch officer, Dirk Klop, died of his wounds the same night.

Best recalled passing the next hours in a daze. There was a dreary sleepless night in a cell at Düsseldorf, then Best, short-sighted because his monocle had been taken away, managed to focus on a sign saying Hanover as the car sped down the Reichautobahn.

He dropped off to sleep again, sustained only by an apple that one of his captors thrust into his mouth. His hands were numb and swollen from the handcuffs and he was unable to draw on the cigarette he had been allowed.

Hanover was left far behind and soon the signs were reading Berlin.

The car stopped outside a large gloomy building and there was a moment of agony as Best, now with a hood over his head, was dragged up a flight of steps and into an office.

Heinrich Mueller had seldom encountered so important a prisoner. He was determined to relish every moment of the triumph of having in the Prinz Albrechtstrasse one of the chief spymasters of the British secret service.

So Mueller thrust his face within an inch of Best and screamed: 'You are in the hands of the Gestapo now. Don't get the idea we will show you the slightest consideration. The Fuehrer has already proved he is invincible. Soon he will liberate England from Jews and plutocrats like you. You're in the greatest danger of your life and if you want to

124

go on living you had better be careful.'

Earlier, Naujocks had confided to Schellenberg: 'That Best is a nasty looking customer. I didn't know they bred that type outside Prussia.' Now Mueller was encountering an Englishman who refused to cower or in any way be intimidated by him.

Best stared straight into Mueller's face with its rapidly flickering eyes and said mildly: 'I have something the matter with my eyes too. Could I perhaps have my monocle?'

For a moment Best was sure that Mueller was going to hit him. The other man turned puce with stuttering rage: 'Don't you worry about glasses or anything else. You will probably be dead before morning.

'I don't seem to be able to get through to you the seriousness of your position. You are in the headquarters of the Gestapo. We can do *anything* with you here.'

Best still refused to be impressed. Plainly here was no common run of Gestapo prisoner to be dragged snivelling to the basement. Maybe somebody higher up could instil some respect into this extraordinary prisoner.

Best needed no introduction to Reinhard Heydrich. Blown up photographs of the head of the RSHA hung in most of the rooms of the Prinz Albrechtstrasse. Best's first impression was of a man far too young to be wearing such a dazzling uniform.

Heydrich forthwith launched into a tirade: 'So far you have been treated as an officer and a gentleman, but don't think this will go on if you don't behave better. You have two hours left in which to confess everything. If you don't, I shall hand you over to the Gestapo, who are used to dealing with such gangsters and criminals. You won't enjoy it.'

Best stared at Heydrich as if he were some choice specimen in a zoo. Then he turned to Mueller and enquired mildly: 'Who is this excitable young officer?'

If Mueller's rage had been spectacular it was nothing to Heydrich's display. As Heydrich clutched the air and literally foamed, Mueller dragged the recalcitrant Best out of the room.

But neither Best nor Stevens were to end up as shambling relics of humanity broken and bruised by Gestapo interrogators. Himmler was convinced, given time, they would be persuaded to volunteer a lot more about the workings of the British secret service.

In addition, the Reichsfuehrer-SS still had to contend with Hitler's unshakeable conviction that the two men were behind the beer hall attempt. The Fuehrer was pondering an eventual painful and bloodthirsty revenge. But, as it turned out, he was going to have to wait.

11

On the evening of 8 November 1939, two German police, carbines at the ready, stood before the frontier post at Constance on the Swiss border.

Behind them, a radio blared out Hitler's beer hall speech. Both men froze at the sight of a lone man attempting to slip past them and make for the frontier. They unslung their weapons and closed in.

The border pass of Johann Georg Elser, a thirty-six-year-old cabinet maker from Württemberg, was out of date. He was marched to the guardhouse and ordered to empty his pockets. The search revealed a handkerchief, a pocket-knife, some bills and coins, a clock spring, some small cogs, a tiny aluminium tube – and a picture postcard of the interior of the beer hall.

This was obviously no ordinary attempt at frontier evasion. The two guards forthwith marched their prisoner to Gestapo headquarters at Constance.

Criminal Inspector Otto Grethe stared menacingly at Elser, who was wearing a dark blue suit, a brown pullover and black shoes. He looked inoffensive enough, but the postcard was enough to put Grethe on his mettle. He switched off Hitler's speech on his own radio and began his questioning.

*

The small hillside farmers of the village of Königsbronn in the Swabian Alps were far too preoccupied with scratching a living to bother overmuch with politics – even of a brand as revolutionary as National Socialism.

Hitler's new paradise left Georg Elser's parents indifferent and unaffected; Georg's mother was more concerned with feeding two sons and three daughters, not helped in the slightest by a husband whose main preoccupation was getting drunk seven nights of the week. One of the sharpest of Georg's earliest memories was pulling off his father's boots each evening – and getting a drunken beating for his pains.

Inevitably, the family was riddled with debt and Elser's smallholding and timber business had to be sold off. Georg, whose main school qualifications were in drawing and geometry, went out to work early.

He started as an apprentice turner in a local iron factory, keeping up his evening classes. He absorbed much about the treatment of crude metals, but work in a foundry began to affect his health. After two years, he left to become apprenticed to a carpenter. In the early 1920s, he established his own well-equipped workshop where he built and repaired furniture, locks and clockwork machinery.

What he knew and subsequently learnt about clocks – at Constance he was to work in a clock factory for seven years – was to prove invaluable.

With Germany already showing signs of an aggressive nationalism and the economy lurching towards disaster, it was perhaps inevitable that sooner or later Georg, unlike his totally indifferent family, would be drawn into politics.

He was no armchair theorist and readily admitted to his friends that reading, other than the newspapers and trade journals, quickly bored him. Politics for him had to mean practical action. Only the Communists promised that. By 1929 Georg Elser had joined the Rotefrontkampferbund, a militant Marxist group founded some years before.

Unlike millions of others, the slump was not to prove too disastrous for him. He was able to get work in clock factories in various towns on Lake Constance.

As a skilled carpenter, he had an added advantage: he

127

could make extra money repairing furniture.

Meanwhile, the siren song of nationalism was beginning to beguile the German people with a vengeance. The shrill voice of Adolf Hitler could not be wished out of existence, even by the most politically indifferent.

Among his fellow Communists, there was talk of the evils of the Munich Agreement and Hitler's designs on the Sudetenland. Above all, there was the depression of workers' wages. The untold riches promised for those who toiled in the Nazi state had not been forthcoming. The Reich labour laws had made it an offence to change one's job; Communists had been rounded up; children were seduced into the Hitler Youth.

But so many of his fellow Communists were prepared merely to rail against tyranny and do nothing whatever about it. Georg itched for action. It was the offer of a seemingly unpromising menial job which enabled him to plan long-term for the beer hall bomb.

The work was as an unskilled labourer in a Heidenheim armament factory. Within months he had worked his way up to a fairly responsible post in the firm's despatch department. What interested him was not so much the job but the merchandise he would be handling – rifle and small cannon ammunition and fusing devices.

Johann Georg Elser began stealing explosives.

Soon he was asking himself: where could he be absolutely sure that Hitler would appear without fail on a certain date? There could be only one answer. At the famous Bürgerbraukeller in Munich on the evening of 8 November of any year.

It was plainly too late in 1938 to carry out an attempt. But a first reconnaissance was obviously called for. On 8 November he inspected the hall. Security, he discovered, was remarkably lax. It was perfectly possible to get in; all the public rooms were easily accessible except in the very small hours.

The next morning, he joined the milling crowds eager to get a glimpse of the Fuehrer. He waited until Hitler had finished his speech and left, surrounded by his cronies.

Then he casually entered the beer hall, ordered a meal

and had a quick look around. The best place to plant an explosive became obvious: in a pillar with wooden panelling and a filling of brick and cement immediately behind and above the speaker's rostrum. It would clearly have to be a time bomb which would go off during Hitler's speech and be detonated not by a fuse but by a clockwork device.

To steal any more explosives where he was working was becoming increasingly risky. Security was rigid. He picked a fight with his supervisor and managed to get himself sacked. On 4 April, he was back at the beer hall. This time, he walked through the main entrance, past the small dining rooms and through the swinging doors into the big main hall where Hitler held his meeting. The doors were not fitted with locks. Swiftly, he whipped out a pocket rule and took the dimensions of the centre column and made a few quick sketches.

Ideally, a job right inside the beer hall would be the answer, but nobody seemed anxious to give him one. Dispirited, he returned to Königsbronn and went to the Nazi labour office to apply for a job as hod carrier with a local stone quarry. The work was crucifying to a scrupulous, studious craftsman and Elser nearly broke under the strain. But it was worth it: the quarry stored gratifyingly large amounts of explosives and detonators. He was able to supplement the store he had already stolen.

Elser managed to secure a key to the storage bunker which contained virtually everything he needed in the way of explosives. Throughout the summer of 1939, he made four or five visits a night between the hours of ten and one to remove small quantities of Donarit and Gelatine. The Gelatine was packed in small paper cartridges, while the Donarit was in compressed tablets. He smuggled out the supplies and hid them in his room, later building a special locker. When his landlady became inquisitive, Elser explained smoothly that he was working on a secret invention which was bound to make his fortune.

The planned assassination now became an obsession which filled all his leisure hours. In a garden, he worked on various kinds of detonators which could be hitched to a time clock. The actual design mechanism was worked out in an endless series of elaborate sketches.

The armament at his disposal became formidable. He could now call on an assortment of wood planes, hammers, set squares, tin shears, graving tools, a compass saw, a precision ruler, scissors, pliers, wood clamps and assorted rasps. There were 50 kilograms of high explosives together with six clock movements, insulated wire, and a six-volt battery. The explosive would be enclosed in a 180-mm brass artillery casing.

On 5 August, Elser left Königsbronn for Munich. From now on, it would be necessary for him to become a well-known figure in the beer hall – a friendly regular whose presence would be accepted without question. It was an appalling risk, of course; the likelihood of later identification was virtually certain. But short of working at the place, which had proved impossible, there was no real alternative.

Each night, forever conscious of his dwindling savings, he would eat a modest meal in the restaurant, staying at his table until closing time. Then he would hide in a small store-room off the dining-hall gallery until the last guest had gone and the place was locked up.

Slowly and laboriously, he had to remove and hinge an eighty centimetre square section of panelling, and chisel and gradually enlarge a hole in the cement filling. Not so much as a pinch of dust could be left behind; each time all tell-tale rubble had to be removed.

All the explosive containers had to be encased in envelopes of scrap metal. The panel door had to be lined with tin; there must be no risk of damage from a chance nail snapping into the panel. Two clocks were used, their loud ticks masked by a layering of cork.

The hours of burrowing began to tell. His knees were stripped of their skin, the inevitable wounds turning septic. These had to be treated by a doctor – one more potentially dangerous witness.

And there was one horrible moment of near discovery. Elser sighed with relief as one particularly taxing night's work was nearing its end. Suddenly, the main doors of the hall were flung open to admit a waiter. Elser saw the man coming and dived for some empty boxes stored behind the pillars. The waiter was not alone. During his various meals, Elser had befriended a large dog. Now it bounded in and made straight for the intruder.

The waiter stared Elser full in the face, then turned and ran. Elser fought a moment of panic, then followed the other man until he came to a table where he sat down, trying to appear calm and absorbed in a writing pad.

The beer hall's owner came bustling up. snapping: 'What are you doing here so early in the morning?'

Elser said humbly: 'I needed somewhere to write a letter privately.'

'Well, you can't do it here,' he was told sharply. 'Go into the garden.'

He shrugged, picked up his sack full of tell-tale rubble and wandered outside. The desire to run for it was overwhelming, but he knew that would ruin everything. He ordered a cup of coffee and tried to appear as unconcerned as possible. He took his time over paying the bill and left as large a tip as he could afford.

Agonisingly, the days and nights inched towards 8 November 1939. Work on the column went on by night, but during the day there was no sleep. Days had to be spent working on the machinery which would trigger the explosive charge.

Mercifully, by 1 a.m. of 6 November, he was able to install the device and set it for sixty-three hours and twenty minutes.

Elser then left Munich for Stuttgart, where he spent the Monday night in the apartment of his sister and her husband. He told the couple that he intended to leave illegally for Switzerland. They asked no questions. They agreed to look after his clothes and possessions and lend him thirty badly needed Reichmarks.

But when he left it was not for Constance. Georg Elser was above all a perfectionist, a professional prepared to leave nothing to chance. His reason argued against it, but a voice was telling him persistently: go back for a final look.

At the beer hall, he made a final inspection. All was well. Within a few hours, he was on the train to Constance.

Adolf Hitler's motorcade, wrapped in its cocoon of steel, streaked through the Munich streets.

At first, Inspector Grethe could get nothing out of his suspect at Constance except a polite insistence that he was not attempting to jump the Swiss border illegally. His story was that he had been on the way to see a friend and got lost.

Then the policeman was handed a telegram: it gave a few sparse details of the bomb explosion and a warning to all frontier posts to be on the lookout. Suddenly, it all made sense: the clock spring, the aluminium detonator part – and of course the tell-tale postcard.

Inspector Grethe reached for the telephone. By next morning, Georg Elser was on his way to Gestapo headquarters in Munich.

To Schellenberg, the suggestion that Georg Elser, the obsessive clockmaker, had been in league with Best and Stevens was patently absurd.

But Hitler would have none of it. He stated: 'All three will be tried together after the war. It will be a great public trial.' It was all to be a show trial for the cleverness of the Nazis in bringing the would-be assassins to book.

Hitler's pride had been hurt. It would never have done to suggest that one single man could have penetrated Hitler's elaborate security and come within an ace of killing him. Some triumph must plainly be manufactured; a public tribunal would be an unrivalled spectacle.

Schellenberg greeted a desperately tired Heinrich Mueller in the Gestapo cellars and repeated his doubts. Mueller reluctantly agreed but commented: 'It's no good trying to shift the Fuehrer. Himmler and Heydrich got precisely nowhere. It's not worth trying and you could burn your fingers.'

Schellenberg said: 'Is *anyone* behind Elser? Or did he act entirely by himself?'

Mueller held out one of his enormous hands; the knuckles were crushed and bleeding. He said meaningfully: 'Elser has added nothing to his original story – even with a little persuasion. He admits that he wanted to kill the

Fuehrer and would have been very happy if he had succeeded. Apart from that, nothing.'

He massaged his damaged knuckles and added with great emphasis: 'I've never had a man in front of me yet whom I did not break.'

Despite himself, Schellenberg shuddered. Mueller noticed and said: 'If Elser had been given some of the medicine he has had from me earlier on, he would never have tried this business.'

Elser had indeed learnt what Gestapo interrogation could mean. Intensive grilling had included injections of truth serum and sessions of hypnosis. But always the story had been the same. He had never heard of Best and Stevens, knew no one in the British secret service and had no connection with any Communist organisation. These preliminary examinations with their negative results were forwarded to Himmler, who exploded with rage. The Reichsfuehrer-SS decided to fly to Munich and confront Elser personally. What happened at the meeting was recorded by Dr Bohme of the Munich Gestapo:

'With wild curses, Himmler drove his boots hard into Elser's body. He then had him removed by a Gestapo official and taken to the lavatory where he was beaten with a whip until he howled with pain. Elser, still handcuffed, was dragged back at the double to Himmler, who once more kicked and cursed him. In addition, the Gestapo arrested his mother and various other relations, but Elser refused to change his testimony.'

Dark suggestions were also made that he was in the pay of Otto Strasser who had offered him 40,000 Swiss francs and a free pass to Switzerland. The Gestapo, backed by a posse of hypnotists, were unable to prove anything.

The Gestapo ordered a short-term clampdown by the German press on Elser's arrest until a complete confession had been secured. It was merely stated that Elser was the prime suspect as the instigator of the beer hall explosion and a substantial reward was offered for his arrest. It was all clever propaganda window-dressing. A few days later, Himmler announced that, since the arrest had been made

133

by the Gestapo, the reward was forthwith cancelled.

Himmler had no problem when it came to controlling his own newspapers, but he could not stop speculation and downright cynicism in the foreign press. In the British *News Chronicle* on 23 November the writer A.J. Cummings asked pointedly: 'What evidence is there to show that Strasser and the British Intelligence Service were connected with the explosion? Himmler so far has offered none.'

The newspaper tracked down Otto Strasser to Paris where he stated: 'I don't know Elser: and moreover I am certain he is not one of my men. I have never known Best or Stevens, the two Englishmen mentioned by Himmler. If the Gestapo has decided that it will be useful to launch an accusation against our Schwarze Front that convinces me of the power of our organisation. It shows the Gestapo recognises the widespread character of our action in the interior of the Reich.'

Whatever Elser may or may not have told the Gestapo, on one subject he was positively garrulous.

When he was questioned about his bomb he became a man transformed. To his astounded interrogators, he launched into a minute exposition of the problems involved in constructing the weapon. Mueller placed an entire carpenter's shop at Elser's disposal and he was ordered to rebuild the bomb and make a wooden pillar identical with the one in the beer hall. Without any further prompting, Elser readily described how he had concealed the bomb. He was back in the world he understood.

As for Hitler, he stuck to his own conspiracy theory. On Tuesday, 21 November, all the German papers had published the results of the enquiry into the explosion. The Nazis' own mouthpiece, *Voelkischer Beobachter,* carried Elser's picture next to news of the arrest of Best and Stevens. The implication was obvious.

Himmler was ordered to confine Elser to solitary imprisonment at Sachsenhausen-Oranienburg concentration camp where Best and Stevens, who went on to survive the war, were also held.

Georg Elser did not survive to defend himself in a dock

or anywhere else. In 1944, he was transferred to Dachau. By then defeat stared Germany in the face and Hitler had been robbed of the trial of which he had dreamed.

On the morning of 5 April 1945, came an order from Himmler to Eduard Weiter, commandant of Dachau. Elser was to be liquidated.

The carpenter was accompanied to the crematorium by two SS guards who had told him he was to repair a door. Elser suspecting nothing: he had often been used for odd jobs around the camp.

As he entered the crematorium, a sudden blow from behind smashed his skull. Then there was a succession of bullets to the nape of the neck. The bloodstained body was stripped and placed on an iron trolley.

Along with two others who had been similarly de-spatched, the corpse was quickly tossed into the flames.

Schellenberg was less than satisfied with what had been achieved at Venlo. He remained convinced that, if nego-tiations had proceeded normally, he could have found out a lot more about the intelligence apparatus of the allies in the Netherlands.

Nevertheless, the Nazi propaganda machine exploited gleefully every aspect of the capture of the two agents. It was claimed that Schellenberg and the Gestapo chief in Dusseldorf had wrenched a confession from Lieutenant Klop before he died. Klop, it was alleged, had admitted the existence of plans 'actively supported by the Dutch General Staff in continuous consultation with the British General Staff' to overthow the Nazi regime. It was but one useful pretext for the German invasion of Holland, which was followed by the onslaught across Belgium and France.

Almost certainly no such confession existed. It scarcely mattered. The activities of two top agents had been smashed. Britain's plans for contacting would-be resisters to Hitler in Germany had been set at naught.

There was kudos also for individual Gestapo agents. Schellenberg and Naujocks, along with others, were sum-moned to the heavy splendours of the Reich Chancellery.

Hitler entered with his characteristically imperious

stride. He was glaring and Naujocks found himself suddenly wondering if he was in for a dressing down.

Then the Reich Chancellor was speaking: 'I am profoundly grateful for your achievement,' he said. 'The British secret service has a great tradition. Germany cannot even begin to hold a candle to it. You have shown resolution, initiative and courage. Consequently, I intend to present decorations to members of the German secret service for the first time.'

Naujocks, resplendent in dress uniform, felt Hitler's fingers on his breast pocket and the tiny click of the pin of the Iron Cross First Class.

There were more words of congratulation, followed inevitably by the brisk Nazi salute. The investiture was at an end.

Schellenberg, the eternal bureaucrat, came inwardly as near ecstasy as was possible for him. In his memoirs, he was to write primly: 'I must confess that at the time I was most impressed by the whole ceremony.'

12

Although the Gestapo tightened its iron grip increasingly on every aspect of German life, in the early days it was still possible, given dumb acquiescence, to lead a relatively normal existence in Hitler's Germany.

But from September 1939 all that changed.

Arrests suddenly became arbitrary. Any person as much as suspected of listening to foreign broadcasts was at risk. False 'for sale' advertisements were placed by the Gestapo in newspapers, offering powerful second-hand radios fitted with earphones. The Gestapo had already confiscated all stocks of earphones at dealers' shops, then questioned those buyers whom they could trace and seized their purchases.

It occurred to Mueller to cast his net wider. Those ill-advised enough to reply to the fake advertisements were promptly arrested and put on the list of 'suspected persons'. Often those picked up were paraded through the streets. Behind them strode the Gestapo agents, ostentatiously displaying the offending radio sets.

It was also announced that anyone found with a leaflet dropped from a British aircraft would be shot. Propaganda communications rotted in fields and woods all over Germany. Few were picked up; there was the ever-present risk of informers.

The maintenance of a total police state was soon providing Himmler and Heydrich with an acute manpower problem. Himmler began drawing on other sections of the SS for Gestapo agents. There was no shortage of volunteers. Scores of SS men reasoned that it was better to carve out a career terrorising one's fellow Germans than risking life on the battlefield. In their new role, Gestapo conscripts showed remarkable zeal.

Even so, preparations were well ahead for the role of the Gestapo in those countries not yet crushed by the invading armies.

And nothing, it seemed, could stop the Wehrmacht riding on its high tide of triumph to the Channel ports and beyond.

After four days of fruitless resistance, the Dutch capitulated on 14 May 1940. Hitler had knifed through to Rotterdam – undefended except for a few anti-aircraft guns which attempted to grapple with German Stukas.

The defence plan of General Winkelmann, commander-in-chief of all defence forces, to give up the northern and eastern parts of the Netherlands and stand fast within Fortress Holland, had crumbled. Nine million people passed under the Nazi yoke.

The hurricane of steel blew on into France. By 14 June, the OKW issued the following communique:

'As a result of the collapse of the entire French front between the Channel and the Maginot Line near Mont-

137

medy, the French High Command has abandoned its original intention of defending the French capital. While this communique is being broadcast the victorious German troops are entering Paris.

And into both the Netherlands and France went the whole cumbersome bureaucratic apparatus of the SD and Gestapo.

In Holland, Dr Arthur Seyss-Inquart, an Austrian and a Nazi party member since 1931, took over as Reich Kommissar. Obergruppenfuehrer Hans Albin Rauter was Seyss-Inquart's right-hand man and was to serve during the occupation of the Netherlands as Höhere SS Polizeifuehrer (Higher SS and Police Leader) and General-Kommissar für das Sicherheitswesen (General Commissioner for Public Safety). As such, Rauter was in charge of the entire police force in Holland, and had under his orders the heads of the most important branches of the German police.

At first the conqueror's approach was misleadingly bland, even benevolent. Seyss-Inquart announced: 'From today, I have taken over the highest civil authority in the Netherlands. The magnaminity of the Fuehrer and the force of German arms have made it possible that only a few days after the catastrophe that was brought about by the former leaders of the Netherlands, order is being restored to public life. Certain measures will be taken, but only in so far as the circumstances will make them necessary ...' Restaurants, cafés and cinemas were reopened and the prohibition on alcohol lifted. Seyss-Inquart added: 'It is expected that the population will show their appreciation for these favours by continued good behaviour.'

But the Dutch were left in no doubt that they had in fact been crushed by the armed fists of the Nazis. Seyss-Inquart delivered his address of inauguration in a Teutonic blaze of splendour. The setting was the ancient Hall of the Knights at The Hague where Queen Wilhelmina used to open the winter session of the government in solemn ceremony. The fact that a new regime was indisputably in control was sharply underlined by the presence of the orchestra of the Cologne Broadcasting Station, specially imported for the day.

Some Netherlanders heaved a sigh of relief. Their country had suffered appallingly, of course. But at least it seemed that the Germans did not intend to launch a programme of wholesale repression. Seyss-Inquart's other remarks had been encouraging: 'We are to build a new Europe based upon the foundations of honour and common labour. We all know that the ultimate purpose of our Fuehrer is peace and order for all who are of goodwill.'

But already harsh decrees had been issued from Gestapo headquarters in Amsterdam. Dutchmen were ordered to listen only to German-controlled radio stations. All radios capable of receiving foreign stations would be confiscated. Hilversum radio had announced: 'No Dutchman is allowed to buy more than one day's minimum food supplies. Clothes-buying must be restricted for an indefinite period. German treasury certificates are legal money and must be accepted at one-and-a-half marks to the Dutch guilder. Anyone found possessing firearms without written permission of the German military authorities will be shot.'

By 5 June, there were more ominous signs. A new official journal, *Verordeningenblad*, was launched. It announced that four General Kommissars were to be appointed as assistants to Seyss-Inquart 'with the special task of supervising and directing the various government departments'.

Behind the scenes, Rauter was busy. He planned that the Security Police (Sicherheitspolizei), which included the Gestapo, would concern itself with the detection of all who committed political offences. The SD remained, as in Germany, the very heart of the police state with power over every department. Dutch undercover agents, known as V-men (Veterauensmanner), were given the job of infiltrating underground organisations. Augmenting the activities of all these groups, including the Gestapo, were the notorious 'Green Police' who, in conjunction with the Gestapo, would carry out arrests, mass raids, deportations, actions against strikes and executions. Here was the very incarnation of Nazi police terror.

One aspect of the SD and Gestapo's task was to prove

comparatively easy. The Germans found in Holland a rich vein of shamelessly willing collaborators.

In pre-war days, the National Socialist Party of the Netherlands (Nationaal Socialistische Beweging) attracted few followers, but its founder, village schoolmaster's son Anton Adriaan Mussert, was a man with a dream – and two idols.

In the early 1920s, he had been drawn first to the raucous bellicosity of Benito Mussolini, the charismatic conqueror of Abyssinia. Rejected by the Liberal Party as a candidate, the neurotic Mussert was now determined to found his own political party on rigidly authoritarian lines. Impatiently, he began to look for a ready-made model and seized on Hitler's pronouncements in *Mein Kampf*. By this time he had attracted a number of fellow thinkers – a ragbag of hotheads which included one or two disgruntled intellectuals, among them a university professor who undertook to work out the party programme.

By 1934, the year after Hitler came to power, the movement had imperceptibly gained respectability and the Dutch government was seriously alarmed. Hitler's strident warnings against the rising red tide of Bolshevism prompted sympathisers among Dutch businessmen to start covertly backing the NSB. Just before the outbreak of war, the party could boast a membership of some 40,000.

At a meeting in Utrecht, the besotted Mussert cried: 'Adolf Hitler is the man who to the entire Germanic world is a gift of God such as is made only once every thousand years.' Theo van Duren, a member of the Dutch resistance, recalled after the war: 'We began to see the uniforms of the Dutch National Socialists. The party had existed since 1933 but had always been forbidden to wear uniform. Now they were strutting around in their black outfits and jackboots, more insolent even than the Germans.'

Two years after the occupation, Seyss-Inquart made a momentous announcement. The Fuehrer had recognised the Nationaal Socialistische Beweging (or NSB) as the only bearer of political life in the Netherlands and had appointed Anton Mussert, the NSB chief, as leader of the Netherlands' people. Seyss-Inquart declared: 'He and his party will henceforth be consulted on all important matters concerning the administration of Holland.'

Right from the start, the Gestapo had a valuable ally – and the Dutch two sorts of enemy.

Elsewhere in the vassal states of the Third Reich there had been no soft introduction to the rule of terror.

The police services had entered Austria, Czechoslovakia and Poland at the same time as the fighting troops. Himmler had brushed aside the protests of certain sections of the OKW. The SD Einsatzgruppe (combat groups), subdivided into Einsatzkommandos (extermination squads) under the direct control of Heydrich, were authorised to carry out 'house cleaning' in Poland to be directed against Jews, intelligentsia and nobility.

Heydrich had unveiled his plans at a top meeting at RSHA headquarters in the Wilhelmstrasse. One of those who attended was an ambitious young Nazi who had started his career in the old days of the SD as a filing clerk.

But he had not regarded the job as a lowly one. Far from it. Here was a born organiser to whom an efficient bureaucracy was one of life's noblest concepts.

Heydrich entrusted to this paragon Amt IV-A4B, one of the Gestapo's six sections. This particular one dealt with 'churches, sects, Jews and gypsies', taking in 'Jewish affairs, evacuations, recovery of goods held by "Enemies of the people and the Reich", forfeiture of German nationality'.

Encapsulated, the function of Amt IV-A4B was nothing less than to mastermind the 'final solution' of the Jewish problem.

The section was staffed by some twelve senior officials. But history remembers only one of them: his name was Adolf Eichmann.

Heydrich announced bluntly that he was far from satisfied with the present rate of Jewish deportations to Poland. The Einsatzgruppe leaders present at the meeting were ordered to step up by at least another four hundred thousand, in addition to those seventy-eight thousand already accounted for. The deportations, death marches and mass shootings forthwith went into top gear.

In France, the situation was to prove rather different. The OKW, faced with Hitler's operational plans for the west, protested volubly against the employment of the sort of slaughter machines suffered in the east. Hitler was forced to yield to the insistence that no police unit, no SD Einsatzkommando, was to accompany the army in the advance through France. Police powers were to be under the sole control of the army.

It was an ultimatum which threw Himmler into a blind rage. The army establishment, who regarded him with something less than contempt, had won. It was a direct blow to his authority. Like a child robbed of his toys, Himmler sulked – and did so in the presence of Heydrich.

The head of the RSHA was reassuring. He had the glimmer of an idea.

The invading armies swept into Paris at 5.30 a.m. on 14 June 1940. The troops of von Kuechler's 18th Army entered the city by the Porte de Villette. At dawn, formations advanced towards the Eiffel Tower and the Arc de Triomphe. Generaloberst von Stutnitz, first Kommandant of 'Greater Paris', was installed in the Hotel Crillon.

Among all the bustle, it is doubtful whether much attention was given to just twenty men who entered Paris in a few light vehicles with little armament. A Sonderkommando (special commando group), they wore the uniform of Geheime Feld Polizei, the secret military police.

Heydrich was careful to see the vehicles displayed military number-plates; they were able to reach Paris unchallenged.

The Gestapo presence was deliberately kept sparse; Mueller's representative was an old crony Sturmbannfuehrer Boemelberg, a former policeman of commendable efficiency and homosexual proclivities.

At this stage, however, he had little power. His instructions were to keep eyes and ears open and wait.

Boemelberg was able to move around Paris with fair ease. He had studied maps and information on France at Gestapo headquarters. Heydrich's files had bulged, not

142

just with dossiers on individuals, but minute documentation of the cultural, religious and political workings of France. Gestapo agents in Berlin had, in addition to looking after their own area, responsibility for shadowing 'Region V' – the codename for Paris.

Boemelberg, installed in considerable comfort at the Hotel de Louvre, rose early on his first morning in Paris. There was a hurried meeting. Within hours, a Gestapo representative was at the Prefecture. Tersely, he demanded forthwith the complete dossier on German emigrés and Jews, together with the names of anyone likely to be hostile to the Nazis.

Meanwhile, Helmut Knochen, Heydrich's senior representative on the Sonderkommando, was equally busy. Knochen belonged to that little group of SD that Gestapo Mueller had so openly despised all those years back in the presence of Schellenberg. With his mop of auburn hair and considerable charm, he looked less like an SS thug than a junior diplomat with a bright future, except for the wide slash of mouth and the penetrating eyes of cold marble. He had been one of the brains at Venlo and a recipient of the Iron Cross First Class. 'One of Heydrich's intellectual thugs,' sneered a colleague who had less than love for him. It was not at all a bad description.

But Knochen and the rest fully realised the strength of the army that ultimately held power. The SD and the Gestapo had entered Paris by subterfuge and had to tread warily.

Knochen could be skilfully charming and tactful. He set out to woo the army by positively exuding reasonableness. He let it be known that he had no intention of interfering with the army of occupation. He would confine himself purely to dealing with such tiresome elements as Jews, Freemasons and Communists. Knochen also courted the military police with considerable skill. He stressed to its chiefs that they alone would have the power of arrest. His men would merely provide the necessary evidence and call on assistance from time to time.

The army was fairly happy. After all, this fellow Knochen had a mere twenty men under his command. He was unlikely to be too much of a nuisance and seemed perfectly prepared to submit to military discipline.

But Knochen had established a bridgehead with the skill of a military tactician. Within weeks, the number of Sonderkommando increased dramatically as Heydrich sent in reinforcements.

The days of the velvet glove were coming to an end. The time had arrived to try something more dramatic.

A series of deafening explosions ripped through the streets of Paris during the night of 2/3 October 1941. By 2.30 a.m., the synagogues were blazing fiercely. An hour later, a charge erupted in the rue Notre Dame de Nazareth. Next it was the turn of the large synagogue in the rue de la Victoire.

In all there were seven dramatic incidents. Jews were not the only ones to suffer. There were victims among Wehrmacht patrols, and damage to neighbouring buildings was extensive.

Frustration and impatience the previous year had driven Knochen into seemingly senseless violence which harmed the occupying Germans every bit as much as the people of Paris.

Knochen's attempts to infiltrate the SD and the Gestapo into occupied Paris had one implacable opponent throughout. General von Stuelpnagel, head of Militärbefehlshaber (military command in France), was utterly opposed to the very presence of the agents of Himmler and Heydrich. Icily, von Stuelpnagel pointed out that the Sonderkommando was interfering in virtually every section of the occupation machinery. For example, they had no business dabbling with matters of security and military intelligence. That was the business of military intelligence – Abwehr.

Von Stuelpnagel proceeded to block Knochen's means of communicating with Heydrich in Berlin. Furthermore, Knochen was forbidden to mastermind the activities of the Gestapo and the secret military police.

It was a serious blow. Knochen might be given the cold shoulder by the military but he reflected that fortunately he had another ally.

Brigadefuehrer Dr Thomas, who arrived in Paris as Heydrich's personal representative to supervise all Sonderkommando, had been one of Heydrich's constant companions around the fleshpots of Berlin. A broad, powerful blusterer, Thomas did absolutely everything to excess. He womanised with almost mystic dedication. His drinking bouts were legendary. Crippled every morning of his life with appalling hangovers which rendered him all but sightless, he was physically incapable of sound administration. The workings of an intelligence machine he understood not at all and treated with a cavalier contempt.

But his carousings were not entirely self-indulgent. In the half-light of the fleshy cabarets of the Place Pigalle and the Champs-Élysées he was able to make fruitful contacts with possible collaborators. Thomas was roped in by Knochen on the Paris cocktail circuit. Both men soon became privy to all the lively gossip of Paris, picking up frequently scandalous details about statesmen and politicians and, of even more value, likely resistance groups and their offshoots.

Thomas was also fuelled by a commodity even more potent than alcohol: hatred of the Jews. He courted assiduously undercover movements sympathetic to the Nazis, most notably the rabidly anti-Semitic Mouvement Social Revolutionnaire (MSR).

The suggestion that a number of attempts should be made against Paris synagogues came from the MSR leaders. It would be a useful supplement to a campaign against the Jews currently run by certain newspapers who had been in receipt of German funds, channelled in their direction by Thomas himself.

Obersturmfuehrer Hans Sommer of Amt VI of RSHA was detailed to liaise with MSR and arrange for the explosions at the synagogues.

Thomas and Knochen were ecstatic at the result. But for von Stuelpnagel the whole affair smacked of appalling irresponsibility. He was jealous of the prestige of his occupation army and had no intention of allowing Heydrich's gangsters to put it in jeopardy. In a fury, he fired off a salvo to Berlin. The letter, addressed to Heydrich as head of

SIPO-SD in Berlin, concluded:

'The responsibility for the measures taken by the Sonderkommando of the SIPO-SD and for the behaviour of this Sonderkommando is assumed by its leader, even if it is not admitted that the latter participated directly in the affair. There must, however, be a change in the leadership of the Sonderkommando by reason of the political implications on the position of the German administration. For this reason, the commander-in-chief of the German army demands that SS-Brigadefuehrer Thomas be relieved of his post. The OKW takes it for granted the Berlin authorities are in agreement that Dr Knochen and SS Obersturmfuehrer Sommer should no longer be employed in occupied territory.'

Heydrich was a man quite prepared to make initial compromises, provided his long-term objectives were not unduly threatened. He reasoned that if one lamb had better go to the slaughter it might as well be his old tippling companion, Thomas.

Within days the Brigadefuehrer announced that he had 'asked to be relieved of his duties'. He was sent complete with hangover to the newly occupied territories of Kiev as head of the SIPO-SD.

There could, however, be no question of Knochen leaving France. He was altogether too valuable to Heydrich.

Von Stuelpnagel considered that he had won at least half a victory. The military authorities believed strongly that the French themselves must ensure the administration of their country, under the direction and control of the occupying forces of course. But back in Berlin, the philosophy was very different. The grip of the Gestapo, far from being lessened with the departure of Thomas, was soon to intensify.

Increased power was now vested in twenty-seven-year-old Bavarian Theo Dannecker, who was nominally under Knochen's authority but in fact received orders directly from Adolf Eichmann, who had personally appointed him as his representative in Paris.

Thomas's hatred of the Jews had been brutal and unsubtle. With Dannecker, the loathing was sadistic and pathological. In his role as French head of Amt IV A4B in Paris, he was constitutionally incapable of understanding why even the most ardent pro-German French insisted on regarding the Jews as Frenchmen first and Jews afterwards.

He became absolute master of that section of the Gestapo concerned eventually with the rounding-up and deporting of French Jews to the concentration camps and gas chambers.

Dannecker possessed power which even Thomas, responsible only to Heydrich, could never have dreamed of.

His supreme authority was Eichmann, who had the ear of Himmler and ultimately of Hitler himself. He was determined to use it.

Indeed, if he wanted to survive it was vital that he did.

Murmurings filtered back to Germany that von Stuelpnagel's occupation policy overall was too soft.

He was ordered to go over to a hard line. The result, on 22 August 1941, was a decree that all Frenchmen detained by the German authorities were to be considered as hostages and could be shot 'according to the gravity of the acts'.

It was a start, but it was not nearly enough to satisfy the sinister trio of Himmler, Heydrich and Eichmann. The Gestapo was still forced to maintain its muted role, but behind the scenes Knochen was busy shaping his miniature RSHA into the Berlin model.

There was, however, to be one essential difference: a healthy leaven of recruits would be drawn not from Germans, but from only-too-eager Frenchmen.

147

13

The pitiful group of French refugees shambled dispiritedly along a southbound road hopelessly choked with a chaotic knot of carts, trucks and tired, defeated troops.

Out of the quiet skies catapulted the Stukas with their terrible whine of menace. Machine-guns and bombs tore into the defenceless convoys.

Henri Chamberlin and three of his companions were to be lucky on that June day in 1940. The four men disentangled themselves from the appalling roadside carnage. Ducking low, they ran zigzag for nearby woods.

It was a situation common enough in every country subjected to German invasion, but on this day, on the road leading to Montargis the miraculous escape of Chamberlin and his friends was rather different.

For a start, none of the men had the slightest sympathy for the victims of the slaughter they left behind. Indeed, even as they ran they blessed the Germans for giving them a break for which they had never dared hope.

Tall husky thirty-five-year-old Henri Chamberlin had been arrested recently on a criminal charge and sent to Cepoy prison. Those who joined him now in the woods were already undercover Abwehr agents, previously in the custody of the French.

At the time of the Stuka raid, all had been under armed guard. Through diabolical luck all had been spared. It was to be a fortunate gain for the Gestapo.

Chamberlin, born in the Paris slums, had a background steeped in crime. During World War I, he had scrounged and thieved in the teeming markets of Les Halles and eventually ended up in a reform school. Later, he had been in and out of jail on a succession of petty charges. In 1939, his bid to enlist in the French army was turned down. Under the cover name of Henri Normand he next took a job as a car salesman, but the authorities soon swooped down with a warrant for his arrest. Life had looked singularly black on that road to Montargis.

Nobody paid attention to the four nondescripts who eventually found their way back to Paris. The honour of France had been dragged in the mud. The capital reflected the general mood of a people betrayed. Parisians were in mourning under grey skies. The only sound to break the silence was the blaring of the German band on its daily progress down the Champs Élysées.

One of the agents, a Swiss named Max Stocklin, made his way swiftly to the Hotel Lutetia on the Boulevard Raspail, headquarters of the Abwehr. Chamberlin, he told his superiors, would be an ideal recruit. A criminal rejected by his own army would surely make an admirable collaborator. Apart from that, his obvious contacts in the underworld would obviously be invaluable.

There was another pressing reason for seriously considering this rather unpleasant opportunist as a recruit. The Abwehr was anxious to be underway with a scheme which entailed nothing less than the systematic looting of France. It seemed a form of activity admirably suited to the twisted talents of Henri Chamberlin.

Chamberlin (or Henri Lafont as he was now calling himself) was promptly put in charge of one of the numerous purchasing offices through which the German military command looted France of almost anything that could be bought, stolen, confiscated or extorted. In cases where purchase was thought desirable, the Vichy government was on hand with impressive sums of 'occupation francs'.

Lafont took to his work as middle-man with eagerness and considerable success.

Then one day came the summons to the Hotel Lutetia and an interview with Abwehr Hauptmann Radecke. The German stared in silence at the elegant well-dressed young man who but a short time before had been in rags and was lucky not to be rotting in either jail or quick lime.

He said coldly: 'You have done very well. Now perhaps

149

you would like to try something else. It is considerably more important and delicate than your previous work.'

Lafont smiled inwardly. He knew perfectly well that there was no 'perhaps' about it. Refuse the Abwehr its slightest whim and his career would be over with one swift bullet.

Radecke went on smoothly: 'For the last six months, we have been trying to lay the leader of the Belgian resistance by the heels. His name is Lambrecht and so far he has eluded us. Find him, my dear Lafont, and you have a very bright future indeed.'

The Frenchman decided swiftly that the only way to deal with a man like Radecke was to treat him as an equal.

He replied firmly: 'To take on that sort of job, I need organisation and money. Without staff, I would be dead within days because the Belgian resistance would undoubtedly kill me.

'I know where there is some useful manpower. Behind bars at Fresnes prison. It's the best talent in France.'

Radecke looked at the other man with admiration. It was a brilliant idea to empty the jails but horribly risky. It was unlikely that the stuffy Stuelpnagel with his old fashioned ideas of Prussian propriety would ever countenance such a thing. It would have to be done quickly or more than a few heads would be on the chopping block. He said mildly: 'Well, what are we waiting for? I think we should pay a little visit to Fresnes.'

By evening, Lafont had personally selected twenty-five of the most dangerous men in the country. Not all, he reasoned, would take part in this one mission, but they would be extremely useful later.

Although he did not know it at the time, Lafont had just recruited the nucleus of France's inner Gestapo.

The unfortunate derelict Belgian mumbled drunkenly at the corner of the Bordeaux bar, buttonholing anyone who would listen to his rambling stories of the brutal Germans and how as a true patriot he would do anything to get even with them. But with each glass of wine Lafont in fact became steadily more sober.

And he kept his ears open, straining for the slightest hint of the whereabouts of his quarry. Several bottles and sleazy bars later, he learnt that the resistance leader was in hiding in Toulouse. Another whining hard luck story and he had the address of Lambrecht in his pocket.

It was just after dawn when the big car with five men pulled up quietly in front of the house in Toulouse. All wore German uniforms. Lafont told his men to wait; this particular coup was going to be for him alone.

Lambrecht, lather covering his face, jerked round in fear as the bathroom door was flung open. Then the fist crashed into his face and he dropped senseless to the floor. Lafont pinned the man's arms behind him and dragged him down to the waiting car, which soon screeched its way to the headquarters of the local Gestapo.

Lafont still saw himself as the hero and he insisted on conducting the initial interrogation personally. Then the questioners were changed every four hours. Only the means of persuasion were constant – whippings, blows with the fist, clubbing and kicks.

Lambrecht took the appalling assault on his broken body for two days. Then he talked and in doing so betrayed a network of cells in France, Belgium and Holland. As a result, the Abwehr was able to make over 600 arrests.

News of Lafont's success spread far beyond Abwehr circles. The official Gestapo in France was both envious and annoyed. Its rivalry with the Abwehr had grown steadily more bitter. What a marvellous coup it would be if the Geheime Staatspolizei could snatch away the brutal young recruit from military intelligence!

Lafont secured an introduction to Boemelberg and was quick to press his suit with the maximum of flattery. Boemelberg mentioned that he was particularly fond of French cooking. The next day some of the choicest dishes from a leading Paris restaurant were delivered to his office. Lafont went even better. Two agreeable youths were told to present themselves at the Hotel de Louvre.

Soon a delighted Boemelberg was enthusing to Knochen: 'This young man must not be wasted on the Abwehr.'

A subtle wooing campaign was instituted. As well as money, Lafont received weapons, police identification cards and unlimited petrol.

He also had his own headquarters at 93 rue Lauriston, a grey house with large rooms in a discreetly wealthy district. Here he was soon joined by Pierre Bonny, a former police-man who had tarnished his reputation by taking bribes.

Bonny was to help transform the house from a mere collaboration cell to a thriving department of the occupying power, a Gestapo within a Gestapo. Shrewdly emulating Teutonic thoroughness, Lafont was soon forwarding regular reports to his German paymasters.

It was as the scourge of the secret army of the resistance that Lafont and Bonny were to be of such special value to the Gestapo. Their agents penetrated the opposition time and again. Victims were dragged to the filthy cellars of the rue Lauriston. Through a haze of pain, they heard Lafont's curiously girlish high-pitched voice, screaming at them to talk. And then the ever-present whip would crash into their faces, buttocks and kidneys.

If any of Lafont's collaborationist butchers had a twinge of conscience there was always a generous pay packet to compensate. Besides, the feeling of a German-authorised police card in the pocket was wonderfully reassuring.

The lights from the glittering chandeliers of the Ritz Hotel in Paris shone on one of the most lavish social events the capital had witnessed in years. Reinhard Heydrich had been determined to make his visit to Paris in style. A party was always a good way of softening people before suddenly changing the mood and springing unpleasant news on them.

For anyone present at the Ritz on 7 May 1942 it seemed that the clock had been put back most agreeably a year or so. Representatives of French society circulated as they had always done. But even euphoria induced by excellent champagne could not blot out the sight of all those German uniforms.

And there was a newcomer. Heydrich was in Paris to introduce with appropriate splendour his latest protégé, pink-cheeked misleadingly benevolent Brigadefuehrer Karl Albrecht Oberg.

By rights, Himmler should have been present. Oberg was the product of a long wheedling campaign which the Reichsfuehrer-SS had conducted with Hitler. Himmler had pleaded that the occupying powers in France had grown soft. The army's influence over the police was really quite intolerable. It was high time the SS had one supreme boss.

Hitler gave in and Heydrich moved fast. Oberg was his appointee and he had no intention of allowing his pigeon-chested myopic chief to steal the thunder and announce the appointment from behind some dreary office desk. Heydrich was determined to grab all the kudos for himself with a dash of style. It was quite out of the question, Heydrich insinuated, for the Reichsfuehrer-SS to leave Berlin at this time. His presence in the centre of the Reich was quite indispensable. Himmler, not for the first time, succumbed to flattery. Heydrich went to Paris.

Karl Oberg was an almost classic career Nazi. He had fought on the Western Front as an Oberleutnant in World War I and had been decorated with the Iron Cross, both First and Second Class. But like so many, he had soon learnt that medals neither paid bills nor guaranteed a job. The depression wiped out the savings of the middle-classes and the Oberg family was no exception. By 1930, Karl, with a young wife, was existing precariously as the proprietor of a tobacco kiosk in his native Hamburg.

In June 1931, he joined the National Socialists as party member no. 575205. Rules dictated that he had to attach himself to one of the NSDAP's numerous organisations. Oberg would have agreed profoundly with Schellenberg's admission in his memoirs: 'In the SS, one met a better class of person.' He approached Heydrich, who not only approved his candidature but took him into the SD.

After that, his rise, both in intelligence and military work for the SS, was rapid. By September 1941, Oberg was SD und Polizeifuehrer at Radom in Poland where he took part in the Jewish pogroms.

Yet outwardly he appeared reassuring to the apprehensive guests at the Ritz Hotel that day. What they saw was a fair-haired pink-cheeked man in early middle age with a pot-belly. He had his counterpart all over the world: the not over-ambitious middle-class suburbanite devoted almost equally to family and weekend gardening.

The workers of Poland would have told a different story. And soon the French were to learn. For this ponderous, kindly father of three, when a Vichy official came to complain about the kidnapping of Jewish children from Jewish orphanages in the unoccupied zone of the country, snarled: '*Ein Jude ist kein Mensch!*' ('A Jew is not a human being!')

Oberg's rank was 'Höher SS und Polizeifuehrer', the same as that of Rauter in Holland. His power was absolute. It amounted to total victory of the Gestapo over the German army command in France. Heydrich had come to Paris with a directive from Himmler which gave Oberg sway over 'all police matters and reprisals against criminals, Jews, and Communists implicated in attacks against the German Reich or the citizens of the Reich'.

The army command could only give Oberg orders on matters concerning military operations of German armed forces security in France. All disputes between the two services would be referred to Himmler and ultimately to Hitler.

That was only a beginning. General Heinrich von Stuelpnagel, who had succeeded his cousin Otto as the new German army commander, was not the only one to lose his power. The Abwehr was also absorbed into Oberg's command. Knochen was put in charge of abolishing the Geheime Feld Polizei; its manpower was transferred to the Wehrmacht and the Gestapo and SD. The equivalent of the German RSHA had responsibility for the main towns of France. An executive was installed at Rouen with responsibility for Evreux, Caen, Cherbourg, Granville, Dieppe and Le Havre.

As in Germany, the Gestapo was designated Amt IV. Its task was to combat enemies of the state, saboteurs, terrorists and active counter-espionage. Amt IVA B4 remained under the control of Eichmann's right hand man, Theo Dannecker.

On paper at least, the Gestapo kept its rigidly defined

role under the banner of the RSHA. But, as in the past, it continued to dabble in every aspect of life during the occupation. The concentration camps, for instance, were officially under the control of the WVHA (Wirtschaftverwaltung Hauptamt), a branch of the SS. But this in no way inhibited the Gestapo from keeping them under constant surveillance.

Within the camps, it also organised its own internal spy system with the recruitment of stool-pigeons. The army's role had by no means been extinguished but it had become shorn of much of its power.

When a decision was taken to execute hostages, three reports were drawn up by the Feldkommandtur, the Gestapo and the Abwehr. Reports from the three armed services were also included. These would determine which services had suffered from the activities of saboteurs. Stuelpnagel gave the final judgement on the number of executions. Then the Gestapo stepped in. It was Oberg's job to see that the killings were carried out.

Heydrich, leaving Paris never to return, bequeathed to Oberg a clear mandate of terror.

It was to carry with it, however, the seeds of its own destruction. It fuelled a hatred for the Gestapo which was to find its most valiant expression in the accelerating growth of heroic resistance.

The head of the RSHA, now on his way to fresh triumphs in Prague, was to meet that resistance face to face.

14

Organ strains from the Handel concerto drifted lazily across Prague's Cathedral Square which had been under a soft white carpet of snow since the early dawn.

It was a scene of almost Christmas card festivity. But such an idyll was crudely shattered by the grim presence of the machine-gun mounted on a low squat dais and pointing directly into the square. Out of place also was the small wood and canvas pavilion containing five heavily carved chairs and flying the swastika flag on its roof.

The privileged spectators of the day's drama would be looking into a square which had been cordoned off with red, black and white rope. Each corner of the cordon was dominated by a gigantic medallion on which was embossed the eagle and swastika of the German Third Reich.

On the ground had been painted 100 yellow discs; a labourer from the Highways Department had been detailed to be on hand with a broom to keep the snow from obliterating them. It was little touches like this which Obergruppenfuehrer Kurt Schact-Isserlis regarded as important – so important in fact that he had recorded them for posterity.

But posterity was not his immediate concern on 15 December 1941. The Thuringian Schact-Isserlis was carrying out a specific job on the orders of Reichsfuehrer Himmler and he was absolutely determined that his chief was going to be wholly satisfied. And not only Himmler. Another distinguished personality would be among those in the pavilion – the newly promoted Obergruppenfuehrer Reinhard Tristan Eugen Heydrich, recently appointed Deputy Reich Protector of Bohemia and Moravia.

Schact-Isserlis felt a twinge of regret that soon the sweeper would have to be removed from the square, so that it would be impossible to guarantee the visibility of the discs at the last moment.

He strode across the square, straightened one of the chairs in the pavilion and then crossed to the guardroom on the other side. The time was just after 11.45 and the final instructions had to be given to the guard of honour.

Within minutes, there was a shout of command. The obedient automatons of the Waffen-SS lined up at lightening speed in two ranks facing each other across the main approach road to the square.

Two open Mercedes flanked by outriders carried the celebrities to the pavilion reception party headed by Schact-Isserlis.

All took their places promptly at mid-day. As the clocks all over the city struck, the door of the guardroom opened to admit into the square those who were about to die.

There was nothing particularly remarkable about any of them: a cross section of housewives, labourers, clerks, students. But the Gestapo with its familiar methods had branded them traitors, as dangerous individuals who had 'attempted to subvert the regime'.

A network of informers had been placed in houses, apartments, factories and offices right from the very moment that Hitler was the new master of the Czechs. The beloved files of Hitler and Himmler had been crammed with every relevant detail about subversives, many of whom had shown the temerity to grumble openly about the presence of the Germans. It was reasoned that if a bunch of them were put out of the way, that would encourage the rest to toe the line.

Schact-Isserlis, whose scrupulous records of the day's work were to fall into the hands of the Allies at the end of the war, was able to recall some of those who had been condemned to death by the hastily assembled courts and were now on the edge of annihilation in the Cathedral Square on a winter's morning.

There were two old women who had shawls over their heads, while some of the young girls wore men's boots. The men had been allowed to keep their caps with warm earlaps and peaks, but others were shivering. One in a bowler stood out from the rest, presenting an oddly ludicrous figure.

Schact-Isserlis waited until the 100 condemned were each standing on top of a yellow disc. Everything seemed to be progressing admirably. Attention to detail might be sneered at by some, but covering every eventuality was essential – even down to having the neatly typed names of every malefactor pasted to a board and varnished over in case there were smudges from the snow or rain.

It was that board which Schact-Isserlis was now gripping. He leant forward and whispered to Himmler: 'Does the Reichsfuehrer wish a roll-call?'

Himmler, he noticed, looked deathly pale as he

swallowed and shook his head.

Heydrich was giving a signal. Schact-Isserlis rapped out an order to the SS-Oberscharfuehrer.

The greatcoated executioner walked across the square with more than a suggestion of swagger. He was well aware that all eyes, both of the curious and of the terrified, were riveted on him.

He took his place behind the machine-gun on the dais and waited for his orders, But the members of the Waffen-SS received theirs first. They were marched off in brisk order to the guardroom and in a few minutes they had their noses pressed against window panes like children outside a sweetshop.

It was 12.15 and the snow was beginning to fall, which irritated the executioner because it made aiming difficult. As for the condemned, they barely seemed to notice the flakes and stared ahead with a stunned detachment. There was no panic. Indeed, one or two faces wore proud smiles as if their owners were ready for the very worst the Germans could do.

The Oberscharfuehrer's right hand was raised now, his left horizontal with his chest so that the wristwatch was clearly visible. At 12.15 the clocks chimed the quarter.

At that precise moment, the hand was brought down sharply.

The arc of fire swept steadily into the defenceless crowd. Some stumbled over like abandoned dolls; death was clearly instantaneous. But there were those who had to live a little longer with tortured heads, chests, abdomen and limbs. Then they too were despatched on the return sweep.

With the air of an artist keen to savour his work, the executioner suddenly ceased firing. The full extent of the horror was revealed.

Death even then had not come to everyone. There were men – horribly mutilated parodies of men – who screamed and groaned and picked at the inert bodies of those who had died quickly.

But these were not the sights and sounds to grip the attention of the executioner and his fellow Germans in the pavilion and guard house.

Momentary distraction came when Heinrich Himmler slumped back in his chair in a dead faint.

With a gesture of irritation, Heydrich tore his gaze away from the spectacle in the square and took in his chief's deadly-white face, the askew rimless spectacles, the lips drawn back from the teeth in the parody of a grin.

Schact-Isserlis's account stated:

'There was a look of contempt of Heydrich's face. Together with the chief of police he caught at Himmler's shoulders and thrust his head down between his knees. His glasses fell off and the clicking sound they made on the floor was simultaneous with the sound of the machine-gun as the executioner swept his gun from left to right again, from right to left . . .'

This time there were no survivors. The rattle of the machine-gun had barely died away before two five-ton trucks drove rapidly into the square. A small squad of prisoners, under the eyes of carbine-toting Waffen-SS, were ordered to get down.

The cordon was dismantled, then the corpses were heaved into the back of the lorries as if they had been sacks of potatoes. Schact-Isserlis was not sure precisely who they were and did not particulary care – doubtless Sudeten Jews who were quite inured to such work and would eventually be despatched themselves since they obviously knew far too much to be allowed to live.

But by now the Obergruppenfuehrer had all but forgotten the executions. The primary task was to look after Himmler, who still appeared groggy and was being supported by Heydrich, mumbling now about: 'Something to hang on to.'

Himmler studiously avoided looking into the square, climbing down unsteadily as he made his way to his Mercedes.

As for the newly promoted Obergruppenfuehrer Reinhard Heydrich, the policing of his new kingdom had been most ruthless and speedy.

After all, it was under three months since the top-secret

teleprinter in Berlin had rattled its urgent message on 27 September 1941 to Adolf Hitler on the Russian front.

It had read:

'Mein Fuehrer,

I dutifully report that this afternoon, in accordance with today's Fuehrer decree, I took over the Acting Leadership of the affairs of the Reich Protector in Bohemia and Moravia. The official take-over follows at eleven o'clock tomorrow, with the centre of operations in the Hradcany Castle.

All political reports and messages will reach you by the hand of Reichsleiter Bormann.

Heil Mein Fuehrer!

(SGD) Heydrich. SS Obergruppenfuehrer.'

The former offshoot of the Austro-Hungarian empire with its ethnic chaos of Czechs, Slovaks, Ruthenians, Poles and Germans, had been the subject of the Fuehrer's wrath at a speech at the Reichstag on 20 February 1938. No longer, he thundered, would the German people tolerate a situation where millions of their brothers lived in oppression. Now it would be the turn of exiles in Czechoslovakia – more specifically, those living in the region known as the Sudetenland which bordered the German frontier and virtually surrounded Bohemia and Moravia.

Already Hitler had his ready-made puppet, a former instructor named Konrad Henlein who had created the Deutsche Heimat Front, the Patriotic German Front. Ostensibly, Henlein was attempting to create autonomy for the Sudetens within the embrace of the Czech state.

But the SD soon took a hand, insinuating its agents not only into the secret service, but into as many local and regional organisations as possible.

The files positively bulged with detailed information on the political, economic and military situation within the country.

Hitler had followed with a violent speech which accused President Benes of ill treatment and persecution of Sudeten Germans. There were large-scale arrests of

Schellenberg   Mueller   Heydrich

Above: Wreckage in the building used as a Gestapo Headquarters in Copenhagen, which was attacked in daylight on 21 March 1945, by Mosquitos of RAF 2nd Tactical Air Force.

Below: Visit to German War Cemetery, Norway.

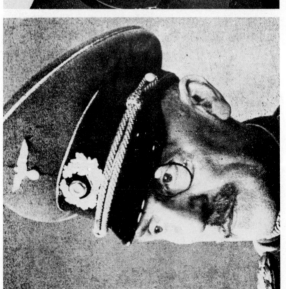

Joachim von Stülpnagel.

With the ceremonial handshake Prime Minister Goering bestows upon Himmler, Reichsführer of the SS, his new post as Chief of the Gestapo.

Above: Armed Forces Day 1935. Hitler with his senior commanders. Left to right: Goering C-in-C Air Force; Von Blomberg, Supreme Commander; Von Fritsch, C-in-C of the Army and Raeder, C-in-C of the Navy.

Below: Beer Hall.

Above: THE GERMAN INVASION OF RUSSIA 1941
Jews in Kovna working for the Germans, towing a Mk I tank, guarded by Lithuanian militia, 27.6.41.

Below: SA action rounding up suspects.

Dr Freisler, Secretary of State in the Prussian Ministry of Justice (later this man was the judge in the notorious People's Court).

Kaltenbrunner.

Count Helldorf, President of the Prussian Police in Potsdam.

Dr Diels has been named as Inspector General of the Gestapo.

Portrait of Reinhard Heydrich August 1940.

Hitler and his good friend and Cabinet member, Hermann Goering (right), were photographed during a trip to the Bavarian Alps with Gregor Strasser (second from left) and Ernst Roehm (third from left).

*Grateful acknowledgements are due to the Imperial War Museum for the use of all illustrations except **Portrait of Reinhard Heydrich August 1940** and **Visit to German War Cemetery, Norway**, for which thanks are due to the Historical Research Unit.*

Czechs. The conference at Munich on 29/30 September 1938 had proposed the peaceful evacuation of the Sudetenland. The fate of Czechoslovakia was sealed. On 14 March 1939, Dr Joseph Tiso, the Slovak premier, proclaimed the founding of the autonomous Slovak Republic, having previously agreed that it would come under German protection. This was followed immediately by the Nazi occupation of Czechoslovakia.

Schellenberg, who was there, wrote in his memoirs:

'In order to be the first to arrive at the Hradcany, the ancient and historic castle in Prague, Hitler, with his entourage and SS guards, raced through the night at breakneck speed over icy roads, passing the advancing German columns on the way. When we got there I had to select suitable offices and lebensraum for Hitler in the castle.

The SD and German Security Police at once took over control of the police, working very closely, however, with their Czech colleagues. The Czech police was an exceptional organisation, the men having been most carefully selected and given excellent training. This greatly impressed Himmler. "Exceptional human material!' he exclaimed. "I shall take them all into the Waffen-SS." '

The SD and Gestapo went into action immediately, as did the notorious Einsatzgruppen. At the Nuremberg Trials after the war, defendants went to great lengths to prove that the action groups were no concern either of the SD or the Gestapo. When it was pointed out that certain of the leaders of the action groups were members of the SD, it was claimed that they had resigned the first office and had been seconded.

An unsigned draft instruction of the SD from that time read:

'The SD should prepare to start its activity in case of complications between the German Reich and Czechoslovakia ... Measures in the occupied regions are carried out under the leadership of the senior officers of

161

the SD. Gestapo officials are assigned to certain operations staffs . . .'

In November, an anonymous journalist from a neutral country, posing as a German, managed to penetrate the notorious Petschek Palace in Prague. He was accompanied by a Gestapo agent who was in charge of the son of a Czech political leader, accused of uttering 'impertinent' criticism of the new regime.

The reporter later filed a story from Paris for the British newspaper the *Yorkshire Post* which ran it on 22 November.

The report stated:

' . . . A young man of about twenty came up and without a word slapped the Czech on both cheeks. Then he pushed him into a corner, and forced him to keep his hands up while he began a long conversation with us. He only interrupted his speech to slap the Czech when he had cramp.

After a long time, Stachlecker, Chief of the Gestapo in Prague, entered the room and began questioning the prisoner, accompanying his words with slaps and blows, as well as insults to the Czech nation.

When the examination was over, the prisoner was taken down to the basement of the palace, formerly the safe room of the bank, and thrown among twenty other prisoners, unshaven, white-faced and clad only in shirt and trousers. I asked my guide what would be the fate of the young man and he answered: 'He will be beaten just enough not to die.'' He added that if the prisoner was lucky he would be freed in sixteen days, and he would certainly not be kept in prison, as there was no more room.

He said that since the mass arrests of 28 October there was no more room in the concentration camps or the prisons, and prisoners were obliged to spend three days and three nights standing in the corridors of Petschek prison. ''We could not kill them all,'' he added, ''but we have kept the names of those we freed.'' '*

*By courtesy of the *Yorkshire Post*.

This was but a mere taste of what lay in store for the Czechs for the next six years.

At the time Heydrich took up his appointment, the situation in what Hitler regarded as the Czech lands of the historic German Reich was in danger of getting out of hand.

As Reich Protector, von Neurath had been both inefficient and in failing health. Resistance groups were not being combated with sufficient severity; the most appalling rumours had been allowed to circulate that Germany was doing badly on the Russian front and could even lose the war. Von Neurath was a mere puppet in the hands of anti-Nazis and should be removed before the resistance did serious damage.

What was clearly needed was a clout from an iron fist. And who better to give it than one of the Gestapo's most sinister lieutenants?

At first, Heydrich was highly suspicious of the offer. There was a real danger that if he left Germany, his entire RSHA could be infiltrated by rivals. Then the knives would really be out and flashing.

Despite the glitter of his new appointment, Heydrich had absolutely no intention of relinquishing his security appointments. His job as RSHA chief with all its ramifications would remain; he planned to have two aircraft on permanent standby in Prague so that he could commute to Berlin.

On the morning of 27 September 1941, Heydrich, complete with staff of RSHA and SS, flew to Prague. For the Czechs, it was the start of the long night of barbarism.

Heydrich was barely installed within Hradcany Castle before he delivered a two-prong attack. First of his victims was the Czech Prime Minister, General Alois Elias. He was known to be in contact with the exiled Benes government in London. He had also been a protégé of the disgraced von Neurath. It was enough. Elias was handed over to the Gestapo, who extracted a confession within hours. Elias was then hauled before a German court and sentenced summarily to death.

The Gestapo went on to tackle know centres of resistance. Most of these had previously been penetrated by undercover agents of the SD.

Legal niceties dictated that those arrested should be brought before special convened courts. But Heydrich was determined to show that a terrible new broom was sweeping through the country. In charge now was the Gestapo, not pettifogging lawyers. Frequently Heydrich bypassed the courts altogether and handed those arrested straight over to the Gestapo. Many were murdered on the spot, others found their way to the extermination camp at Mauthausen.

The very name of Heydrich was enough to inspire hatred and fear. From now on he was known as the 'Butcher of Prague'.

But Heydrich was no mere thug with a liking for sadism and the taste of blood. His own instinct told him that there had to be a time limit put on the policy of mass arrests, shootings and imprisonments. It would do no harm for information to be leaked to the government-in-exile that Czechoslovakia not only accepted German subjugation but actually liked it.

With total cynicism, Heydrich proceeded to stand his previous policy on its head.

The butcher began to behave suspiciously like a Social Democrat Father Christmas. With a considerable fanfare, he declared that political persecution would stop. The fat ration was raised for two million Czech industrial workers and luxury hotels were commandeered for them as holiday homes. The Czech social security system was completely overhauled.

Reinhard and Lina Heydrich acted as benevolent hosts receiving a stream of Czech delegations at the Hradcany Castle. Of course, deportations and executions continued, but the killings were handled with more subtlety than in the past. Most shootings, Heydrich gave out, were of dangerous saboteurs who had threatened the safety of the state and who had attempted to escape.

As the months wore on, Heydrich began increasingly to

revel in his new job. And not simply because of the power it brought. The greatest joy was to be rid of Himmler and the miasma of intrigue which surrounded him. There had been no greater intriguer in his time than Reinhard Heydrich but, now in his late thirties, he had come to tire of it. There was no time now for the former womanising and carousing. Besides, even these seemed to have lost appeal.

And most unappealing of all was the Hradcany. Soon Heydrich had selected for himself a suitable country seat, an enormous white mansion in the style of a French chateau.

Life seemed good among the clipped lawns and the magnificent gardens. Here it was possible to forget that other life in Prague – or would have been save for the ring of steel of SS bodyguards.

The policy of a spoonful of sugar had to have its limits. The Czech population would only be treated benevolently up to a certain point. The campaign of terror could be started again any time. The stick and the carrot kept the 'Czech Germans' usefully bewildered.

Anxiety gripped the Czech government-in-exile in London. A flexible occupation policy by Heydrich was clearly a subtle way of undermining the resistance. That was something that could not be tolerated.

London began laying its plans. Its first move was to secure the co-operation of the RAF and fly in General Ingr, a special agent who would report on the present situation in the Protectorate. The scheme was a humiliating failure. Within two weeks, Ingr was picked up by the Gestapo.

Now there was only one course left. Elaborate plans were made to kill Reinhard Heydrich.

Feelers were put out to the British intelligence service. Under a cloak of maximum secrecy two Czech NCOs, Jan Kubis, a farmer's son from Moravia, and Josef Gabeik, a locksmith from Slovakia, were selected for special training at a school for spies near Manchester. Then there was further training in sabotage in Scotland and final briefing at another intelligence centre at Dorking in the south of England.

Speed was of the essence. All the signs were that Heydrich's policy of repression would soon flare up anew.

Indeed, this was confirmed on the very day of the assassination bid. Himmler sent a flash telegram to Prague ordering the arrest of 10,000 hostages from among the Czech intelligentsia. Orders were also issued that 100 of the most important of these should be shot that very evening.

These latest instructions had an air of desperation; the Russian campaign, which Hitler had confidently proclaimed would be over in seven months, had suffered reverses. All had been well until the assault on Moscow. Then the mighty Wehrmacht machine had ground to a halt in the unspeakable winter and the frozen troops had been left to stare wistfully at the towers of the Kremlin.

True, that would put heart into the resistance. But, reasoned Czech exiles, it would also mean a terrible new wave of terror for the Czech people. If Heydrich was killed, that would surely be a cue for a triumphant uprising. As a fillip to morale, it was widely believed, the death of the Reich Protector would be of incalculable value.

At the beginning of 1942, Kubis and Gabeik were dropped into Czechoslovakia.

Life continued agreeably enough for Heydrich. Spring dawned and the mansion of Jungfern-Breschan received a stream of visitors. Even Himmler, previously detested by Frau Heydrich, unbent to the extent of coming to stay. So did Admiral Canaris. Relations between the Abwehr and the Gestapo were scarcely cordial but Heydrich had a sentimental regard for his cunning old mentor. All the signs were that a number of hatchets were being buried.

Jungfern-Breschan had other visitors that spring, but neither Heydrich nor his SS bodyguards were aware of them. In the hedges and fields around, Kubis and Gabeik logged every move of the Reich Protector. His departures each morning were minutely observed.

The agents toyed with the idea of wrecking Heydrich's special train between Prague and the Czech border, but the Protector's travels by rail were too irregular. Eventually, it became clear that the attempt would have to be made somewhere between Heydrich's country house and his

Prague office. It was noted that it was his habit to sit for the journey completely unprotected in the front of his open car.

The sun shone brightly on Prague that May morning with the merest suggestion of a mist hanging over the Ultava valley. Heydrich was reluctant to leave and spun out the last precious moments playing with his three children.

His mood was particularly relaxed. The previous night there had been a performance of his father's chamber music in the Waldstein Hall. It had brought back poignant memories of happier days. Somehow, the prospect of a day's drudgery had little appeal.

The three-and-a-half-litre Mercedes convertible pulled up at the front door of Jungfern-Breschan. There were last lingering good-byes, then Heydrich took his usual seat in the front. For a while, the car was unobserved. First to spot it taking a sixty-degree turn towards Valcik was a member of the Czech resistance, another of the parachutists from England who carried a boy scout's whistle. At the corner of the pavement where tramlines almost touched the footpath stood Josef Gabeik and Jan Kubis.

Gabeik nervously fingered the British army Sten gun while his companion gripped a British hand grenade. That would be a back-up weapon if the bullets failed to connect. Heydrich was due at the hairpin bend at just before half-past nine.

But there was no sign of him. The road ahead was empty and stayed that way for an agonising eternity. What no one realised was that Heydrich had changed his plans. He was making for the airport, where he was going to pilot his own plane for Berlin.

It was not until 10.30, one hour after the hoped-for rendezvous, that Valcik was able to put the whistle to his mouth.

The Mercedes, sporting two pennants on the mud-guards, the SS flag and that of the Reich Protector, was being driven fast. The chauffeur, Klein, slipped skilfully into third gear and took the bend to the river. There in the front passenger seat was a familiar figure in the field grey uniform of an SS Obergruppenfuehrer.

A sudden sound distracted Kubis. He swore softly. There, trundling in his direction, was a tram and all the signs were it would reach the hairpin corner at the same time as the Mercedes. The car was very near now. Gabeik dropped the raincoat which concealed his automatic weapon and brought the sten to his shoulder. Heydrich was just about level.

Gabeik heard Kubis shout: 'Now!'

Gabeik squeezed the trigger. Nothing happened. The Sten had jammed. All he had was the utterly useless automatic weapon – and, my God, Heydrich had seen it!

The Protector uncoiled from his seat, his hand snaking towards the pistol in his holster. Heydrich bawled at Klein: 'Stop!' It was a fatal mistake to be made by someone as experienced as Heydrich.

The car swung hopelessly round the corner and it was Klein who next worsened the error. Instead of keeping the Mercedes moving, his feet flew towards the brakes. The car screamed like a tortured animal and bucked past Kubis, who lobbed the grenade at the nearside front panel.

There was a violent flash. The car was totally immobilised, its back nearside tyre wrecked. The green coachwork looked as if it had been punched by an almighty fist.

But Heydrich was still in the fight and quick on the draw. Kubis caught a glimpse of the furious Protector before the bullets sang past him. Then Kubis was running, darting between two tramcars. A bicycle had been placed nearby as part of the original preparations. Kubis leapt on and snaked downhill. The shouts of Heydrich and Klein grew fainter.

For the moment, Gabeik stood rooted to the spot. Then Heydrich moved towards him, still firing. The Czech was running now, zigzagging in and out of the astonished but mesmerised group of people which had inevitably gathered. Heydrich kept on firing.

He stood alone and isolated now, but seemingly unhurt. Then he began to sag, his hand straying almost in disbelief towards his right hip. He half staggered, half crawled back to the Mercedes, screaming at Klein: 'Get after the bastard. Get him.'

Klein, built like a barge, was not able to move fast
enough and his ample bulk made an ideal target for
Gabeik, who managed to wing the chauffeur during the
short fruitless chase.

The last conscious hours of the Reich Protector of
Bohemia and Moravia passed in excruciating agony. First
he tried to clamber back into the wrecked car, wheeling to
and fro in the road like a hopeless drunk. All the time the
crowd watched, not with particular satisfaction but with a
mild curiosity. No move was made to help the wounded
man.

Then the Czech policemen flagged down a baker's
delivery lorry and ordered the driver to take Heydrich to
hospital. The lorry started none too gently. Heydrich
screamed and in a frenzy of agony crawled his way out of
the driver's cab, staggering round to the back.

As he crashed on to the floor a dark crimson stain
trickled down and mixed in with flour and bacon fat.

Beside Heydrich sat one of the policemen. He stared at
the writhing, whimpering man with total indifference.

He felt no compassion at all. He had been present in the
cathedral square that Christmas when 100 of his fellow
countrymen had been mown down for the most feeble acts
against the state.

Heydrich's unceremonious arrival stirred the Bulovka
Hospital into a frenzy of activity.

Medical Director Dr Diek was swiftly on the line to
Hradcany Castle. He asked to speak to Secretary of State
Karl Hermann Frank.

He was told coldly: 'That is quite impossible. There is a
list of people to whom the Secretary of State will speak. It
does not include you.'

'In that case,' said Diek dryly, 'perhaps someone will tell
me what to do with Obergruppenfuehrer Heydrich who is
currently in my hospital after an assassination attempt.'

'Are you mad?' the voice snapped back. 'The Protector
is currently flying to Berlin.'

Diek knew that he must at all costs hang on to his temper.

'SS-Obergruppenfuehrer Heydrich is unlikely to fly anywhere ever again. He is here in this hospital. And it is my duty to tell you that his chances of recovery are not rated highly.'

Diek sensed a change of attitude. A hand was put over the receiver and he heard muffled instructions.

Seemingly within minutes, the Bulovka was surrounded by SS. Patients deemed considerably less important than the Protector were bundled unceremoniously out of their wards so that Heydrich could have a completely isolated room plus accommodation for the Gestapo investigators.

Surgeon Dietrich Hohlbaum carried out a preliminary investigation and prepared to operate.

His discoveries were grim. Lumps of wire, felt, leather, horsehair and glass were firmly embedded in Heydrich's back and side. They had lodged in spleen and liver. Removing them would be a daunting task; if infection set in and spread, a virtually impossible one.

News of the attempt on Heydrich's life threw both Prague and Berlin into panic.

Not for the first or last time, a crisis induced initially in Himmler a state of mental paralysis. When he emerged into something like rationality, his only contribution to the prevailing chaos was to make things worse.

Himmler contacted all the leading doctors and surgeons in the Reich and the occupied countries and ordered them to rush to Prague with advice and practical help. This was not what was wanted. Urgently needed were generous amounts of penicillin. But this was 1942 and medical supplies were badly stretched on the Russian front.

Meanwhile Heydrich's temperature soared to 102 degrees Fahreinheit.

As for Hitler, his rage was monumental, but unlike Himmler he was able to think rationally and act with terrible swiftness. The Fuehrer stormed: 'I always said this soft business of a Protectorate was nonsense. I'll send those damned Czechs somebody a great deal worse.'

Karl Daluege, chief of the uniformed police, was forthwith sent to Prague as caretaker Protector.

But Daluege had no power. All that was vested now in the daemonic figure of Karl Hermann Frank, a man with a fanatical hatred of the Czechs.

Immediately the baker's cart taking Heydrich had left the scene of the shooting, the crowds melted away.

But some were not quick enough. First to reach the scene after the two policemen was a platoon of German infantrymen who had been on a fieldcraft exercise. What they saw puzzled them – a wrecked Mercedes and, by it, the unfortunate Klein, who was by now practically incoherent with fear, only able to babble something about the Protector having been shot.

The officer in charge promptly reported to headquarters by field radio. His instructions were precise: arrest anyone in sight and await instructions!

The round-up was completely random. Men, women and children were held near the Mercedes by carbine-toting Wehrmacht and told: 'Orders of the Gestapo.'

On to the scene now strode Karl Hermann Frank who doubled his job as Secretary of State with that of civil police chief.

Frank invariably carried a whip. And he cracked it as if bringing dogs to heel.

He indicated nearby buildings and snapped at the head of the platoon: 'Bring out everyone.' The occupants of houses and flats were dragged out to join the rest.

Frank added: 'March them down to the Council House and keep them there until I give further instructions. The Reichsfuehrer-SS will no doubt have the Fuehrer's orders by now.'

And he had. Hitler's rage and spite were still spilling over. He stormed: 'If we don't know precisely who the assassins are, it doesn't really matter. We'll simply kill every single Czech and that way we'll get those responsible just the same. The entire canker at the heart of the Protectorate will be torn out.'

Hitler put only one brake on Frank's activities. Production workers at the huge Skoda armaments factories had to be spared. Heydrich or no Heydrich, there was still a war to be fought.

Prague was swiftly sealed with road blocks. A curfew was slapped on the city and all public transport forbidden. By special trains, SS and Gestapo poured into Prague.

Uniformed SD men swept through shops, restaurants and bars demanding identity cards and papers. Plain clothes Gestapo spies listened for the very slightest hint that might betray the assassins.

An announcement was broadcast that a reward of a million crowns – then about £200,000 – would be paid to persons or organisations giving information leading to vital arrests.

As for the assassins, they were by now activating the first of their escape plans. This was to make for Resslova Street where, in the crypt of the Karel Boromaeus Greek Orthodox church, they would meet up with other members of the resistance.

They would then be given forged papers and fresh clothes that would turn them into bargees. They would travel downstream to the point where the river Vitava joined the Elbe. After that, they were on their own.

Karel Curda, a member of the resistance ring which had made the attempt on Heydrich, had taken refuge in the loft of the family farm. But soon news of arrests and executions reached him. The sheer weight of names was appalling. Sooner or later, they would all be rounded up and taken to Gestapo headquarters.

Curda had no intention of being among their numbers. He made the journey to Prague and confronted the lieutenants of Gestapo chief Dr Otto Geschke.

He told them: 'You don't need to waste your time arresting innocent people. The killers are a certain Gabeik from Slovakia and Jan Kubis, whose brother is an innkeeper from Moravia.'

But where were they?

This was one question Curda could not answer, but, once having embarked on the path of betrayal, he found it impossible to stop.

He let drop more names. Among them was the Moravec family, whose twenty-one-year-old son Ata was known to be a resistance activist.

Four in the morning had long been a favourite hour for Gestapo swoops. Large black saloons screeched to a halt at the Bishop's Road sidewalk in Zizhov suburb.

Gestapo Inspector Oskar Fleischer led the rush to the front door of the Moravec apartment. The entire family was dragged out into the corridor. The order was to face the wall with their hands above their heads.

Then Fleischer set about the flat. Papers, documents and the entire contents of wardrobes and cupboards were rifled.

Nothing was found. The Moravecs were too experienced resistance hands for that.

Interrogations of the family began. They knew it was only a matter of time before they were taken. And Mrs Moravec had a serious heart condition.

Suddenly, she requested to go to the lavatory. Fleischer had strictly forbidden it. She asked again. A guard relented and accompanied her.

As she walked in front of the German, her hand played casually with the medallion on her necklace. It was a matter of a moment to extract the small inconspicuous brown pill she was never without.

The guard waited outside. Mrs Moravec came out of the door, walked a few steps and suddenly began to sweat and quiver. Then she sank slowly to the ground; froth was detectable on each side of her mouth.

Two men leapt on her with a feverish attempt at artificial respiration. It was too late. The mother had killed herself to escape the ignominy of betrayal under torture. But she could not know the psychological repercussions of what she had done. From now on, her grief-stricken son, Ata, was in a state of mind to tell the Gestapo anything.

Ata was starved and brutally beaten. But mere fisticuffs produced sullen indifference. Fleischer next resorted to dragging the boy to view his mother's body at all hours of the day and night.

Eventually, he gave in. A gleeful Fleischer now had the identity of a certain Greek Orthodox church.

173

The area was rapidly encircled by 400 SS and Gestapo. Other contingents raced into the sexton's apartment, forcing him at gunpoint to lead them through a side entrance to the church.

Oberhauser, one of the SS, kept his pistol pointing at the sexton's back as they edged towards the altar. The sexton was just pointing to a carpet covering a concrete slab leading to the crypt, when a fierce fusillade zipped down into the church from the members of the resistance in the choir loft.

Oberhauser, grabbing the sexton, backed out of the church shouting: 'There are three of them up there.'

From windows of neighbouring buildings and from a school across the street, retaliatory German fire raked the church's fabric.

But Geschke realised that this would merely mean counter-productive confusion; there were too many plain-clothes Gestapo milling around. They could easily be mistaken for members of the resistance. He called off the fire. The SS men were regrouped and issued with hand grenades. Then they went back into the church.

It was an heroic but ultimately futile stand by the three beleagured Czechs in the choir loft. They were attacked with gunfire and grenades and one of the trio took the full force of a grenade in the leg. Maddened with pain, he turned his weapon on himself.

The other two had no chance. Severely wounded, they were dragged out of the church by the SS. The body of the dead Czech was left outside while the other two were rushed to hospital so that they could recover sufficiently for the Gestapo to start questioning.

Now the Germans were able to examine without opposition the concrete slab above the crypt. When they lifted it they were greeted with a volley of fire and were forced to retreat.

An order was shouted: 'Give yourselves up. You are surrounded.' There came the riposte: 'We are Czechs – we will never give up.'

And again came the shower of shots. Even tear gas bombs lobbed into the crypt had no effect. Next, a fire hose was wedged into the entrance. It was cut to pieces. Hastily, a machine-gun was inserted. There was silence. Plainly, the Czechs had been forced into the back of the crypt.

Another hose was tried and water began to pour into the refuge, which now had turned into a veritable death trap. As well as the water, more grenades were used. Then two men were ordered down into the crypt. Gingerly they made their way down the steps. There was no answering fire. An officer followed, pistol at the ready. Soon there came a shout: 'Fertig' ('finished').

The remaining corpses – Gabeik and Kubis were among those who died that day – were dragged upstairs and out into the street. Their faces were bloody, the corpses saturated. Some had fallen victim to the grenades, others had shot themselves and tumbled into the water which had risen in the crypt.

Those who watched and waited over Heydrich's unconscious body veered between optimism and despair. For a time, the specialists believed that Heydrich might recover.

His temperature fell, the wounds began to discharge freely. But on the morning of 4 June, one week after the attack, there was a relapse; Heydrich died.

After lying in state at the Hradcany Castle, Heydrich's swastika-draped coffin was conveyed to Berlin under heavy guard, first to RSHA headquarters and from there to the Reich Chancellery. Following an elaborate ceremony – including the obligatory Funeral March from Wagner's Götterdämmerung – the funeral procession made its way to Invaliden Cemetery.

Hitler, more visibly distressed than most people could remember ever seeing him, returned immediately after the ceremony to his private office.

Himmler professed himself shaken by Heydrich's death. But for possibly different reasons than ones of personal grief. He was extremely worried about what would happen to the late RSHA chief's private files. If they fell into the hands of some of Heydrich's sworn enemies – party secretary Martin Bormann or the detested von Ribbentrop, for instance – the outcome could be awkward. The very deepest secrets of the top Nazis were contained in those dossiers.

It was not until early in 1943 that Heydrich's successor as RSHA chief was to be appointed. In the interim, Himmler lost no time in getting to grips with the RSHA and, of course, the array of filing cabinets which nourished it.

Hitler now commanded that the time had come for *Vergeltungsaktion* – reprisal action – for the killing of Heydrich.

One of its results was to be the appalling massacre of the innocent people of the small village of Lidice some thirty kilometres from Prague.

Here the population was forbidden to leave the village. Men and youths who were over sixteen were locked up in barns and stables. The children and women were imprisoned in the school. SS Hauptsturmfuehrer Max Rostock, commanding a detachment of the SS Division Prinz Eugen, took out men in groups of ten and shot them. By the afternoon, 172 men of the village were killed. Nineteen men of Lidice who worked in the neighbouring mines were taken to Prague and executed along with seven women. The rest of the female population were sent to Ravensbruck concentration camp, while their children were either murdered or sent to Poland. Pregnant women were aborted before going to the gas chambers. Photographs were taken of the dead of the villages where they lay. Later, every house in the village was set on fire and dynamited. The village of Lidice ceased to exist and its name was removed from the land registers.

Karl Frank, who had masterminded the Lidice massacre and who was to be publicly hanged in Prague after the war for his crime, later stated in a report to Hitler that the exercise had been necessary: 'because the inhabitants gave assistance to the parachutists from England.'

A communiqué also stated:

'Underground literature, stocks of weapons and ammunition have been found as well as the existence of a transmitting set and an illegal depot containing large quantities of rationed food.'

No evidence connecting Lidice with the harbouring of Heydrich's assassins was in fact ever found.

After the war, the Czech government built a new village at Lidice at the hillside which is close to the mass grave. A nearby museum, containing personal possessions and pictures of those who died, forms a permanent memorial.

Executions elsewhere in Czechoslovakia continued long after Heydrich's death.

People were murdered even in the prisons. A total figure of 360,000 had been quoted as the number of Czechs who suffered under Nazism before the Germans pulled out of the country.

News of Lidice spread within months far beyond the confines of the Third Reich. It fuelled resistance movements in scores of countries which were to be persecuted by the Gestapo for another three long years.

15

One of the jobs of the duty radio officer on the dawn shift at the Kranz monitoring station in East Prussia was to track the output of a small transmitter belonging to the Norwegian resistance. It was tucked away in the mountains and operated by a small group of partisans. At 3.48 precisely each morning contact was made with London and a message of some ten or dozen coded groups transmitted.

The operator knew that a team of German experts had flown to Norway in a bid to find the offending transmitter. Those mountains had proved one of the best allies for the

Norwegians; they acted as a screen and made the signals harder to pinpoint. All sorts of ingenious direction finders had been built into the Fieseler-Storch aircraft, but as soon as it approached the fjords, the transmitter went dead. It happened time and again and the crew swore as they flew around for as long as there was enough fuel. Then they had to make for home to the impotent wrath of their chiefs and soon start the whole fruitless search over again.

To the operator, it had all become dull routine. Automatically, he turned the receiver to 15,465 kilocycles, the frequency used by the Norwegians, and waited for the call sign.

Suddenly, he was jerked out of his lethargy. There was a call sign, all right. But not the usual one.

'*KLK from PTX . . . . . . KLK from PTX . . . . . . KLK from PTX . . . . . . AR 50385 KLK from PTX*'

Then followed the message, which was made up from several cypher groups. The operator reported his puzzling new discovery and listed the frequency. The time was 3.58 a.m. on 26 June 1941.

The Reich's most highly qualified radio experts working in counter espionage wrestled in vain to decode the message. Within hours of it being received, teleprinters were rattling out an order to all Wehrmacht direction-finding stations.

'*Essential discover PTX schedule. Night frequency 10 363. Day frequency unknown. Priority 1a.*'

The answer when it came disconcerted the Abwehr and every section of the German secret service. Call sign PTX was beamed straight to Moscow. And, to make matters worse, the intercept service was soon reporting no less than seventy-eight similar transmitters.

Just how effective shortwave radio could be as a deadly weapon in the intelligence war had been fully realised by Russia and Germany way back in the 1920s. The Russian navy had pioneered communications between naval staff ashore and ships on high seas. Then it had been the turn of the air force. By the end of the decade, shortwave radio was generally accepted for all important spheres in the Soviet Union.

Hitler's Germany raced to keep up. The Abwehr began developing radio for counter-espionage. Radio technology was soon advancing to the point where it would be possible to hunt down and eliminate the transmitters of enemy agents.

Father of the intercept service was Oberst Buschenhagen who, with a small cipher staff, had formed an evaluation office in the Friedrichstrasse in 1919. Within seven years it was able to boast a section running intercept stations in six of the major German cities.

By no means everyone in the Abwehr was starry-eyed about radio. To many of its more cautious officers, it all sounded uncomfortably like something out of those lurid thrillers Reinhard Heydrich was in the habit of reading.

As for the chief of SD and Gestapo, he had been quite prepared to encourage the Abwehr in its horse-and-cart thinking; gaining control of a radio network for his own interests would be that much easier in consequence.

It turned out to be something of a battle. SS-Obergruppenfuehrer Kurt Daluege, boss of the Ordnungspolizei (ORPO), was a man with ambition. Small transmitters, he reasoned, would scarcely be of use to the military. He would make a name for himself by using such sets for police work.

Daluege instructed his staff to perfect a para-military organisation to be called the Intelligence Communications Agency. It grew with remarkable speed. Daluege was soon in command of around 2,000 men with seven direction-finding stations and a number of shortwave sets.

Daluege's impertinence threw Heydrich into a rage. Unless Daluege was put in his place, he would be encroaching on the SD and Gestapo with his damn new toys. What Daluege could do, Heydrich reckoned he could do better. A Security Police and SD radio training school was rushed into being.

Suspicion flared inevitably between the two branches of the SS with, slowly and almost imperceptibly, the control over radio as an arm of espionage slipping away from the Abwehr.

On the outbreak of war, the Wehrmacht entered the

lists, arguing that radio was simply another weapon and should be under the control of professionals. In the end, the squabble was settled by compromise. An outfit called Radio Abwehr and Signal Security was set up. It sounded impressive and kept the Abwehr happy; control in fact belonged to the military.

Heydrich had to seethe in silence. The Gestapo, however, was destined for an important role in radio espionage though Heydrich was not to live to see it.

Admiral Canaris, as head of the Abwehr, had to hand over his entire coding and intercept service to a new division, Wehrmacht Intelligence Communications (WNV was its shortened German initials). The head of WNV had the task of supervising communications between the individual services and was also responsible for those between OKW and the various theatres of war.

In June 1941, Hitler put the seal on the new arrangement by directing that the Wehrmacht was the competent authority in all questions of radio monitoring. The Fuehrer had barely ceased to pronounce before there came the first of the mysterious transmissions to Russia.

Problems abounded for the radio experts. A lot of their equipment was painfully inadequate. Short-range direction finders were of little use until they homed in on the enemy's location. Short-range sets were far too bulky to approach a clandestine set unnoticed.

But all the talk about the pros and cons of the ironmongery was somewhat academic. Codes being used by the Russians continued to keep their secrets.

Nevertheless, the new service doubled its efforts, the inadequate direction finders concentrating above all on locating the call sign PTX. Monitoring experts were uncertain whether it was operating in North Germany, Belgium, Holland or France. It was all infuriatingly vague.

Then came something much more promising – three transmitters had definitely been located. And they were right in Berlin.

The first reaction of Hans Kopp, head of Signals Security, was total incredulity.

He gasped: 'Surely no one would run such risks in the

heart of the Reich.'

He was told: 'That's precisely what they are doing and they're being confoundedly cheeky about it. They're changing call signs, frequencies and schedules constantly.'

Goering's Luftwaffe possessed the most effective monitoring equipment at the time. Kopp ordered up some of the best.

The Berlin street looked normal. Uniformed post office mechanics were ripping up the road. Hans Coppi, who happened to be passing by, would not have given them a second glance, but he found himself staring at the post office truck. Anything else but a quick glance would have been foolhardy and Coppi, whose instinct was to run, forced himself to continue on his way casually.

It was the truck's number-plate which had made him cold with fear. It contained the initials WL – Wehrmacht-Luftwaffe.

Unaware that they had been spotted, Hans Kopp's men, their equipment hidden in workmen's shelters, took bearings from tunnels in the subway system or from anti-aircraft positions on the roof.

The men edged their way forward with their direction finder and receiver. But the transmitters continued to operate for annoyingly short periods or, almost as if they had some forewarning, would start from a totally different area of the city.

Then all at once they ceased completely.

Hans Coppi, in addition to being a skilled radio operator, was a loyal Communist. His advice to his Russian masters was that traffic to Moscow from Berlin should be cut off for a while.

The hunt switched by December to Belgium and the task of detecting the elusive transmitters was turned over to a former cavalry Oberleutnant and anti-tank commander Harry Piepe.

He had little taste for the drudgery of espionage and, more serious, scant knowledge of how to tackle Communists. Agents were despatched to the taverns of Bruges to

181

pinpoint likely Reds but, not surprisingly, they had little success.

Berlin's patience quickly gave out. Hauptmann Hubertus Freyer, who commanded the radio company at OKW headquarters, was sent to Bruges, together with experienced operators and the very latest direction-finding equipment.

Freyer also came with an order. He was to team up forthwith with Kriminalkommissar und SS Hauptsturmfuehrer Karl Giering of the Gestapo. Giering was an old-style policeman in the Mueller mould; he had been conspicuously conscientious during the beer hall investigation and had gained Hitler's admiration thereby.

Initial investigations by Piepe, Freyer and Giering were promising. Flights were made over Brussels and it had been possible to listen to PTX transmitting. Even better, the point of transmission was located in the Etterbeek quarter of the town. It looked as if the spy network was becoming careless. The operator was on the air for something like five hours between midnight and five a.m.

A curfew was promptly slapped on the street. The direction finders narrowed the search to the rue des Atrebes: more specifically to houses numbered 99, 101 and 103. No. 103 was found to be empty. In No. 99 was a Flemish family. That left 101, believed to be occupied by South Americans.

It seemed an obvious scheme to storm the empty house, but Giering pointed out that they would have only one chance; if the initial assault was in the wrong place then the spies would quit in a matter of hours. The sensible thing was to set up a listening post nearby and try for some more bearings.

Soon the experts were in no doubt: the offending set was in No. 101, the house supposedly occupied by the South Americans.

Twenty-five men of a garrison battalion, ten men from the Feld Polizei and a sprinkling of Gestapo cordoned off the three houses. Each man wore socks over his boots. Torches, axes and fire hoses were on hand. Then came the signal to attack from Piepe. The contingent hurled itself at the three houses.

Then came the call from 101: 'Here! Here they are!'

A succession of shots fractured the night. Piepe's torch ribboned on a fleeing figure. By now Piepe had got to 101 and was brushing past a dark-haired woman in a dressing gown and making for the first floor.

The transmitter stood on a table. Beside it were papers on which a number of figures were scawled. The operator's chair was empty.

On the second floor, a woman lay in bed weeping, but Piepe had no time for her now because of the scuffle and the shouts below. Soldiers and policemen were struggling with a man who said he was Carlos Alamo, Uruguayan citizen, born in Montevideo. The woman said she was Annette-Anna Verlinden. The other gave her name (truthfully, as it turned out) as Rita Arnould, the housekeeper.

Rita was badly scared. She not only admitted to being the courier for the Brussels spy ring but identified Alamo as Mikhail Makarov, the Russian radio operator, and Anna Verlinden as a fellow Russian, Sophie Posnanska. Another of the ring, Anton Danilov, who had been responsible for liaison between the Russian embassy in Paris and the groups in Belgium and Holland, was gathered into the net when he arrived an hour later.

A search of the house revealed a secret door leading to a dark room faced with a complete forger's den with passports, official forms, stamps and invisible inks.

Piepe picked up two pictures of men he did not recognise and took them to Rita Arnould. She shrugged: 'One is the picture of the man we know as the Grand Chef. The other is his deputy the Petit Chef who gives us orders.'

Piepe departed with the prisoners, leaving two Feld Polizei in charge of the house.

There was a knock at the door. The two policemen found themselves staring at a filthy tramp who enquired petulantly for the lady of the house.

One of the policemen snapped: 'There's no one here. On your way.'

The tramp shambled off, not daring to look back but allowing himself a little self-congratulation for swift thinking.

Even so, he might not have been so lucky if Harry Piepe had still been in the house. It had been the very narrowest of escapes for Leopold Trepper, alias the Grand Chef.

Leopold Trepper had been steeped in revolution right from his teenage days as an impoverished Polish Jewish shop-keeper's son in Zakopane. Crippling poverty had forced him to abandon studies at Cracow University. He had drifted from one futile manual job to another. Almost inevitably, he became a Communist and at twenty-one he engineered a strike in the Galician town of Dombrovka.

After that, he was on the wanted list of the Polish army. To be a Jew was equally dangerous as to be a Communist. The Zionist organisations smuggled him out of the country, to a kibbutz in Palestine.

Communism for Leopold Trepper did not mean dialectic discussions in the pink parlours of the radical middle-class. It had to be the revolutionary battlefield. The most logical next step from Palestine was the Comintern, the Soviet secret service.

More specifically, there was an opening in the Razvedupr, better known as the State Police Administration of GPU.

The Russians sent Trepper by way of probation to Paris as an informer in a chemical factory. When his particular cell was rounded up, Trepper, with a natural talent for survival in the treacherous moral twilight of world espionage, managed to escape.

His Soviet spy masters were impressed. They sent for him and eventually groomed him as their agent responsible for the western European circuit – the Grand Chef of the spy cadre of the Rote Kapelle (Red Orchestra).

His task was to build up the circuit in Belgium which was under the control of Johann Wenzel, known as 'Hermann'. Later contact was to be established with the Berlin group run by Harro Schulze-Boysen and Arvid and Mildred Harnack.

The organisation which Trepper was ultimately to control amounted to a breathtakingly comprehensive espionage network within the Third Reich and the countries it had overrun. The organisation – dubbed 'orchestra' by the Abwehr who referred to operators as 'musicians' – extended from Norway to the Pyrenees, from the Atlantic to the Oder, from the North Sea to the Mediterranean.

Harro Schulze-Boysen and his attractive wife, Libertas, were, on the surface, conventional members of the German ruling class, many of whom voted for Hitler, not out of love for Nazism, but as a bulwark against Communism.

Harro, whose mentor had been Goering, had secured a job in the Civil Aviation Ministry and then gravitated to the Research Office through the attaché section of the Luftwaffe. He and his wife had irreproachable social qualifications. Harro was the grandson of Grossadmiral Tirpitz and Libertas Haas-Heye was the daughter of Countess Eulenberg, another of Goering's close friends.

But there was another Harro Schulze-Boysen – the dashing gold-haired idealist and fanatic who in the early 1930s had started an extreme left-wing newspaper, *Der Gegner (The Opponent)*.

On the streets, red and brown shirts squabbled over the rapidly expiring corpse of the Weimar Republic. Although muffled by the arrogant crunch of the Nazi jackboot, the voice of Schulze-Boysen called for a completely classless society to which bourgeois youth could rally. Conventional Communism at this time was spurned. A third force was the dream, an alignment of both left and right which would sweep away democrats, totalitarians and the establishment – but above all the Nazis.

Different party manifestos were produced every day. Opposition to Hitler appeared to many to be just about the only consistent aim of the third force. Many sections of the radical intelligentsia wrote off Schulze-Boysen as a muddled idealist. Even as late as 1939, he confessed that he knew little of even the most elementary tenets of Communism and had hastily to borrow the works of Stalin and Trotsky.

Whether Schulze-Boysen was muddled or not was scarcely the concern of the Nazis. They saw him and *Der Gegner* as potential threats.

Hitler had barely assumed power before a Gestapo flying

squad swept down on the editorial offices of *Der Gegner* at No. 1 Schellingstrasse. The procedure was familiar: the place was wrecked and all available copies confiscated. As editor, Schulze-Boysen and two friends, Adrien Turel and Henry Erlanger, were arrested. The Gestapo could do little about Turel, who was Swiss, and he was soon released.

Schulze-Boysen and Erlanger were hustled to a detention camp. Two ranks of SS were drawn up in the courtyard. Each man carried a whip loaded with lead. The prisoners were nude. Schulze-Boysen was kicked and beaten and slashed with whips as he ran the gauntlet the regulation three times.

Then Schulze-Boysen astounded his captors by insisting on coming back for the fourth time. Half-fainting and dripping with blood, he clicked his heels and shouted: 'Reporting for duty! Order carried out plus one for luck.'

The SS were impressed. One man called out: 'Good Lord, man, you belong to us!'

Schulze-Boysen's family, appalled at his arrest, frantically pulled strings to secure his release. Senior Nazis were nervous at possible repercussions of keeping a member of the Tirpitz family in prison. Pale and still racked with pain, Schulze-Boysen, his hair cut with garden shears and every single button on his suit ripped off, was released.

Erlanger, on the other hand, had been a half-Jew; the Gestapo beat him to death.

It was then that Schulze-Boysen vowed to throw in his lot with Communism, which alone could provide the shock troops of revolution. But he was prepared to bide his time. To a friend he confided: 'I have put my revenge into cold storage.'

It made sense to find a secure power base. And what could be more secure than the armed forces? He would be in among the watchdogs of Nazism – the best possible cover. His choice eventually fell on the Luftwaffe. Promotion was slow, but what transformed Schulze-Boysen's prospects was the meeting with Libertas Haas-Heye with her impeccable lineage as the granddaughter of Prinz Philipp zu Eulenburg und Hertefeld, who had been the favourite of the Kaiser.

The stormy and unstable marriage of Harro and Libertas started as a love match. But Schulze-Boysen, the fanatical revolutionary, was only too aware that her family had the entrée to the very inner circle of Nazism – in fact, to Hermann Goering himself. Libertas's mother, the Countess zu Eulenburg, had a family estate near Goering's ostentatious palace, Karinhall.

Goering was a witness at the wedding. He was also able to secure Harro a job in the Reich Ministry of Aviation. He worked in the press department, where he turned out to be a tireless desk officer. He was an obliging young man prepared to do anything – and that included writing Nazi-tailored articles for the controlled press on such subjects as the evils of Bolshevik expansion. His future looked bright.

Slowly he was able to edge his way even further into the secret departments of the ministry with an eye on the Research Office, the nerve centre of Goering's telephone-tapping network.

Schulze-Boysen's intelligence cell now numbered precisely six disaffected artists and intellectuals united by little beyond a fierce hatred of Nazism. It was not ideal, but it would have to do for the first espionage mission of the Schulze-Boysen group. Moscow, harsh task-masters as always, were beginning to demand action.

That was provided by the conflict of the Spanish Civil War which all over the world acted as a powerful magnet for the revolutionary left.

Schulze-Boysen knew that the Reich Ministry of Aviation had formed a 'Special Staff W' to direct German help to General Franco. There were secret links from the ministry to Franco's partisans fighting the left-wing republic.

All possible information was gathered about Special Staff W. This consisted of details about German transports to Spain, how many officers and men were involved and the nature of the Abwehr's activities. The assembled information was forwarded to the Soviet trade delegation in Berlin. It all sounded fairly elementary espionage. But Schulze-Boysen's group went further. The Gestapo had sent in a number of its agents to infiltrate the International

Brigade. These men were rounded up by the Republicans in Spain and shot.

Soon the Schulze-Boysen network expanded; latest recruit was National Socialist Party member No. 4,153,569.

To all appearances, Arvid Harnack was a fervent Nazi of impeccable credentials. He was a scientific assistant at the Foreign Policy School of Dr Rosenberg. The Nazi masters of this earnest bespectacled civil servant may have known that he had visited Moscow in 1933 as the member of an innocuous-sounding Society for the Study of Soviet Planned Economy. What they certainly did not know was that Harnack was recruited in Russia as a Communist agent.

Harnack had a spell in America on a two-and-a-half-year Rockefeller fellowship at the University of Madison, Wisconsin, where he met and eventually married an American lecturer in literature, Mildred Fish.

Harnack's Soviet control in Germany was a member of the staff of the Soviet trade delegation who went under the cover name of Erdburg. It was his plan to combine the Harnack spy network with that of Schulze-Boysen.

To Harnack, Communism was a companion of his nights and days. The precepts of his masters were to be followed absolutely without question. The necessity of leading the double life of a spy, no matter what sacrifices and deceits it entailed, was highly justified.

He immediately regarded Schulze-Boysen with distaste and distrust. The man, he reasoned, was a bottle-party Communist – of considerable courage and resource, no doubt, but with a recklessness and innate lack of discipline that could spell disaster. Above all, his puritanism revolted at the knowledge that Harro and Libertas, their marriage heading for disaster, were embarking on a series of hectic affairs. Sexual licence, reasoned Harnack, was only justified if it furthered the cause of Communism. But the instructions given by Erdburg were quite clear and there could be no question of the two networks not merging.

The addition of Harnack's single-minded expertise galvanised the Schulze-Boysen network. Soon it was extending right into the Nazi Foreign Office, pulling off a highly successful coup in netting a first secretary named Rudolf von Scheliha, who was passing information to the Russian secret service. His Berlin apartment was already a salon for a sizeable part of the diplomatic colony. The titbits picked up on the embassy cocktail circuit rapidly found their way via Schulze-Boysen to Moscow.

On 22 June 1941, Operation Barbarossa, the invasion of the Soviet Union, was unleashed by Hitler's Panzer armies. Swiftly, Erdburg contacted the senior German agents. They were ordered not to assemble in one place; instructions were given in underground stations and at tram stops. Erdburg went to each rendezvous carrying a suitcase containing radio sets. Every Berlin member of the spy ring had previously been given a cover name known to Moscow headquarters, and the organisation was divided into two parts.

Encoding would be done by 'Arwid' under Harnack The informer group was 'Choro' controlled by Schulze-Boysen, the overall leader. Other cells, master-minded by the Grand Chef and the Petit Chef, existed throughout western Europe.

Rote Kapelle was being mobilised and sent into battle.

16

Harro Schulze-Boysen continued his career in the Luft-waffe unsuspected and completely trusted. At the start of 1941, he became a member of the First Echelon of its operating staff with complete access to the top secret sections, including the command post of Goering's Signals Service. His days in the press group were long behind him. As an intelligence officer he now had a sight of all diplomatic and military reports which originated from the air attachés in German embassies and locations.

Infiltration was also stepped up inside Oberkommando

des Heeres (OKH), army headquarters. The star informant here was radio operator Horst Heilmann, at one time an ardent Nazi, who had become completely dazzled by the Schulze-Boysens. They instantly realised what a valuable contact they had netted, for Heilmann was a member of Decoding Section East, which was eventually to be responsible for unscrambling the messages sent to Russia by the Rote Kapelle.

Other contacts were no less useful. Oberleutnant Herbert Gollnow was a young officer whose particular attraction was his job in the sabotage section of the Abwehr. He worked closely with Canaris's office and knew a great deal about the activities of agents infiltrated by the Nazis into Russia.

Gollnow was ambitious; he particularly wanted to improve his knowledge of languages and placed a newspaper advertisement for a tutor.

It was obligingly answered by Mildred Harnack. Since information had to be gathered with care, interrogation was gradual and subtle. Herbert Gollnow became Mildred Harnack's lover. Later, when questioned on this by the Gestapo, she said simply: 'I was ordered by my husband.' Completely unaware of the truth, Gollnow was to prove a useful source of information without suspecting that it had literally been seduced from him.

Moscow became merciless in its demands for a constant flow of information on the progress of the Russian invasion. 'Choro' section bled its contacts dry for such information as the number of dive bombers being produced by the Luftwaffe each day and the extent of German air losses on the eastern front. The Russians learnt that Allied convoys between Iceland and Russian ports had been destroyed because the Abwehr had managed to secure British code books in advance.

Also forwarded to Russia was the armament of the latest Messerschmidt. On the military front Rote Kapelle was able to supply the Soviets with part of the offensive plans proposed by Army Group B for 1942 in the Voronezh area. Unguarded titbits of gossip were passed on, including the general feeling in OKW that 'the Russians have thrown everything into the present offensive and have no further reserves.'

The bosses of the Russian secret service had every reason to be satisfied when they looked at the cluster of flags on their situation maps. Each denoted a Rote Kapelle cell. Particularly effective was Brussels, centre of a network which spawned Soviet informers and agents all over Germany. One of the brightest and most effective of Russian recruits was Brussels chief Victor Sukulov-Gurevich alias Vincente Sierra, otherwise the Petit Chef.

Sukulov-Gurevich was one of those characters who seemed to spring directly from spy fiction. In one sense, he did that quite literally, because soon the Russian was calling himself Kent – simply because he had once read a novel in which the spy hero was a certain Edward Kent. It was characteristic: Sukulov-Gurevich lived and breathed the never-never world of the fictional secret agent. He was an assiduous womaniser, dressed expensively and had a lifestyle to match.

He also happened to be a ruthless and resourceful professional spy who was nothing less than the brains of the GPU in central and western Europe.

With the invasion of Russia, the cryptographers, agents and couriers of the man known as Kent processed a torrent of information pouring in from a score of countries. Moscow headquarters received within hours every scrap of intelligence it demanded.

The call sign from Brussels was PTX. The Rote Kapelle's Brussels headquarters was 101 rue des Atrebes.

Piepe, Freyer and Giering turned in their reports to their superiors in the Abwehr and the Wehrmacht. The scooping up of the cell in the rue des Atrebes was highly satisfactory, of course. But still the messages kept their tantalising secrets. The key to the codes had not yet been secured.

Then came a stroke of luck. A fragment of an encoded message was found in the fireplace of the house at Rue des Atrebes. Fear of the Gestapo worked wonders with the housekeeper Rita Arnould.

Schellenberg's Amt IV took over the interrogation. Within hours, the Germans had the information they wanted. According to the woman, Kent's men had been keen readers, but not for relaxation.

Key sentences had been used in certain books to construct a code. Schellenberg's agents were instructed to ransack bookshops throughout Belgium and France. At first the experts could only crack one word in the code, but it was enough to suggest that French books were involved. But which?

Schellenberg's cypher experts worked unceasingly on the laborious process of combing through some dozen books in search of a single word. But it was well worth it. A key sentence was isolated; the decoding section of OKW did the rest.

What they discovered was devastating for the conspiritors. The workings of the European network lay exposed. Worse, the code name of Gilbert (used by the Grand Chef) was revealed along with 'Choro' and 'Arwid'.

The Gestapo was edging ever nearer to Rote Kapelle.

The mood in Moscow changed abruptly. There had been a tailing off of radio traffic from Berlin and Kent received an order to find out what was wrong.

It did not take long. Coppi had realised right from the moment he had seen the disguised post office truck that Nazi counter-espionage was closing in.

Oberleutnant Wilhelm Vaux, chief decoder for signals security in the Luftwaffe, snatched up the ringing phone in the adjoining empty office.

The voice at the other end said: 'Is that you, Horst?' Vaux replied: 'He's not here at the moment. Can I take a message?' Harro Schulze-Boysen gave his name and directed: 'Tell him I called.'

Vaux was suspicious now, but all he could think to say was: 'Do you spell Boysen with a Y?' Even as he was asking, another question was framing in his mind. Why was Harro Schulze-Boysen, already a suspect as a member of the Rote Kapelle, trying to get in touch with Heilmann so urgently?

The caller rang off. Vaux dashed back to his own office, picked up a phone and swiftly dialled RSHA headquarters.

A badly rattled Moscow at last lost its patience. The message Russia sent to Kent in October 1941 ordering him to reactivate the Berlin network had contained the address of the leading agents in Germany whom Kent was to contact.

The Russians had taken a criminally dangerous risk. Possibly they were not aware that code after code used by Rote Kapelle was being deciphered. One man who knew just how much the Gestapo was learning was Horst Heilmann, who in his job worked closely with Vaux, the crypto-analyst. Frantically, Heilmann had attempted to contact Schulze-Boysen.

It was an act of foolish courage that could only have one outcome. Hans Heilmann was dragged from his apartment and thrown into the Prinz Albrechtstrasse cellars.

The black Gestapo cars sped through the deserted dawn streets. Schulze-Boysen himself was next, then Libertas, who had attempted to flee by train to friends in the Moselle.

Gestapo agents burst into the breakfast room of the Fischerdorf pension on the Kurische Nehrung in East Prussia and arrested the Harnacks on holiday.

The arrests continued over the weeks, prisoners filling the cellars of the Prinz Albrechtstrasse to such an extent that the RSHA set up a Rote Kapelle Special Section. Interrogations were turned over to Kriminalkommissar and SS-Untersturmfuehrer Johann Struebing.

Struebing was a conventional policeman. The methods of torture habitually employed at Prinz Albrechtstrasse were anathema to him. He objected to them not so much on humanitarian grounds, but because he believed them to be untidy and inefficient.

Schulze-Boysen, who was allowed to keep his uniform, was interrogated by a somewhat abashed Struebing. The whole thing, said the policeman confidentially, was doubtless a regrettable mistake. He was quite prepared to believe that Schulze-Boysen and his friends had merely discussed politics and the arts at their meetings.

Schulze-Boysen agreed readily that there had been nothing treasonable in their activities.

Struebing frowned. 'There is just one thing that puzzles me,' he said reasonably. 'Just what exactly are these?' He pushed photostats of decoded messages from Moscow across the table.

Still the prisoner kept his nerve and admitted nothing. Arvid Harnack was equally tight-lipped. Struebing was prepared to wait.

Predictably, Libertas Schulze-Boysen was the first to crack. She knew full well the evil reputation of the Prinz Albrechtstrasse. Struebing had only to give the merest hint of the horrors frequently committed there. Libertas was then left to her thoughts and instructions were given that she was to be asked no further questions.

Instead, Struebing encouraged a typist from the RSHA to make friends with the prisoner. The neurotic, badly frightened Libertas first poured out to the other woman the unhappiness of her marriage. The typist, duly primed, elaborately avoided any reference to Rote Kapelle.

Struebing, in simulated anger, forbade Libertas to talk to the other woman any longer. But soon he found some pretext to bring them together again.

The typist was a good listener. The confidences poured out of Libertas tearfully and gratefully.

The Gestapo, after very little work, soon had in their hands virtually the complete list of the Berlin network.

As the weeks wore on, the Gestapo hardened its methods. The prisoners were handcuffed all the time and forbidden to write letters. Females were placed in darkened cells.

All the standard tricks of interrogation were employed. Gestapo stoolpigeons, posing as prisoners, were introduced into the cells. If prolonged torture, as distinct from sporadic beatings-up, was not employed its threat was always there and liberally talked about. An interrogator would say to a prisoner: 'I don't think you will be able to stand physical persuasion as well as Coppi.' In fact, Coppi had not been tortured at all. The merest hint was enough to open a lot of mouths.

Most of the Rote Kapelle members were idealists and intellectuals. Few had the steely lack of passion of the professional agent. They had not been trained in the special Moscow spy schools which would have demonstrated tricks of survival under torture.

One by one, they gave in and confessed. They even betrayed each other.

The gallant Horst Heilmann, on the other hand, was one of the very few to be proof against the threats of the Gestapo. He proclaimed: 'I wish to die at Harro's side.'

Soon Mueller was assuring Himmler that, for practical purposes, the network was all but broken. What should be done next? Himmler, as was usual when any decision was expected of him, went trotting to his Fuehrer.

Hitler stormed: 'What is to be done next? The next step is to string them up rightaway. There must be no delay.'

It was suggested to the Fuehrer that a trial could be stage managed, film cameras and all, before a rubber stamp People's Court. Himmler was beside himself. The People's Court would be his province; the Gestapo would gain marvellous prestige from such a trial. Then it was reasoned that, since a number of the more important prisoners had belonged to the Luftwaffe, the matter was logically the responsibility of Reichsmarschall Goering. Himmler took few pains to conceal his disgust.

Disasters were now heaped thick and fast on Rote Kapelle.

A devastating blow came early in 1942 with the capture by the Germans of the chief operator, 'le Professeur', otherwise Johann Wenzel, together with his set in Brussels. Wenzel had also been an invaluable contact man with Dutch and French Communists whom he had trained in radio.

For Trepper stuck in Brussels, all links with Moscow had now been severed. Kent, in France, already sensed the eyes of the Gestapo on him and was lying low. That left the Dutch circuit, code named Hilda. From this group, Trepper managed to secure a decidedly ancient battery-operated radio set: the tenuous link with Moscow had been re-established.

The success of the mop-up in the rue des Atrebes the previous December had intoxicated Harry Piepe and Karl Giering. Nothing could stop them now from pursuing the rest of the Belgian network. Both pinned their hopes on a key member, a Jewish Polish forger named Abraham Raichman, codenamed 'the Manufacturer'.

Raichman had served Rote Kapelle conscientiously. After all, it had given him an opportunity to indulge in the twin passions of his life – making virtually foolproof passports and rubber stamps. He had little interest in espionage; all he asked was to be given the facilities to carry on the work he did best.

A realist, Raichman reasoned that there could be a job for life for him in a sophisticated modern state. Right or left, political complexions meant little. There would always be a market for the bureaucratic tools of deceit which he could provide so expertly.

It did not take much effort to persuade him to throw in his lot with the Gestapo.

First to be betrayed by 'the Manufacturer' was a Rumanian agent, Konstantin Yefremov, a leading figure in the Dutch circuit. No subtle methods were used on him. He was told either he could collaborate or forthwith face a firing squad.

Once Yefremov started talking he found it difficult to stop. One of his traitorous revelations particularly interested the Gestapo. The Grand Chef had, in addition to his other activities, a business interest in a firm called Simexco with offices in the rue Royale, Brussels.

Gestapo and Abwehr researches revealed little. Simexco, it seemed, was a perfectly above-board enterprise; its directors and shareholders were Brussels businessmen who would have little taste for espionage.

One thing struck the investigators as odd. Señor Vincente Sierra, a member of the board, seemed to spend most of his time out of the country. It was only a supposition, of course, but what was to stop Simexco being a cover for espionage? A tap put on the firm's telephone disclosed a large number of calls to Paris. Most of them were to a firm called Simex.

Piepe, Giering and twenty Gestapo officials moved to France.

They took Abraham Raichman with them. His instructions were to contact known agents of Rote Kapelle and tell them to get in touch with Trepper, as Raichman wanted to contact him urgently. But nailing the Grand Chef was not going to prove quite so easy; Trepper was far too canny to fall for such a suspicious ploy as that.

Piepe and Giering realised that if they wanted to capture the chief, they would have to do it themselves. Both were convinced that the answers lay in the offices of the mysterious Paris firm of Simex, whose managing director was Jean Gilbert, living in the Boulevard Haussman. A photograph soon identified Monsieur Gilbert as Leopold Trepper, Grand Chef of Rote Kapelle.

But Trepper had gone to ground. Sooner or later, the Germans reasoned, he would have to contact Simex. Once again, it was a question of patience.

The break came when the wife of one of the company's directors mentioned casually that Monsieur Gilbert had recently been suffering from toothache.

Giering pounced. He and Piepe were soon in the waiting room of Dr Maleplate, practising as a dentist in the Rue de Rivoli.

The two men demanded to see the dentist's list of appointments. Maleplate told them: 'My patient Monsieur Gilbert is due at two o'clock today.'

Outwardly casual, the two Germans withdrew. A swift telephone call from a nearby café ensured reinforcements and an armoured car. Giering and Piepe returned to the consulting room in good time and ordered Maleplate: 'Put your patient in the chair and prop up his head. We'll then arrest him.'

Within a few minutes, the Grand Chef was staring down the barrels of two revolvers. Trepper was perfectly calm. He assured his captors: 'I'm not armed.' Smiling slightly as the handcuffs clicked into place, he said to Giering: 'I congratulate you. You've done your work well.'

Señor Vincente Sierra, the director of Simexco, had been traced to a Marseilles apartment. Five French police, instructed by the Abwehr, burst in. Sierra and his girlfriend, Margarette, were taken by a Gestapo squad first to Paris and then to Brussels.

It was in Belgium that the saga of Rote Kapelle had begun. Somehow it seemed appropriate that with the arrest of Sukulov-Gurevich, alias Kent, alias Vincente Sierra, the story should end there.

Seventy-five members of the main Rote Kapelle cells were tried before the main tribunal, a specially convened Reich Court Martial, an offshoot of OKW.

Dr Manfred Roeder, the Judge Advocate General and presiding military legal officer of Air Region III of the Luftwaffe, was to be the trial's Special Commissioner.

Roeder was a man with a fanatical hatred of traitors. It soon became clear that the majority of the defendants were doomed. But only fifty of the seventy-five in the dock were condemned to death.

This suited Hitler not at all. In a stormy passion, he demanded that the remaining prisoners were to suffer death by hanging. Furthermore, the women were to go to the guillotine.

Death by the noose did not mean judicial hanging as the legal systems of more civilised countries required. There was no scaffold at the prison of Berlin Potzensee. Hitler gave clear instructions that no conventional gallows was to be constructed. There would be no drop.

A prison official recorded:

'The executions took place in a single room but in separate compartments divided by curtains. The hangman stood on a stool. The prisoner was lifted up, handcuffed and lowered. As far as I could see, complete unconsciousness came at the very instant when the noose tightened.'

In fact, the majority of the prisoners died by slow strangulation. Harnack's last words were: 'I regret nothing. I die a convinced Communist.'

As the women were guillotined, the execution chamber reverberated with the screams of Libertas Schulze-Boysen as she pleaded in terror: 'Let me keep my young life.' Her decapitation, like the others, took just seven seconds.

The executions ground on remorselessly into other prisons throughout Germany and the occupied countries where Rote Kapelle had operated. Just how many perished either by gallows, guillotine or firing squad will never be known. Many of Trepper's agents disappeared into concentration camps. The lucky ones lay low until after the war, giving themselves up to the advancing Russians.

Rote Kapelle was very far from being dead. Indeed now there were two clandestine networks. One was being operated by the Gestapo with turned-round agents. An enthusiastic collaborator now was Kent, the extreme opportunist to whom the spy game had been worth playing for its own sake. In his memoirs, Schellenberg claimed: 'Finally, about sixty-four transmitters were sending misleading information to Russia.'

The Gestapo had to play its new game cunningly. A sprinkling of genuine information was sent to the Communists to allay suspicion. The 'shadow' Rote Kapelle had one over-riding purpose, of course. The Russians unknowingly revealed to the Gestapo the names of still more agents.

As for the Grand Chef, the Germans made a speedy decision to keep him alive. As a turned-round agent, he would clearly be invaluable.

Trepper desperately wanted to keep what remained of Rote Kapelle in business. But he was not sure how long he could withstand the inevitable torture if he refused to co-operate. On the other hand, he had no intention of betraying the network. He decided to string the Gestapo along, hoping forlornly for a break.

On his arrest, he was taken to German headquarters on the rue des Saussaies. One of the first to turn up and gloat was the fat head of the Gestapo, Boemelberg. He enthused: 'At last we have him, the Russian bear!'

Giering, however, remained firmly in charge. He told his prisoner: 'You've lost twice over. I can either have you shot as an enemy of the Third Reich or turn you over to the Russians.

'We would of course, tell them that you, along with a lot of your friends, have given away Rote Kapelle. After that, the Russians won't hesitate to shoot you. Either way, your outlook isn't exactly bright.'

The interrogation went on into the small hours. Throughout, Giering exuded friendliness, admitting frankly that the Gestapo, masterminding the shadow Rote Kapelle, badly needed Trepper's co-operation.

It might have been secured by torturing him, but this was not Giering's way. His idea was to keep Trepper's arrest a secret. Only by hoodwinking the Russians into thinking that the network was still flourishing, would the Germans be able to gather further names of agents who could then be rounded up. A Trepper bruised and beaten by Gestapo thugs would scarcely be of much use as a turned-round agent.

Trepper realised that, although a prisoner, he held the trump cards. The Germans could not afford to do without him; the network had to be kept going. The longer Trepper was away from his old haunts and not communicating either with the French Communist Party or Moscow, the greater would be Rote Kapelle's lack of credibility.

On the other hand, it would be foolish to give into the Gestapo too soon. But of one thing Trepper was absolutely determined: he would tip off his Russian masters that he was in the hands of the Gestapo.

But how?

As the interrogations wore on, Trepper built up a relationship of friendly rivalry with Giering. The atmosphere relaxed. Trepper expressed himself anxious to brush up his German and asked for a dictionary, a pencil and some paper. The request was granted.

Trepper set to work. He pleaded insomnia and asked to be allowed to read at night. Under the eyes of the guards and cover of the dictionary, he scribbled furiously, putting together a full report of his arrest and what he knew of the shadow Rote Kapelle. The information obviously had to be as difficult to decipher as possible.

In tiny letters, often on scraps cut from a newspaper, he scribbled feverishly, using a cunning mixture of Hebrew,

Yiddish and Polish.

In his memoirs, *The Great Game*, Trepper wrote:

> 'To convince the Centre, I had to recapitulate every-
> thing . . . I drew up a detailed list of the arrests, specifying
> dates, places and circumstances. I told everything I
> knew about how the members of the network had be-
> haved after their arrests. Next I listed all the transmitters
> that had fallen into the hands of the enemy, the des-
> patches that had been discovered, the codes that had
> been broken.'

When the report was finished, Trepper decided on the
most dangerous gamble of all. He would activate Operation Juliette.

Madame Juliette Moussier was an elderly woman who ran a
confectioner's shop in Paris which since 1941 had been used
as a mailbox for despatches from the French Communist
Party. These messages, packed in tiny tubes, were handed
over the counter by a succession of Juliette's 'customers'.

It was a dangerous game at the best of times. Now
Juliette was going to be used for the most perilous mission
of her life. Leopold Trepper, alias the Grand Chef, was
aiming seemingly to betray her to the Gestapo.

Giering was delighted with the information Trepper gave
him: he reasoned that excellent progress had been made
since his prisoner seemed only too ready to toss one of his
key agents to the wolves.

But Giering had no intention of arresting Juliette Moussier yet. She could be used as a courier for bogus messages
of military intelligence designed to mislead the Russians.
He forthwith sent a number of turned-round agents to the
confectioner's shop.

The ploy was a total failure. Juliette told them all coldly
that she would deal only with the Grand Chef in person.

Trepper protested to Giering: 'After all, it's natural. I've
been under arrest now for two months. I've not been able
to make contact with anyone. If you want me to collaborate, you've got to trust me completely. The use of inter-
mediaries is bound to invite suspicion.'

Giering was worried. He was under no illusions of what his fate would be if it got to the notice of Himmler that without permission of higher SS authority he permitted his star prisoner directly to contact a fellow agent. He expressed his dilemma to Trepper.

The Grand Chef decided to get tough. He snapped: 'That's your problem. If you want to deceive Juliette and Moscow into thinking that I'm still at liberty and at work there is no other way. The game will collapse and the results for the Gestapo will be precisely nil.'

Giering, although still worried, saw the point. He took the first plane he could to Berlin. He came back with the personal go-ahead from Reichsfuehrer Himmler.

He told Trepper: 'If you betray us and pass any message to Juliette I will personally see to it that all Rote Kapelle prisoners in France and Belgium are executed.'

The threat left Trepper unmoved. He had no intention of passing his report to Juliette on the first meeting. That would come much later.

The black Citroens of the Gestapo edged into the numerous side streets near the confectioner's shop. Nazi agents were ordered to shadow Trepper every inch of the way. Many Gestapo men posed as customers, as Trepper, with a message from the shadow Rote Kapelle in his pocket, walked into the shop. His report for Moscow remained cunningly concealed back in his cell.

Quickly, he embraced Juliette, whispering that he would be back with a message later that was to be passed on.

Juliette Moussier was a nerveless professional. Her expression did not alter as she took the money for the box of chocolates which Trepper bought. He strode straight out of the shop and into one of the Gestapo cars parked round the corner. He still had Giering's undelivered message.

To Giering he explained that Juliette was suspicious at first and regarded the initial contact as a test. She had refused to take any message, but agreed to do so at the next meeting.

For how long would the suspicions of the Gestapo be lulled? Trepper realised the risks he was running, but sensed that impatience would ruin the whole scheme.

The second meeting with Juliette Moussier was fixed for the last Saturday in January 1943.

The choice of a weekend was deliberate, for Trepper planned to whisper hastily to Juliette that her work for him was at an end and she was to disappear. The Gestapo would remain blissfully ignorant until they discovered that the confectioner's shop remained closed on the following Monday.

Leopold Trepper had bunched his report into a handkerchief. As he entered the shop, he blew his nose noisily. To anyone watching, it seemed as if he had only handed over one message. He kissed Juliette warmly and whispered: 'Get out as quick as you can. The work is done.'

Giering expressed himself satisfied. He had not told Trepper that a number of his own men had watched his every move. There seemed no doubt now that the Russians thought that the Grand Chef was free. The Gestapo officer was less pleased when he discovered that Juliette had vanished. Anxiety gnawed. Had Trepper after all managed to tip her off? Plainly, it was too late to do anything about that now. What mattered most of all was the reaction of Moscow.

Trepper's impatience was every bit as great as that of the Gestapo. Both sides sweated throughout most of February. Then came the day when a smiling Giering came into Trepper's cell, brandishing two despatches.

The first read:

'On the anniversary of the glorious Red Army and of your birth we send you our best wishes. In appreciation of your great services, the directors have decided to ask the government to award you a military decoration.'

The second despatch was worded:

'Otto, we have received your despatch, sent through the intermediary of our friends. Let us hope that the situation will improve. We feel it necessary, to insure your security, to discontinue the liaison until further orders. Make contact direct with us. Detailed directives

203

will follow regarding the work of your network in future.
Director.'

If Giering was delighted, so was Trepper. The Grand Chef knew that Moscow wanted the war of nerves to continue between Russia and the Nazis. In his report, Trepper had appended a note saying that, if it was Moscow's wish to carry on, the reply should include congratulations for both the anniversary of the Red Army and Trepper's birthday.

Trepper could now seemingly do no wrong in the eyes of the Germans. He was the star performer of the shadow Rote Kapelle. But his only dream was escape – perhaps to Moscow, where they would undoubtedly allow him to carry on the struggle. So far he had survived and, as he was to insist after the war, had told the Gestapo nothing and had not betrayed a single agent. But for how long could he go on playing cat and mouse?

Still the Gestapo appeared to be trusting. Too trusting, perhaps. One day in September 1943, Trepper asked to be driven to a pharmacy for some medicine. His Gestapo guard waited outside.

Trepper disappeared through the doors of the Pharmacie Bailley. He walked the length of the store and out of the back entrance. Soon he was melting into the crowd, making for the nearest Métro station. He reckoned he would have perhaps forty minutes before rue Saussaies was at a state of alert. Trepper managed to remain under cover in France until Allied tanks rolled into Paris the following August. A plane eventually took him to Moscow.

The shadow Rote Kapelle had been discredited, thanks to Trepper. But the work of resistance flared anew. Soon there were new transmitters in Brussels, Antwerp, Copenhagen, Stockholm, Berlin, Budapest, Belgrade, Athens, Istanbul, Rome, Barcelona and Marseilles. The detector vans homed in. The arrests and executions continued until the end.

And the Grand Chef? He naturally expected to arrive in Moscow a hero. Instead, Stalin denounced him as a traitor and had him thrown into jail. Eventually, he was released to return to Warsaw.

There were those who maintained that Trepper had simply been a victim of one of Stalin's numerous anti-Jewish pogroms. Many favoured another explanation, that the Nazis had convinced Moscow that Leopold Trepper had been working for Germany all along and had deliberately betrayed his own agents. They let him go to suffer the punishments of the cause he had in reality served so courageously.

It could be that Himmler and the Gestapo, in revenge for their own approaching death agonies, so arranged things that they had the last cruel laugh on Leopold Trepper.

17

Everything about Ernst Kaltenbrunner seemed calculated to evoke a potent mixture of distaste and fear.

There was the slash of a mouth in the rough hewn brutal face which might have been the work of a deranged sculptor. Although the eyes were brown, it was hard to be sure since they were almost completely covered by the heavy tissue of the lids. The shoulders were massive but what really caught the attention were the small and delicate hands – nature's obscene joke in the creation of a monster.

This was the man who in 1943 was appointed the successor of Reinhard Heydrich as head of the RSHA. Under him were the Security Police (SIPO); the Gestapo; the Criminal Police (KRIPO) and the Security Service (SD).

Hitler regarded Kaltenbrunner with affection. The Fuehrer proclaimed: 'The man is nothing but a gangster.' It was meant as a compliment.

Schellenberg had originally been put forward as a likely successor to Heydrich but Hitler would have none of it. Schellenberg was clever, doubtless. But not only was he too young, he was also an intellectual. Such people, Hitler believed, were likely to be emotionally unstable and, when it came to the crunch, of questionable loyalty. To the Fuehrer, there was only one way to think and that was with an eternally hovering jackboot.

Kaltenbrunner, on the other hand, was fanatically loyal. He was also, like Hitler, an Austrian. Indeed, in 1935 he had been the leader of the Austrian SS. His devotion to Nazism was absolute.

He was fond of proclaiming that German women should keep on having children as long as possible. Husbands no longer able to father the future citizens of the Reich should be replaced by SS studs. He believed in the opposite course for inferior races; the Jews should be exterminated and the Slavs gradually die out by way of sterilisation and the annihilation of their leaders.

As far as intelligence work was concerned, Kaltenbrunner was completely useless. He was indeed the head of German espionage on paper, but in fact Schellenberg fulfilled the function, continuing to be under the direction of Himmler.

From the very start, Kaltenbrunner was a dangerous adversary of dubious efficiency, not least because he was almost permanently fuddled on champagne which he had shipped from France.

Schellenberg wrote:

'I would find him in his office at eleven o'clock in the morning, having risen hardly more than half an hour earlier, his small eyes dull and empty. With the joviality of a drunkard he would reach under his desk, or bellow "Orderly!" and pour out a glass of champagne or brandy for me. Then when he became too obstreperous, I would take a nip or two to pacify him and pour the rest on the carpet. Usually he did not notice this, but once when he did, the veins in his face became so swollen with rage that I thought he was about to have a stroke.

This was the man who proclaimed that Allied parachutists should be lynched and, furthermore, that the enraged populace should be encouraged by the police. When Heinrick Mueller asked him what should be done with twenty-five French prostitutes who were suffering from syphilis, Kaltenbrunner stormed: 'Machine-gun them, of course.'

For a man with a killer mentality there was plenty to do in the occupied countries.

There now came under Kaltenbrunner's control the various Einsatzgruppen (action groups), which were a legacy of Heydrich. They had been used against the Czechs as an instrument of repression, but by 1941 Heydrich had drawn up plans to use them as killer squads.

After the war, the army might shudder fastidiously at the very mention of the Einsatzgruppen and protest that they were regarded as beyond the pale and had nothing whatever to do with the Wehrmacht. But the fact remained that in 1941 Heydrich had ordered Mueller to negotiate an agreement with the military on how the Einsatzgruppen were to work. A directive of 13 March 1941, which carried the signature of Generalfeldmarschall Keitel, stated that by order of the Fuehrer Einsatzgruppen were to carry out special duties in Russia, acting on Himmler's own authority.

On 4 April, six weeks before the attack on Russia, the quartermaster-general of the army, Eduard Wagner, started negotiations on a written agreement with the RSHA which was drafted by Schellenberg. The army agreed that the Einsatzgruppen would be given food, transport and communications facilities by the army. But directives for the missions for these groups would be the responsibility of the RSHA.

The arrangements were completed early in May. Rear echelons were placed under the Reichsfuehrer-SS. The RSHA realm of terror in the east was expanding fast.

Each Einsatzgruppe consisted of 1,000 to 1,200 men who were divided into a number of Einsatzkommandos. Out of 1,000 men there were to be around 350 members of the Waffen SS (armed SS), 150 drivers and mechanics, 80 members of the auxiliary police, 130 of ordinary police, 40-50 from the KRIPO – and between 100 and 135 from the SD and Gestapo.

The latter two groups were also to help supply back-up

services, ranging from interpreters and radio operators to teletypists and clerical staff, including women.

Within one month of being set up, the Einsatzkommandos were in action. One of their most spectacular atrocities in 1941 was at Riga, where some 35,000 people were murdered. SS-Obergruppenfuehrer Erich von dem Bach-Zeleswki, a veteran Junker officer and former Reichstag deputy, was able to boast: 'There is not a Jew left in Estonia.'

Eyewitness accounts of the activities of the killer groups abound; one from Poland must do duty for hundreds:

' ... They assembled mainly elderly male Jews, and all of them were put in the great synagogue in Mielicz; there they were slaughtered – almost all the Jews were killed. Those who tried to escape through the windows were shot from the outside. In the morning, units of black and green uniforms surrounded the place, and they took us out of our homes and ordered us to the market place. People who could not run, the sick, were shot sometimes in their beds; others were later placed in the centre of the market place. Then young men were selected and ordered to step aside; the women, children and old people were roped in a long column and we were in the middle. These were SS, SD people ... When we arrived there they surrounded us with such heavily armed units, the like of which I had only seen at the front. Then they told us that we were setting out on a march and that we had to hand over everything which we possessed – money, gold, silver, watches – only twenty zloty were left to each man. They ordered us not to speak, not to turn around, not to look at or come into contact with each other and said that whoever violated these orders would be shot ...

'Then we were given the order to set out and march. One girl managed to run after the column and she shouted all the time "Father, Mother". Here Chola Chenis, the girl, was taken away. We did not know what happened to her. All we heard was a shot. From time to time, whoever halted and tried to arrange his clothes was told to leave the column and then we heard a shot behind us. That is how we marched in the mud, because this was the heaviest rainy season. It was in December. Then we were already sitting or lying down on the floor, they came and argued with us, and told us that we were to blame for the war. They took all the sacred articles, and they took the two Jewish elders with beards. We heard that others also were taken. We knew that two hundred people were taken away. And we never saw them any more. We did not know what happened to them. We still had hope that perhaps this was not a death march. The next morning we were placed in rows again. But there were only three people to a row now.

Those who were shot were usually taken some kilometres from the round-up and out of sight of the military. Long trenches had been dug in advance. Victims, assembled in groups, were forced to undress. Then they were lined up on the edge of the trench or made to ascend a pile of bleeding corpses, helped on their way by the whips of the SS. Execution was frequently by a single shot in the back of the neck. Then the trench was filled in.'

There was something almost cosy about the weekly lunches which were held in Eichmann's Berlin office. Here, the main architects of the bureaucratic jungle of the RSHA would meet in relaxed conviviality. Kaltenbrunner, his sweaty purple face corrugated with duelling scars, would soak up the champagne and enquire with tipsy expansiveness after Eichmann's family. Himmler attended whenever he could.

It was during a succession of these lunches that the details of the installation of the first gas chambers were discussed, a matter dear to the heart of Eichmann as chief of Section IVb of the Gestapo with, among other things, responsibility for the system of convoys to take the European Jews to the gas chambers.

Here, too, over the cheese and the looted brandy, they discussed the progress of repression by the Gestapo in all the occupied countries. But, as the war progressed, anxiety began taking the place of arrogant confidence.

The supremecy of the Reich was being challenged from within the vassal states. Resistance was on the loose.

In Poland, opposition was carefully orchestrated. On 1 September 1940, Nazi parades were held throughout Poland to celebrate the first anniversary of the outbreak of war.

Nazi soldiers marched and sang in a number of cities. Not a Pole or Jew turned out to watch. All places of entertainment were open but remained empty. Suddenly, in the early evening, hundreds appeared and began a slow silent procession towards cemeteries and patriotic monuments. In Warsaw, the Tomb of the Unknown Soldier was covered by a mass of red and white flowers.

The Gestapo retaliated swiftly against the mild demonstrations. There were mass arrests and house searches in Warsaw and Lodz. Incitement, the Germans were convinced, had come from a knot of thriving underground newspapers. In Warsaw, the printing press of the *Dziennik Polski (Polish Daily)* was seized. The staff and some 200 clandestine workers were rounded up by the Gestapo and shot.

But it was the so-called Polish Home Army which proved the biggest source of opposition to the Germans. Commanded by Bor-Komorowski, this highly organised resistance group, with its sabotage cells and forged German documents, became feared both by the Gestapo and its Polish collaborators, the Blue Police.

The Polish resistance masterminded a string of assassinations of key Gestapo figures, acting often under the radioed orders of the Polish government-in-exile in London, some of whose members operated as undercover agents in Poland itself.

Wilhelm Krueger, Gestapo chief in Cracow, was particularly proud of his expanding empire. There had been twenty-two concentration camps in the area when he arrived; the number soon increased to forty-one.

One of Krueger's notorious specialities was the practice of putting barefoot men, women and children into boxcars which had been spread thickly with wet quicklime.

And Krueger particularly enjoyed interrogations. He invariably began by soothing the nerves of the weary prisoners. He would speak softly and kindly to them like an indulgent father – and then, suddenly thrusting forward with outspread fingers, jab out their eyeballs.

On 12 February 1943, Gestapo vehicles screeched to a halt at each end of a Warsaw street, making a deadly effective barrier from which there was no escape. Seventy passers-by were dragged at random from the pavements and thrown in the back of the lorries.

That evening the Gestapo stuck up notices all over the city announcing that every one of those captured had been in 'ceaseless armed attacks against Germans'.

Each notice carried the signature of Wilhelm Krueger, whose responsibilities as deputy to Governor General Hans Frank extended to Warsaw.

The resistance decided to eliminate the Gestapo chief. It was by no means easy since, like all in his position, he never travelled without a motor-cycle escort and armoured vehicles bristling with machine-guns. Nevertheless, at 9.50 a.m. on 20 April two bombs tore Krueger's car apart in a Cracow street.

Other executions followed swiftly.

Roman Leon Swiecicki, a lieutenant of the notorious Blue Police, was known to be an enthusiastic collaborator with the Gestapo, particularly at hastily assembled courts whose purpose was to do little beyond handing out death sentences.

Swiecicki was shadowed for days by the resistance; it was known that he left his Warsaw apartment each day and took a tram ride to his office.

One morning, two men stood behind him in a queue of commuters. As a tram approached, both emptied their weapons into Swiecicki, then melted away into the rush hour crowds.

Now it was the turn of the resistance to place placards throughout Warsaw. Large red posters were printed. They began with the words: 'In the name of the Polish republic ...' and ended with the signature: 'Directorate of the Polish resistance.' The posters stated that a special court

211

had tried the cases of Krueger and Swiecicki, found them guilty of 'special crimes' and sentenced them to death. The sentence had been carried out.

Each announcement of sentence referred to the violation of laws under the Polish government which existed before the advent of the Nazis: it was a subtle piece of implied resistance.

News bulletins broadcast by the BBC in London beamed news of resistance executions throughout Poland. They helped to maintain the morale of those who listened regularly to the forbidden broadcasts. But it was also realised within the Home Army that such measures were invariably followed by reprisals against the civilian population.

Governor Frank had set up Standgerichte (exceptional tribunals). They were exceptional because they were composed almost exclusively of Gestapo staff members. A clause of the decree stated: 'The exceptional tribunals of the security police must be composed of a Fuehrer-SS from the security police and the SD and two other members of the same service.' The real point of the Standgerichte was outlined in yet another clause which stated that sentences had to be carried out 'on the spot'.

In other words, the process of annihilation was to be speeded up. And it was. In the jails of Cracow alone hundreds of detained Poles were 'judged' and executed.

The resistance became more subtle in its retaliations. Killer squads no longer prowled the streets. Instead, leading members of the Gestapo were kidnapped at night and hustled to fields and woods.

Hangings were then staged as if they were suicides. At gunpoint and at the edge of death, the victims were forced to write final notes, explaining how they could no longer live with their guilt and shame and were taking the only way out.

By 1943, the Gestapo had an iron grip on the Poles – muscle was provided by 60,000 of Himmler's agents, backed by an army of 500,000. The resistance became more desperate and at the same time more highly organised, and the links with the government-in-exile grew closer.

The effectiveness of the Executive of Civil Resistance, a

branch of the underground movement, increased when two Poles trained to kill were parachuted from England into Europe and, through the resistance networks, eventually found their way to Warsaw.

There were a number of targets for execution. One of these was Frank Rutkowski, a civil servant in the municipal waterworks, who, as a stool pigeon of the Gestapo, had terrorised many of his fellow workers into informing and working for the secret police. A decision was taken to kill him.

One of the agents, known as 'Philip', later reported the execution to resistance worker Stefan Korbonski:

> 'The observer tipped us off that Rutkowski was direct-ing the construction of some sewers in distant Grochow. We hired a cab to go there and on the way we decided on a ruse. I had on me a forged identity card of a Gestapo agent, with my own photograph on it. I took Rutkowski aside, showed him the card, and told him that his chief wanted to see him urgently, and that we had come to fetch him. Without a moment's hesitation Rutkowski got into the cab.
>
> During the drive I told him that we had to make an arrest on our way back and that we might need his help. He again agreed without hesitation. As we were driving along in the cab, he grumbled that although he was working so hard, he could not get his children accepted in a German school. That was more than we could stand, so as soon as we reached a desolate spot, we stopped the cab, pulled out revolvers and read the sentence to him on a sheet of paper. He fell on his knees and cried and begged. It was no use ...'

After the war, many members of the Polish resistance were accused of using reprisal methods every bit as brutal as the repressions of the Gestapo. To betray to the Ger-mans the location of an arms dump was enough to incur a death sentence. Poles were shot by their own people for 'subservience to the Germans'.

It was undeniably true, however, that warnings were often sent notifying individuals that they were under threat. The usual result was that they were given Gestapo protection.

It was not always enough to guarantee survival.

In October 1943, the American magazine *Colliers* carried an article 'Revenge in Poland', written by journalist George Creel, who interviewed an escaped member of the Polish resistance, designated 'Mr B'.

The Pole stated:

> 'In Skierniewice, for instance, Kreisfuehrer Buchholz refused to abate his cruelties and was executed on 2 June. Ritter, his successor, also put his faith in the Gestapo, and perished on 25 June. The man who now has the job is much more humane.
>
> In another district, a certain Funk was warned to quit burning villages for the non-delivery of corn. He kept on, however, and met his death as did Vorblicher, another blustering bully. Schoene, the new man, is quite an improvement. Just before I left home, the members of the Warsaw chamber of commerce were warned that all would be killed if they did not stop their confiscation of Polish property. I hear that it has had good effect.
>
> Geist, a brute in charge of the Warsaw labour exchange, was killed after repeated warnings. Keller, his successor, keeps his sadism under control.'

The Chief of Intelligence of the Home Army was, understandably, high on the Gestapo's wanted list. Nerve centre for his agents was a house tucked away in the Vistula district of Warsaw. Bor-Komorowski joined the man codenamed Woodpecker, and five others one day in 1942 for a top-level conference.

Suddenly all stiffened at a violent knocking on the front door. Arrest was expected at any time; already five of Woodpecker's men had been caught. Torture might very well bring betrayal.

Bor-Komorowski and his companions stood mesmerised and listened to voices below. They heard the tones of a man raised in anger.

Then suddenly the owner of the house appeared with a relieved grin. She reassured them: 'There's no need to worry. It was the man to read the meter. He was impatient because I took so long to answer the door.'

One of the group suddenly said: 'Where's Woodpecker?'

Then they heard a groan of pain. Woodpecker stood framed in the door; no one had seen him slip out. Just before he pitched forward on the floor he gasped: 'I've taken poison.'

He had assumed automatically that the Gestapo had arrived. His nerve had cracked.

Woodpecker was smuggled to hospital and his life saved. But it was only a temporary respite. A few days later, the Gestapo caught him. This time he carried no poison. He was tortured and murdered, betraying nothing.

This sort of war of nerves was to be unceasing. But the long night of Gestapo terror was to be lightened by the equal ruthless faith of resistance in ultimate liberation.

And not just in Poland and eastern Europe.

Hitler had a spectacular success with his invasion of Norway and Denmark in April 1940.

The Fuehrer was determined that none of the highly dubious intellectuals so beloved of Himmler was going to get the job of Reichskommissar of Norway.

Forty-one-year-old Joseph Terboven was a short thin totally humourless individual with the charm of a codfish. His credentials were exemplary. He was an old-style Nazi who had joined the party in the 1920s. His street fighting prowess against the Communists had automatically assured him a bright future. By the year that the Nazis took power, Terboven was Gauleiter of Essen. Hitler sent him from there to Norway.

With the enthusiastic support of the Nasjonal Samling party, the pro-Nazi organisation led by Vidkun Quisling, Terboven embarked on a programme of Jewish persecution – and sheltered behind the law to do it.

The Norwegian Constitution of the 1850s, which had forbidden the entry of Jews into Norway, was revived. Terboven was able to proclaim that consequently all Jews already in the country were there illegally. Soon the mass arrests by the Gestapo and consequent deportations began.

Five hundred and thirty-two Jewish prisoners were jammed aboard the troopship *Donau,* which sailed for Germany. There the Jews were loaded on to trains heading for Auschwitz. Among those deported were an eight-week-old infant and an eighty-two-year-old woman.

Deportations were unceasing. By the end of February 1943, some 760 Norwegian Jews had perished in the gas chambers of Auschwitz. Able-bodied men were put to hard labour.

Only twenty-four came back alive: a survival rate of three per cent.

By then, the Norwegians had learnt to hate.

Three months after the invasion of Norway, Winston Churchill had drafted a key memorandum demanding the instant creation of a unique military organisation to carry on the war from right inside Nazi-occupied Europe.

That memo requested the co-ordination of 'all action of subversion against the enemy overseas'. But such dry and official language was soon to be forgotten. What was to be recalled time and again was Churchill's memorable instruction to members of the newly constituted Special Operations Executive (SOE).

It was 'Set Europe Ablaze'.

The Prime Minister went on to sketch out his plans for SOE. The new organisation was not to flinch from unconventional and 'ungentlemanly' tactics; indeed, it was to revel in them.

Dr Hugh Dalton, Minister of Economic Warfare, which was concerned with intelligence, sabotage and propaganda, declared to Foreign Secretary Lord Halifax:

'We must organise movements in enemy-occupied territory comparable to the Sinn Fein in Ireland, to the Chinese guerrillas now operating against Japan ... We must use many different methods, industrial and military espionage, labour agitation and strikes, continuous propaganda, terrorist acts against traitors and German leaders, boycotts and riots.'

Such an organisation ruffled many conventional military minds to whom any form of irregular warfare was

216

anathema. The doubters were swept aside by Churchill and Dalton; nowhere was the conception of SOE more welcomed than among the occupied countries' resistance movements whose members were being hunted unrelentingly by the Gestapo.

Norwegian military resistance, known as Milorg, slowly and perilously evolved. Its members, knowing nothing of underground warfare, were inexperienced and often careless.

British SOE officers later working with Milorg agreed that if the good-natured Norwegians had a fault, it was that they talked too much. A saying soon became current: 'The Gestapo is a bad enemy, but the Norwegian is even worse.'

However, they were soon to learn. The most salutary teacher was, indeed, not to be SOE, but the Gestapo itself.

During the summer of 1940, groups of young Norwegians arrived in England. Under the noses of the Germans, they had braved the perils of the North Sea in fishing-smacks and private boats. If zeal had been sufficient, they would have made the finest resistance workers of all.

SOE was ruthless. Idealism was all very fine; but of questionable benefit unless accompanied by courage and physical endurance. There was some prodigious weeding out.

A hard-trained force of subversives emerged. By 1942, forty-nine SOE agents had been landed back in Norway from fishing boats, together with 150 tons of arms and equipment. Resistance fighters fleeing from the Germans were often taken back to England.

But 1942 was also a black year for resistance forces in Norway. On 23 February, the Gestapo swept down on a fishing vessel minutes before it was due to sail from Alesund in the north-west. The twenty-three passengers were interrogated and tortured; twenty others were betrayed and a ring-leader executed.

The coup had only been made possible because of pro-Nazi forces operating deep within the Norwegian resistance. Most valuable informer for the Germans had been a

Norwegian named Henry Oliver Rinnan. He had infiltrated an 'export' group in Alesund which despatched refugees and volunteers across the North Sea.

Milorg and SOE were still reeling from the blow of Alesund when the Gestapo struck again.

Televaag was a small fishing village nestling near Bergen and an ideal location because it was one of the nearest points to the Shetlands and had a staunchly pro-British population. It was here that many agents began their missions in Norway.

Inevitably, the area teemed with informers. The local police chief was a known member of Quisling's Nasjonal Samling party; he had built up his nest of informers.

Not that it required brilliant powers of deduction to know what was going on. A Televaag resident, no lover of the Nazis, had the national characteristic of garrulity in an acute form. He was heard boasting to friends that he had seen weapons, ammunition and radio sets in the farmhouse of the local Milorg leader.

It did not take long for the Germans to discover that a barn at the back of the house was likely to prove rewarding.

In the early hours of an April morning, the SD detachments edged quietly forward. One of the Norwegian agents of SOE hidden in the barn spotted the Germans and opened fire, killing two officers.

But there was no way out. One of the agents was killed, the other dragged away for questioning, along with the Milorg leader. Both were executed.

It was far from being enough for Reichskommissar Terboven. Reprisals were ordered against Televaag forthwith; it would serve as an example for the rest of the country.

More than 300 houses were burnt to the ground. Cattle were killed and confiscated.

Seventy-six Televaag men between the ages of sixteen and sixty-five – almost the entire male population – were deported. The rest of the population were interned for the duration of the war.

Eighteen young men from Alesund, chosen utterly at

218

random, were executed after torture. Many of them, in their death agonies, gasped out the names of Milorg leaders. The Gestapo was ordered to seize them.

During May and June 1942, the Gestapo, assisted enthusiastically by police officials working for Quisling, rounded up leaders in Bergen, Stavanger, Oslo, Drammen and Konigsberg.

Some managed to escape to England and testified to the royal Norwegian government of what happened to their comrades who had been taken to the Gestapo headquarters in Oslo at 19 Moolergaten or to the four-storey brick building on Victoria Terrasse, the sight of whose curtained windows was said even to make Quisling supporters sick with fear.

One witness told of seeing a fellow prisoner 'taken down into the basement after having denied that he had been engaged in espionage. Here he was burned with a soldering iron on a couple of less sensitive points on the inside of the hand. Afterwards it was explained to him how much more painful it would be to be burned in a more sensitive place. As he still refused to confess, he was first burned on the inside of one of his wrists, which made a wound about the size of a florin, and then burned with the same iron on the other side of the artery.'

Another witness testified of a fellow prisoner:

' . . . The policeman had broken four of his fingers and had pulled out the nails from two of them. Afterwards they had hit him with sticks wrapped in cloth until he collapsed. Then they had turned him on his back and jumped on his stomach. He stated that he had asked his tormentors to shoot him. I myself saw that he was bleeding through the mouth and the rectum and that four fingers had been broken and bent backwards. I also noticed that two nails were missing . . .'

Gestapo units had gone on to crack down on underground groups in the north. Hundreds of arrests were carried out around Kristiansand. Twenty-four agents and Milorg leaders were executed and there were many civilian shootings.

By the end of 1942, the Germans had good reason to be

well satisfied with the situation in Norway.

Gerhard Ronne had been one of Denmark's brightest architects and it was generally conceded that he had done Copenhagen proud with Shellhus (Shell House), the new headquarters of the international oil company.

The building was in the shape of a shallow U. At each of its rounded corners on Kampmannsgade there were gigantic windows lighting the interior stairway which snaked from base to roof. There were five floors of offices in the block and ample attic space. All in all, the Danes agreed that one and a half million kroner had been well spent. The Germans thought so too. But for rather different reasons.

In May 1940, Gestapo headquarters had been in the Dagmarhus in the city centre. But bureaucracy was a hydra-headed monster; the hunt was soon on for new premises. Shellhus, which overlooked water reservoirs and Saint Jorgen's Lake, was taken over.

Denmark's Gestapo chief was Rhinelander SS-Obergruppenfuehrer Karl Heinz Hoffmann. Serving with him were SS-Obergruppenfuehrer Gunther Panks and Otto Bovensiepen, one of Kaltenbrunner's protégés. Crammed into Shellhus were a series of specialised departments: Gestapo clerks laboured away on files concerned with sabotage and resistance. There were alarmingly detailed card indices carrying the names, aliases, descriptions and photographs of Danes suspected or wanted.

In addition to adding new names, existing records had to be updated to accommodate information gained during interrogations.

The clerks were like their counterparts in civil service departments the world over. The only difference was that they were not allowed to penetrate other than the fourth or fifth floors. Not that they minded; few found the sound of beatings and screams particularly conducive to peace of mind or, far more important, executive efficiency.

So, whenever possible, the Gestapo's particular brand of persuasion was conducted in the basement or on floors where few office staff worked.

Shellhus became a notorious torture centre. Punishment

for the unco-operative began with punches and beatings with truncheons and then progressed to prisoners being strapped face down over a table with hands and feet tied beneath. Then the whippings began, with the torturers working in relays.

Senior Gestapo secretaries were summoned to make swift shorthand notes of the agonised whispers of informers.

Soon the Danish underground was able in a modest way to throw the Nazi bureaucratic machine out of gear. When an agent was taken, all codenames, underground addresses and meeting places known to him were changed. It was not much of a victory but infinitely better than nothing.

Escapes from Shellhus were rare but they did happen.

Edith Bonnessen had been a member of the Danish resistance movement since 1941. She had worked for the illegal newspaper *De Frie Danske* and had then been an assistant to Duus Hansen, chief of the clandestine radio network.

Codenamed Lotte, Edith had processed all cipher messages which passed between Hansen's headquarters, which were in the offices of a Copenhagen textile firm, and London, Stockholm and Gothenburg.

But the firm was under suspicion. The Gestapo was waiting for Edith at the offices when she arrived with a parcel of transmitter crystals. They were found after she had been taken to Shellhus.

The crystals were damning enough. Worse, the parcel had been inscribed 'For Lotte'.

Her interrogator was jubilant. He ran into the passage shouting: 'We've got her. We've got Lotte.'

Edith knew what was likely to be in store for her; she had no idea how long she would be able to withstand Gestapo persuasion. At risk was a whole network of underground operatives.

The masters of Shellhus were so elated at her arrest that they became careless. She was left alone in her cell with a single guard, who had been celebrating her arrest and was amorous as well as drunk.

Edith blatantly encouraged his advances, only breaking

off to ask for the lavatory.

Her captor lead her along a corridor, but was so fuddled he directed her to the wrong room.

Edith was alone in the corridor. She checked the desire to panic and run, made briskly for the stairs and descended for all the world as if she owned the building.

At the exit, she faced disaster. She noticed it was impossible to leave the building without showing a pass. She darted smartly into an empty office, snatched up some files, making her way around the building to another door.

Guards came to attention and saluted. Edith swept out with a brief '*Auf wiedersehen*'.

By September, she was safely in Sweden.

Dr Mogens Fog stared uneasily at the outside of the nondescript house whose upper floor had already been used a number of times for meetings of the Danish Freedom Council.

It was tempting fortune to use the same house again but what worried Dr Fog was that from across the street he could see that the letter slit in the front door was empty. A newspaper pushed halfway through it had been the agreed sign of safety.

It had happened before. Fog had promptly telephoned, been given the agreed password and an apology for having forgotten the newspaper. When Fog had then returned to the house the paper had been hastily placed in the door.

This time he arrived late and in a hurry. What the hell was going on upstairs? Cursing, he found the nearby telephone booth and dialled the number of the house.

He snapped: 'What's the matter? Where's the paper?'

The voice at the other end replied in perfect Danish and with a hint of a laugh: 'Nothing. Come on up.'

It was not until he put the receiver down that Fog remembered he had neither asked for nor received the required password.

Was he to go in? There was still no newspaper.

Half way up the stairs, he hesitated and walked down the street. But hesitation could be dangerous so he retraced his steps, making for the top floor. The Gestapo was there, waiting.

At Shellhus, he was beaten up. They took away the 200,000 kroner he had been carrying for distribution to the resistance, together with his return ticket to the village outside Copenhagen where he had his hideout. Then they dragged him off for interrogation.

He was scarcely conscious of the periodic blows and answered most of the questions in monosyllables.

His thoughts were with the train ticket; the destination stamped on it would betray yet another resistance cell.

The men of Shellhus brought in Fog's possessions in a box and laid them in front of him. He was able to palm the train ticket and began to swallow it, hunching over the box so that the movements of his mouth were disguised.

Then, his mind racing, he turned his attention to the contents of the box.

He looked up, feigning surprise. 'But there must be some mistake. These are not my things. They must have come from some other prisoner.' He indicated a key: 'That's certainly not mine.' If he admitted to owning the key it would be only a matter of time before he was tortured again and forced to admit that the key belonged to an apartment of the Freedom Council where a future meeting was due to be held.

The Gestapo official growled: 'Of course they're yours. I suppose you are going to say you don't know anything about the 200,000 kroner.'

Fog replied sulkily: 'Of course I do. They're Freedom Council funds.'

He reasoned that such an admission could scarcely do much harm now. The Gestapo might very well consider that since he had told the truth about one thing, his other replies might be genuine.

None of this saved him from further torture. For three hours the beatings went on.

'Where did the Freedom Council last meet?'

'Where are you living?'

He told them nothing. But for how long could he remain silent? How long would it be before the dreadful pain forced his severely bitten tongue to loosen? How long before the bloodstained lips uttered their betrayals?

They beat him to the edge of unconsciousness, knowing the exact moment to ease off and bring him back from the abyss.

Then they flung him in a cell for three months, throwing him just enough food to keep alive. Prison regulations demanded he be searched every two weeks; it was another excuse for a beating. Then they found the knife sewn in his trousers and the pencil concealed in his sock. They beat him up again and left him.

This time they didn't come back.

In his solitude, a slide into depression was inevitable. The agony of the beatings was replaced by the agony of loneliness and the almost physical oppression of silence.

Eventually, he came to terms with it. And having done that, he settled down to work.

When eventually, the Gestapo took him back for more questioning, its officials found Fog transformed. Here was a man only too willing to talk. Indeed, it was impossible to stop him. He rambled about neurology, his particular interest. He discoursed on philosophy and ethics by the hour. He treated his Gestapo questioners as if they were a classroom of students. In his discourses, he soared on to an intellectual plane that left the Germans gasping.

Gradually, they became infected with the acidity of boredom. Plainly, they believed, their prisoner had gone mad.

Back in his cell, Fog smiled. There, in his loneliness, he had rehearsed his discourses of tedium over and over again. Now he had submerged his tormentors in a sea of verbiage, the only weapon he possessed. But he had not told them one single thing they had wanted to know.

At last, the inquisitors of Shellhus admitted defeat. They left him alone. He had won.

But there was no overall victory for the Danish resistance. At least not yet. The net tightened; there were more arrests.

In the wake of the allied landings on 6 June 1944, saboteurs launched an attack on the Globus factory producing components for the V2 rockets.

Retaliation was savage. It was carried out by Denmark's collaborationist para-military Schalburg Corps which, with its plain-clothes intelligence service, aped many of the characteristics of the Gestapo machine.

But there was a bonus for the resistance. On 31 October, the RAF carried out a successful raid on Gestapo headquarters at Aarhus in Jutland. Much documentation on the underground was destroyed. A large hole had been blown in Gestapo intelligence.

Karl Heinz Hoffmann felt a chill. Aarhus, he knew, could so easily be followed by Shellhus.

18

From behind his desk at 57 Boulevard Lannes in Paris the taste of power seemed increasingly sweet to Gruppenfuehrer Karl Albrecht Oberg in the third year of the occupation of France.

His special powers had gained him complete control over all measures necessary for security and repression. If the military authorities or the Abwehr attempted to interfere he had only to send a swift complaint to the industrious Himmler, who immediately authorised all necessary measures to crush 'dangerous factions'.

Himmler, however, had severe problems of his own. Unthinkable military reverses began to dog the Germans in the east. In a single winter campaign, the Wehrmacht had lost more than a million men.

The desperate search for fresh manpower was on. Himmler was intent on increasing the number of recruits to the Waffen-SS and began wooing sympathetic organisations in the occupied countries.

The Reichfuehrer-SS sent Oberg an urgent order: 'To support to the maximum the pro-Nazi movements.'

Overtures were made by Oberg to the representatives of the Vichy government, which controlled the so-called 'Free Zone' of France in the south which the Germans occupied in November.

Oberg proposed closer collaboration between the police authorities of Germany and France. Many Frenchmen grasped what they thought was an opportunity to buy off the Germans: it might lead to a lessening of Gestapo brutality. In fact the repression became steadily worse.

Elsewhere, in 1942, Hitler suddenly seemed to gain a new lease of life. The debacle for the German armies in front of Moscow was followed by preparation for a new drive in the Caucasus.

At sea, German U-boats inflicted heavy losses on Allied shipping. British convoys, attempting to knife through to beleaguered Malta with vital supplies, were shattered from the air. The world was also getting a taste of Japanese muscle. Burma had been taken; India seemingly lay ahead.

The Germans, over-running the Free Zone of France, swarmed into Vichy. Oberg had his own method of sounding out opposition. The Gestapo went in with false identity cards and combed the Free Zone for secret radio transmitters. Resistance cells were wrapped up in Lyons, Marseilles and Toulouse.

Oberg also had some able new recruits: members of the Milice, often consisting of convicted French criminals quite prepared to become temporary policemen as the price of freedom. The Gestapo's procedures were ominously familiar. In the wake of forces making south went the Einsatzkommandos, talent-picked by Oberg and Knochen. Hauptsturmfuehrer Geissler had been sent in advance with instructions to operate in Vichy itself.

Soon an Einsatzkommando was installed in each capital of the military regions of the south. The SIPO-SD men dug in at Limoges, Lyons, Marseilles, Montpellier and Toulouse.

Gestapo rule was absolute. Paris was the centre of a web which radiated throughout a France now robbed of every single vestige of independence. The tentacles of Brussels grabbed at the north and the area of the Pas de Calais. There were around 130 separate Gestapo offices which included frontier posts and police stations – and that took no account of the entirely separate networks of the Abwehr, the Geheime Feld Polizei and the Feld-Gendarmerie.

Into all these groups, of course, seeped collaborators and informers of every kind.

Propaganda, inspired by both Germany and Vichy France, began to work overtime on behalf of Himmler, desperately anxious to swell the thinning ranks of his armed SS.

The Reichsfuehrer-SS was to get his legions, thus adding to an empire of impressive power. He was to become in August 1943 Minister of the Interior and Public Health. He was the supreme police authority in Germany and occupied Europe. He was controller of the concentration camps. The one-time chicken farmer whose physique was so pathetic that its details had to be faked to gain him membership of his own Waffen-SS, lacked only one coveted office: an army command. He was to get that as well, if only in the closing months of the Third Reich when Germany was a charnel house.

While Himmler was boasting proudly to Hitler about his new legions, for all the world like a small boy with some new toy soldiers, Oberg had to deal with more immediate matters. Or, rather, he delegated them to a certain Sturmbannfuehrer Horste Laube.

Laube was extremely gratified to have his own department, designated Section II Pol. Nevertheless, the fact that it existed at all was something of an admission of defeat for the Gestapo. Section II Pol was to keep an eye on traitorous elements within the RSHA's own ranks as well as among those French who had hitherto shown themselves enthusiastic collaborators.

The growth of the seemingly omnipresent resistance legions of the Maquis (the word described the brushland of Corsica where outlaws concealed themselves) was worrying to the Germans.

In towns and villages, Maquis members were not only attacking and killing collaborators, but actually managing to infiltrate the police. By the spring of 1943, Section II Pol was tracking all transfers, changes of station and promotions of all police officials.

As well as the Maquis, infiltration by the secret army of the resistance from London had been in operation since 5 May 1941, when the first agent from headquarters of Special Operations Executive, French section, had been dropped.

The Free French of General de Gaulle was also active; the RAF had sent in agents. But it was the SOE that was of particular annoyance to the Gestapo. News of its success in Holland and Denmark had spread rapidly.

In the Gestapo building in Paris, Frederic Martin, alias Rudi de Merode, an old crony of Henri Chamberlin, built up a considerable reputation for the singular brutality of his interrogations.

De Merode had done extremely well out of the occupation as an active brain behind the so-called Bureaux d'Achats, one of the numerous black market organisations prepared to supply just about anything at the right price. De Merode and his colleagues also enriched themselves by plundering the houses of suspects: as co-opted members of the Gestapo they enjoyed full protection.

In addition to all this, Rudi de Merode prided himself, because of the excellent facilities available at the rue de Saussaies, on being capable of breaking any man who refused to co-operate.

One of De Merode's more imaginative subordinates was Georges Delfane, alias Masuy, who invented the highly effective bath-tub torture.

The celebrated SOE agent Wing-Commander Forest Frederick Edward Yeo-Thomas, otherwise 'Tommy' and codenamed the White Rabbit, who was parachuted into France and pounced on by the Gestapo at the Passy métro station in March 1944, experienced at first hand most of the more refined horrors of the rue de Saussaies. Yeo-Thomas's biographer, Bruce Marshall, describes in his book, *The White Rabbit*, what happened after the agent had been severely beaten up by de Merode's men.

' ... He was jerked up by the handcuffs which bit deeply into his flesh. At the end of the passage a door opened and he was flung onto the tiled floor of a bathroom, through the open window of which blew in a freezing draught. He was dragged to his feet and two men pulled off his trousers and underpants; his hands were manacled while his jacket and shirt were torn off behind his back.

While Rudi bent and twisted the chain tightly round his ankles Ernst opened the cold-water tap and filled the bath. At an order from Rudi one of the guards left the room and came back accompanied by a crowd of German girls in uniform, who crammed the doorway and laughed and mocked at Yeo-Thomas as he stood naked and shivering in the icy draught.'

His tormentors were anxious to discover the whereabouts of some arms dumps. When Yeo-Thomas refused to talk, an ox-gut whip crashed down on to his chest, raising a weal. He was forced to sit down on the edge of the bath. His tormentor then caught hold of the chain around the prisoner's ankle and gave it a twist and tug. Yeo-Thomas was in the freezing water now and stood facing the jeers of the female spectators.

A fist crashed into his jaw and he was catapulted headlong into the bath, his face under the water and his legs stuck in the air.

His hands were manacled behind his back and he was unable to stop the sudden onslaught of panic. He kicked out in vain; the water acted like a distorting mirror in an amusement arcade and all the faces were stretched and elongated into a fresh menace. When he swallowed, the water splitting his lungs was a totally different agony. It was followed by a sharp curtain of blackness and he felt himself going limp, submitting in tearful gratitude to what he was sure was impending death by drowning.

Noise like bellows magnified a thousandfold kicked him back into consciousness and there he was looking straight into the mocking eyes of Rudi de Merode. The noise was his heart stimulated from artificial respiration on the bathroom floor, where he lay being stared at by the same giggling girls.

'Where are the arms dumps?'

He barely had time to dredge out the disclaimer before they had picked him up again and this time he was flung into the bath so violently that he hit the edge and his last conscious thought was: 'They're not going to let me die.'

He never knew how many times the process was repeated, how many times he was on the edge of finally succumbing before being brought back to consciousness once again. In one moment of disorientation he was convinced that he was already dead and that it was his spirit looking down on the whole tableau – on his own hideously disfigured body, on de Merode and the gaggle of girls cramming the door.

As if conscious that his prize was slipping away, de Merode kicked Yeo-Thomas hard. The agony made him jerk upright from the bathroom floor but he had lost all the strength of his legs and he had to be helped.

For a second or two they supported him on his feet, then there was the rush of air as the rubber cosh knifed into his skull.

He came to in de Merode's office and the same ghastly litany was resumed.

De Merode stared at him in open-mouth disbelief: 'Haven't you had enough?'

Yeo-Thomas said nothing. The other man shrugged, looked at the two henchmen standing behind Yeo-Thomas and nodded.

There were more coshings, steady rhythmic blows all over the most sensitive parts of his body. But still he refused to give away the whereabouts of the arms dumps and each time his intransigence brought a fresh beating.

Again he had thought that he had experienced death, but for a second he came awake and realised that the beating had stopped. With the gratitude of a child who realises his punishment is over, he closed his eyes again seeking release from appalling pain in the bliss of sleep.

But the guards shook him awake and he heard a sharp: '*Nicht schlafen.*' ('No sleeping.')

He was on the edge of tears now, thinking of his wife Barbara and the very special friends within SOE whom he was trying so desperately not to let down.

Yeo-Thomas was not a religious man but now he was praying with an intensity he thought he had lost in childhood. He was praying for de Merode either to kill him at once or leave him alone for just a few hours.

If he killed him, it would be of no great consequence because the SOE network would be safe. If the torture was stopped, even for a while, other agents in the field would be in less danger of betrayal and have time to change covernames, addresses and codes. If torture was resumed after an interval, Yeo-Thomas could in the extreme of his agony let drop something unimportant to de Merode in the confident belief that it would be valueless and out of date.

The worst thing would be for the beatings to start immediately; Yeo-Thomas doubted whether he could survive much longer.

Any diversion, however brief, would be welcome. And it came when he saw his guards guzzling hot coffee and black bread. He croaked that he was cold and thirsty.

With ill grace, one of the guards got him a mug of water. He quaffed it down and felt better, but by now it was dawn and that meant another session with de Merode.

Yeo-Thomas sweated not just with cold but with fear, and again he had the novel experience of discovering that he was praying – no longer for himself and for his own survival, but just for death.

In the afternoon came a change of scene. Yeo-Thomas, accompanied by two SD men, was taken to 84 Avenue Foch. Here was a new interrogator. It made no difference, the question was the same: where were the arms dumps? Did it matter? Why not tell them? But then he knew that initial betrayal was rather like killing your first man in battle. It was hell, but once you had done it, a repeat performance was somehow easier.

Before he knew where he was he would be betraying his fellows and for himself he would have gained little because they would kill him anyway.

He repeated: 'I have nothing to say.'

How long must this go on? How long had he been here? Forty-eight hours was the time agents were trained to hold out. There were still a few agonising hours to go before he could possibly be seen to co-operate. Even that was risky, because one betrayal, however bogus and unimportant, might lead to others. Would they beat him insensible again so that all trace of time was lost?

Time was not something you could buy from the Gestapo, a commodity to be traded. It had to be schemed and cheated for.

Yeo-Thomas realised that he was able to reason with a fair amount of confidence. Was strength really returning? There was only one way to find out.

He was seated facing the window. He calculated the distance of a possible jump. Would he have enough strength to vault the table in the middle? Then what? He would catapult through the glass and from at least four floors up and in his condition there was a fair chance he would be killed instantly.

But could he do it after the punishment he had taken? He tensed every muscle, ignoring the screaming pains attacking every point of his body.

And then he leapt.

To his astonishment, he was able to clear the table with comparative ease. He was conscious that his head had hit the glass and smashed it. But his shoulders were barely through the pane before his interrogator, who had been caught off guard, had recovered and leapt for his legs. Then he was pulled back into the room and was back in his chair.

After that came yet another beating up with rubber coshes, this time dispensed by five thugs whom he had not seen before. They slammed away in the area of his testicles until he fainted with agony.

The interrogation started all over again with another questioner. But now Yeo-Thomas could barely focus his attention on what was being said. He was conscious though that this questioner seemed to be slightly friendlier and less brutal than his predecessors.

The man could afford to be benign. Yeo-Thomas was told that the Gestapo had located the flat which he and another agent, a girl named Suni Sandoe, had used in the rue Claude Chabu. No matter what he said now Yeo-Thomas knew that Suni was blown.

All he could do was plead ignorance of her role in SOE. But there was no time to think of that now. He was escorted back to the rue de Saussaies.

The beatings up and the bath torture continued, but Yeo-Thomas was aware of a change of atmosphere. De Merode was as brutal as ever, but his manner was somehow different – he began showing signs of actual benevolence. That scared his prisoner more than the man's previous menacing demeanour. What was de Merode planning?

To make matters even more puzzling, the tone of the questioning gradually became softer. The tortures and beatings became more infrequent. De Merode was confoundedly pleased with himself, like a man who holds all the cards.

Yeo-Thomas was soon to find out why.

On the way back to his cell in the corridor he came face to face with de Merode's newest prisoner. The Gestapo had caught Suni Sandoe in her apartment in the rue Claude Chabu. Not going into hiding had proved fatal.

There was an uncharacteristic lack of security by the guards. Yeo-Thomas managed a brief conversation: Suni must plead total ignorance of his activities and deny flatly ever seeing any arms in her apartment.

But that was only half the explanation of de Merode's insufferable good humour. Yeo-Thomas was next ushered into an unfamiliar room. There seated on chairs widely spaced out were some dozen members of the White Rabbit's resistance cell.

The Gestapo had netted them all.

Yeo-Thomas had to think fast. Attempt at normal conversation with the prisoners was out of the question. He did not try it. Then he had a sudden inspiration. He began humming the tune 'Madame la Marquise'.

The guards showed little interest; possibly they were unable to understand. With increased confidence, Yeo-

Thomas began singing questions and warnings. Soon everyone cottoned on to the trick. Yeo-Thomas told them when he had been arrested and what he had been able to withhold from the Gestapo.

He and his companions were thrown into the notorious Fresnes prison and eventually sent to the concentration camp at Buchenwald, where many of the resistance were slowly strangled from hooks in the ceiling of the crematorium.

'Tommy' Yeo-Thomas survived; he had told the Gestapo nothing.

By the time of Yeo-Thomas's arrest, the progress of the war had put new heart into the resistance. The Allied offensive in Egypt and North Africa had been successful. The myth of Rommel's invincibility had been shattered and the Italians were out of the war.

But France was also to become the victim of Allied successes: air raids by the British and Americans were stepped up. Service du Travail Obligatoire, forced labour, was introduced.

Recriminations against collaborators became increasingly vicious and executions of pro-Germans and Vichyites were ordered and solemnly carried out. A favourite warning was to push miniature coffins through letter boxes.

Infiltration by agents went on; some were luckier than Yeo-Thomas.

Jacques, an SOE radio operator, did not go free for long after his drop. Picked up in the area of Moulin, he was taken to the Gestapo post near Clermont-Ferrand.

His interrogators demanded his code so that they could take his place and intercept messages. When he refused, they slugged and kicked him. But without result.

The next move was to hold a flame in front of the right eye, jabbing at the same time with a steel bar. Jacques still held out.

Like good bureaucrats, the Gestapo believed firmly that everything, including torture, should stop for lunch. Jacques, now partly sightless, was secured to a chair. His questioners went off to eat.

After knocking over the chair and then smashing it, Jacques reckoned it was worth attempting a jump from the second-floor window. He landed with a crash on a small roof below. Then he ran along the wall. The next leap was into the street. Now he was running with his hands thrust out in front of him, the manacles clearly visible.

Of course the Gestapo had heard him. Men were running from the house, but Jacques was well ahead. Suddenly, he veered off to the right down a side-street, practically colliding with an approaching figure.

SOE training made wits razor-sharp. Jacques jerked out to the newcomer: 'Don't say a word.' Then up came the manacled hands. Jacques snatched off the other man's hat, cramming it on his own head.

Jacques went on moving, but slowly now. What the Gestapo saw when they rounded the corner were two men, one running towards them, the other wearing a hat and strolling away casually. Inevitably, they leapt on the wrong man. By the time they realised their mistake, Jacques had vanished.

He hid out in a back-yard until midnight, then made for the country, anxious to put as much distance as possible between him and Gestapo headquarters.

His eventual link up with a Maquis cell brought the instruction: 'Escape through the Pyrenees and come back to England.'

Jacques refused at first. He wanted to continue his work in France. But London wanted him back and he gave in with a bad grace. Eight months later, London relented and Jacques was parachuted back into the resistance.

The number of underground groups allied to the Special Operations Executive multiplied. By the end of 1943, there had been nearly 400 parachute operations from 120 aircraft at the disposal of SOE.

It was by no means the only form of resistance which the Gestapo were called upon to root out.

For opposition was ripening fast – from deep inside the Third Reich itself.

19

Admiral Wilhelm Canaris was much attached to the somewhat dingy and untidy office he used in Berlin as head of German military intelligence.

The one-time U-boat Kapitan, who was known affectionately to his old shipmates as 'the little Admiral', had nothing but contempt for the pompous Teutonic ostentation beloved of so many of the Nazi leaders.

He sat behind a scarred and distinctly battered desk resting on a shabby, much holed carpet. Books and journals were scattered haphazardly. In any other Nazi office, the presence of a dog basket would have aroused fastidious horror. But Canaris frequently shared the room with a number of favourite dachshunds. The almost obligatory picture of a glaring Hitler was nowhere to be seen; instead, Canaris favoured a signed portrait of an old friend, the Spanish dictator Francisco Franco.

It might have been the study of some amiable, unambitious provincial schoolmaster. But in fact from here was run the Abwehr – or, to be precise the 'Amt Ausland Nachrichten und Abwehr,' the Foreign and Defence Intelligence Service.

When Canaris became its boss on his forty-seventh birthday on 1 January 1934, he had enjoyed Hitler's maximum support and favour. The Fuehrer's admiration for the British military secret service was profound. He made it clear to Canaris that Germany must create something to rival and eventually supercede it. Hitler had somewhat florid visions of 'a holy Order doing its work with passion'.

At first, Canaris had matched Hitler's mood but it was not long before disillusion set in. The gangster tactics of the

Roehm purge and the shabby cynical character-smearing of Generaloberst von Fritsch had disgusted him. To blot out his doubts he took on a ferocious workload, travelling in a souped-up staff car from one end of Germany to the other.

Canaris was sufficiently shrewd and tortuous to be able to conceal his essential hatred of Hitler and all his works under a veneer of brisk executive efficiency, which was more than could be said for his immediate subordinate, dapper fifty-year-old Oberst Hans Oster, a Saxon cavalryman of the old school and a convinced monarchist.

What he saw as the vulgar trappings of the Third Reich frequently invited Oster's contempt and he made no effort to conceal it. When an Austrian intelligence officer reported for duty at the Abwehr he greeted Oster with a vigorous Nazi salute.

The other man shuddered in distaste, ordering crisply: 'No Hitler salute here, if you please.'

Beneath an air of flippancy and almost foppish elegance was a burning hatred of National Socialism. The greatest object of Oster's detestation was Reinhard Heydrich, whose SD was unceasing in its attempts to penetrate the Abwehr and discredit it.

Above all, Oster had one obsessive dream – to bring about the day when Hitler would be removed, put behind bars and, ideally, consigned to an asylum.

But such a task was plainly beyond the scope of the Abwehr; what was needed was practical support from within the army. Oster believed that he knew just where it could be found.

His choice fell on no less an individual than the chief of the German General Staff.

Ludwig Beck had long been an object of suspicion to Adolf Hitler. The fellow was a sound professional soldier, certainly. But he was also another of these confounded intellectuals, much given to quoting Schopenhauer and Clausewitz, but openly lukewarm in proclaiming the virtues of his Fuehrer. In this, he was notably different from the bunch of careerists and place-seekers whom Hitler had hand-picked and with whom he felt most at ease.

Hitler's avowed plan to crush Czechoslovakia came as a malign revelation. Beck had previously proclaimed: 'The General Staff must be the conscience of the army.'

He saw the impending assault as a moral obscenity. It was not just that Hitler was prepared to risk world war by obliterating a smaller nation. His action, in Beck's eyes, showed up the Third Reich as tyrannical and corrupt, as an evil force with utter contempt for the traditional Christian values that Beck espoused.

In vain he bombarded von Brauchitsch, the successor to von Fritsch, with a volley of objections. He even dared to suggest that if Hitler was bent on going ahead with war, the general staff must resign in a block. It was useless. On 21 April 1938, Hitler again ordered the preparation of plans for a strike on Czechoslovakia. Beck was sufficiently diplomatic to realise that he would get nowhere by simply proclaiming his moral objections. He set to work to produce a document which would prove that on tactical and logistical grounds the whole adventure was doomed to failure.

Hitler did not even bother replying to Beck's objections. As for Beck himself, his mind was made up. He would resign. And more. He would plot actively for what he believed was a sacred duty: to overthrow Hitler.

But first he contacted another sympathiser and fellow monarchist, Carl Frederick Goerdeler, the mayor of Leipzig, who had held the job of Price Controller under Hitler. A man of enormous energy and passion, Goerdeler undertook the job of unofficial ambassador for the conspirators.

He travelled to France, England and the United States to drop discreet warnings of the perils Nazi Germany represented.

When Beck eventually resigned as chief-of-staff, he began, with the assistance of Goerdeler and Oster, to canvas more likely talent from the resistance. And the scene of their operations was the unremarkable group of offices housing the Abwehr.

*

Soon Goerdeler came up with a sensational new coup. He had succeeded in the highly dangerous task of penetrating Prinz Albrechtstrasse 8. His Gestapo sympathiser was former civil policeman and Heydrich protégé Artur Nebe.

Nebe was not an attractive character but what he had to offer was of distinct value: the addresses of seemingly innocuous private houses scattered throughout Berlin which were in fact Gestapo sub-stations.

With the help of burly Gestapo member Hans Bernd Gisevius, Goerdeler set about drawing up a list of SS and SD locations that, with the aid of the army, would be seized in the bid to topple Hitler from power.

The list gave startling confirmation of Gestapo influence and power in 1938. Here was information that had been deliberately withheld from the Abwehr: how armed units of SS shadowed practically every institution inside Nazi Germany. These armed cadres were not just Waffen-SS, but undercover groups who could be mobilised within government offices, schools and factories. The SS could call on an army-within-an-army scattered throughout the Reich which could be found even in the most humble village police station.

The seizure of Berlin would be the key to the rest of Germany. The army would have to secure centres like the SS barracks at Lichterfelde and the broadcasting centre at Koenigswusterhausen.

The conspirators soon had another plum: the immensely popular commander of Wehrkreis (military district) III of Berlin, who had a network of loyal forces at his disposal.

Gisevius has left us a pen portrait of General der Infanterie (later Generalfeldmarschall) Erwin von Witzleben:

'. . . a refreshingly uncomplicated man. The Berlin commander was a typical front-line general with his heart in the right place. Probably not too well read and certainly not inclined towards the fine arts, he was nevertheless a man firmly rooted in the chivalrous traditions of the old Prussian corps officers. He liked country life and was a passionate hunter . . . '

Von Witzleben was to prove invaluable to the renegade Gestapo man. Gisevius lived in wholly justified fear of Heydrich's surveillance. To be even so much as seen in the offices of the Abwehr would be unwise; to use the telephone, sheer lunacy.

What was needed was somewhere indisputably free of Gestapo wiretaps. Von Witzleben provided Gisevius with a private office next to his own, airily telling his adjutant that the newcomer was 'a close relative arranging the von Witzleben papers'.

As for Adolf Hitler, plans for his seizure were worked out at the home of Hans Oster. A company of commandos known to be fanatically loyal to von Witzleben would storm the Chancellery. Hitler would be taken into custody. He would then be spirited away to a castle in Bavaria to await trial. The seizure of the head of state would come immediately there was a public announcement of the impending invasion of Czechoslovakia.

Then all at once the whole scheme was in danger of disintegration – but not from Hitler or the Gestapo. The British Prime Minister Neville Chamberlain, the arch appeaser who had at last woken up to Hitler's potential threat, announced his intention of flying to Germany 'to seek an accommodation' with the Nazi dictator.

The news was flashed to every country in Europe. The bulk of Germans, with no stomach for war, greeted it with relief. But not the conspirators. They realised that if Hitler backed down, then the whole impetus for a revolt would be removed.

Chamberlain's meetings with Hitler were at Berchtesgarten, Bad Godesburg – and Munich. Hitler ended up by getting all he wanted in Czechoslovakia without firing a shot. He returned to Berlin a hero.

At von Witzleben's house, the conspirators tossed their secret plans into the fire, only Oster retaining his three-page handwritten draft, which he locked in the office safe at Abwehr headquarters.

The conspirators were not destined to strike again immediately. Less enthusiastic supporters of a coup drifted away in the wake of Hitler's early victories in the west. For many of them, there now seemed a sporting chance that they could share in the spoils.

The situation changed yet again after the invasion of Russia and the first ominous sign of military reverses. By now the aims of the conspirators had changed. At first, the object had been purely to stop a world war. Then it had been thought necessary to arrest Hitler and put him on trial. But now it was recognised that only with the Fuehrer's death would Nazism itself disentegrate.

It had to be assassination or nothing.

Adolf Hitler's four-engined Focke-Wulf Condor was heading for Fuehrer headquarters in Rastenburg, East Prussia, after taking the German Fuehrer on a tour of the Russian front.

He had been to Generalfeldmarschall Eric von Manstein's headquarters in the Ukraine, then to his own at Vinnitsa, followed by a return to von Manstein to offer congratulations on the successful thrashing of a single Russian army corps.

After that, there had been a flight to Smolensk, headquarters of Army Group Centre.

But now he was on his way back to East Prussia, seemingly tireless and spending most of the flight conferring with Generaloberst Alfred Jodl. The rest of the party took the chance of a much needed rest, occasionally staring out of the windows at the reassuring presence of the escorting Me 109s.

Meanwhile, in the hold of the Condor, the contents of an innocuous-looking parcel were behaving precisely as they should.

A slow-burning fuse was working towards the plastic inserted in a canister shaped like a couple of brandy bottles laid one on top of the other. In a matter of minutes the firing pin would be released and the Condor torn apart in the skies.

Hitler had been in high good humour when he had left the Ukraine after congratulating von Manstein. But, in fact, the Fuehrer had no cause for congratulation anywhere else.

241

Rommel's Afrika Korps was in trouble: at Vinnitsa he had begged for reinforcements and supplies. And in Germany, in the towns and cities which Hitler never visited, Allied bombing was cruel and relentless.

By now, the number of plotters against the Fuehrer had widened. Generalmajor Baron Freiherr von Tresckow, who in 1943 was chief-of-staff at Army Group Centre at Smolensk, was among those admitted. A convinced Christian who came from a long line of Prussian soldiers, he had served as a staff officer under Beck.

One of those personalities born to command, it was inevitable that, once drawn into the conspiracy, he would itch to lead it. What at this stage primarily interested men like Beck and Oster was that von Tresckow had access to a useful group of fellow officers equally dedicated to getting rid of Hitler.

In addition, von Tresckow was in constant touch with Beck, Oster and others in Berlin. Goerdeler had made a hazardous trip to Russia at the invitation of von Tresckow to bring pressure on Generalfeldmarschall Hans Gunther von Kluge, the commander of Army Group Centre.

Initially, von Kluge had shown some enthusiasm for the cause of the conspirators, but he lacked the courage to declare himself wholeheartedly. One of those involved in the conspiracy described him with some accuracy as 'only a fair-weather friend'.

Von Tresckow refused to admit defeat. For weeks, he and Fabian von Schlabrendorff, a studious-looking Berlin lawyer and a wartime reserve officer of the Wehrmacht serving in Russia, experimented with British plastic explosives and silently burning fuses supplied by the Abwehr. It struck von Schlabrendorff that the plastic containers or 'clams', when stuck together had the shape of a brandy bottle. The package was made up, stuffed with explosive and fuse and wrapped securely in paper.

Von Schlabrendorff next tackled one of Hitler's aides, Oberst Heinz Brandt.

He said casually: 'I promised to send some brandy to General Helmuth Stieff at Rastenburg. Could you take the packet for me?'

The unsuspecting Brandt took it readily. Von Schlabrendorff had pressed down heavily on the fuse. Within minutes, the Condor rumbled away for take-off

With suppressed excitement, von Tresckow and von Schlabrendorff returned to HQ and put a quick call through to Berlin.

Their message was terse: 'Operation Flash is under way.'

And it was. Inside the packet, the corrosive acid was rapidly eating away at the retaining wire. The Condor hummed its way through the skies.

Then the wire snapped apart and the firing-pin crashed into the detonator.

Generalmajor Henning von Tresckow's already tattered nerves were shredded still further by the jangling telephone.

The message from Rastenburg stunned him into incredulity; Hitler's Condor aircraft had landed without incident.

Now the grim shadow of the gallows fell across von Treschow and von Schlabrendorff with a vengeance. What had happened to the mechanism of the bomb was for the moment unimportant. The cold fact was that the incriminating package was still aboard the aircraft and at any moment could be ripped open by Brandt as the innocent recipient of two bottles of brandy.

Von Tresckow took his courage in both hands. He rang back Rastenburg and asked for Brandt. A wrong package, he explained, had been entrusted to Stieff. Someone would be on the next courier plane to retrieve it.

The task fell to von Schlabrendorff, who passed what was to prove one of the most dreadful nights of his life. There was the very real risk that Brandt's suspicions would be aroused and that he would open the package. If that happened, the Gestapo would be waiting at Rastenburg and there would be no escape from their interrogation and torture.

On arrival next morning, he went straight to Brandt's office and what he saw made his bowels churn. Brandt stood behind his desk, holding the packet. In casual conversation, he tossed the bomb from one hand to the other.

Von Schlabrendorff stared as if mesmerised, conscious that he must at all cost keep his nerve. Somehow, he managed to hand over the real brandy and retrieve the explosive package.

But still fate had not done with him. The infuriating Brandt was in a talkative mood and was in no hurry to get rid of his visitor. Somehow, von Schlabrendorff managed to get out of the other man's office, but he dared not examine the bomb at Rastenburg.

Now there followed fresh agony while a car took him to the nearby railway station at Korschen. On the Berlin train, he quickly locked the door of his private sleeping compartment. With his heart in his mouth and conscious of the need to keep his hands rock-steady, he removed the wrapping paper and extracted the fuse.

The acid capsule had certainly fractured. The wire had eaten through and the firing-pin moved forward. The trouble was the dead detonator. Von Schlabrendorff reflected that Hitler literally had the devil's luck.

Two weeks later, the conspirators tried again. Another officer in von Tresckow's circle, Oberst von Gersdorff, offered to sacrifice his own life while killing Hitler. The idea was that while the Fuehrer was opening an exhibition at the Berlin War Museum, von Gersdorff, his overcoat stuffed with time bombs, would throw himself upon the Nazi dictator.

But Hitler by now was adept at altering his schedules abruptly. His visit to the exhibition was cursory and the cohorts of Mueller were everywhere.

For the moment, there was stalemate and frustration. But the plotters, many of them middle-aged and inhibited by prejudices and cautions they could not conquer, were unaware of another group of patriots prepared impulsively to lift the lid off the burning cauldron of resistance.

20

Bitterness and disillusion burnt away the youth of Hans Scholl.

The advent of Adolf Hitler and the Nazis had promised for Hans and his generation the recovery of honour for a Germany dragged ignominiously into the dust of defeat less than twenty years before.

Youths between the ages of ten and fifteen had grown up in a world where their fathers were mere statistics among a million unemployed and where money was worth nothing. The hypnotic speeches of the Fuehrer seemed like a blow for rebirth.

In the flush of enthusiasm for the siren song of Nazism, Hans and his fellow youth ignored the warnings of their parents' generation, whom they believed had been responsible for Germany's unjust immolation.

Hans's father had cried out at those he saw as 'wolves and deceivers'. But the bellicose injunctions of Hitler stilled the small voice of sanity. The Fuehrer had called for a youth that was 'quick as greyhounds, tough as leather, and as hard as Krupp steel'. The hyperbole had lit a flame. In 1934, at fifteen years old, Hans Scholl had joined the Hitler Youth.

There had been numerous other youth groups in existence before the advent of Hitler. The contemporaries of Hans Scholl had belonged to a number of them, notably the Bundische Jugend (Youth Group), which aimed with rather romantic vagueness at personal freedom steering clear of politics. To Hitler, the very existence of such a group not prepared to dedicate itself wholeheartedly to National Socialism was sheer anathema.

All such organisations were regarded as dissident and

either disbanded by force or subjected to shotgun weddings with Hitler Youth.

Fuelled with indignation at such intolerance and experiencing the first stirrings of doubt, Hans and his friends continued underground meetings with the representatives of banned organisations.

The inevitable happened. Himmler swiftly instituted a Gestapo dragnet. Hans and his friends were rounded up in their homes and flung into prison. The treasures of their fatally naive adolescence – books, photograph albums and song sheets – were confiscated and destroyed.

The Youth leader, Baldur von Schirach, called on Gestapo agents to infiltrate the dissident groups under the guise of sympathisers. Soon the cellars of the Columbia Haus were swollen with fresh-faced youngsters, many of whose group activities had been scarcely more sinister than those of the average scout troop.

Most of them were beaten up and released with a warning. A few were sent to Dachau and others shot. But Hitler was cautious; he realised he would need a compliant youth movement for his new Germany. He could not afford to make too many enemies too soon.

Hans Scholl was among those released. But for a time his rebellion and indignation had to be stilled. He soon found himself conscripted into the army.

In between soldiering in the last days of peace and the swift, breathtakingly successful invasion of France, Hans was able to pursue his medical studies at the University of Munich. But the Gestapo was not to leave him or his family alone.

Ever since his previous arrest, shadowing of the Scholls was unceasing. Hans's father was unwise enough to denounce Hitler as 'a scourge'. The words were heard by a fellow council worker in the town of Ulm. There came the inevitable rap on the door in the depths of the night and summary arrest.

Herr Scholl was eventually let go, but the Gestapo made it very clear that its agents would be back.

News of how his father had been treated acted as the final spur to a Hans white hot with anger. At twenty-four he had come to realise that it was no longer any use merely talking of revolution over endless cups of coffee in the apartments of his friends. Somebody must actually have the courage to speak out publicly. The first real opportunity was to come, not from any of his own generation, but from a distinguished academic at Hans's university.

Dr Hans Huber, one of the university's most popular and liberal leaders, took it upon himself to champion the cause of the persecuted Christian churches.

The seizure of monasteries and the expulsion and arrest of priests and nuns had been entrusted to the Gestapo. Three priests in Lübeck had been seized and executed for distributing the text of sermons. What really incensed Himmler was that these texts had been deliberately circulated to soldiers: such treasonable rubbish could sap the will of the Wehrmacht to fight.

Another outspoken critic of Hitler had been the Bishop of Munster, Graf Clemens von Galen, who deliberately stressed the Nazis' role in corrupting youth – 'the illegal imprisonment, exile and expulsion of the innocent'.

Huber began collecting the most inflammatory excerpts of the bishop's sermon that he could find. He had them printed as leaflets and set about distributing them to a specially drawn-up list of Munich's most influential citizens.

One of the addresses he chose was the house of the Scholls.

For Hans, the remarks of the bishop seemed to be a direct gift from God. Equally important, there was actually someone in Munich brave enough to distribute such literature. What one man had started, he could continue.

The tools of resistance of Hans Scholl were not bombs or pistols. He had no sympathetic cadres within the army or the Gestapo to help him. His sole weapons were a duplicating machine, ink and paper. But they were as much tools of treason as had been the disguised brandy bottles of von Tresckow and von Schlabrendorff. And in some of his fellow medical students he found resisters whose zeal matched his own.

In the evenings, free from their studies, Hans and his

247

group laboured on what they regarded as their testimonial of belief to the German people. Because many of them were so young, they had little experience of their own. They began searching in history for precedents, drawing on classical writers to express their own feelings on personal liberty and the evils of persecution, pressing into service quotations from Goethe and Schiller, and describing the state of Sparta, which had abandoned love and friendship and made the individual totally subservient to the demands of the state. The language was often obscure but the implications were only too clear.

Hans Scholl's sister, the pretty romantic Sophie, a member of the Reich Labour Service for Young Women, was not at first let into the secret of her brother's activities, which by now had been given their own code name, Die Weisse Rose (The White Rose). The name reflected Hans's innate romanticism despite his experiences in the Columbia Haus.

Gradually, the tone of Die Weisse Rose leaflets became more critical and outspoken. The Nazis themselves were not the only ones to be attacked. Hans and his friends were contemptuous of teachers, artists and intellectuals. The young resisters argued that such people were acquiescing passively in the regime: universities were lending out technical facilities, artists were accepting state subsidies in order to be allowed to carry on their work. The language of the leaflets was florid and melodramatic; not only was Hitler the greatest liar in human history, but 'his mouth is the foul-smelling maw of Hell, and his might is at bottom accursed'.

Needless to say, the leaflets were in the hands of the Gestapo within a few hours of their distribution. At first, Mueller regarded them as a relatively harmless irritant. He had neither the men nor the time to spare on a series of massive dragnets of students' houses, apartments and rooms. Duplicating machines were common enough and there was nothing to be gained from examination of the cheap wartime paper on which the messages were written.

But mild concern soon turned to alarm. The leaflets began to turn up in other parts of Germany. It seemed obvious to the Gestapo that there were duplicating and distributing organisations in all the university towns – Hamburg, Bonn, Freiburg and Heidelberg.

Mueller despatched a number of agents to pose as students in the universities, and young Gestapo members spent a lot of valuable time looking for mythical resistance cells.

In fact, much of the distribution was done solely by the tireless Hans. He journeyed to Linz, Vienna and Frankfurt, posting around 1,500 leaflets. Then he returned to Munich and with Sophie, now an enthusiastic fellow resister, scattered leaflets joyfully along the darkened streets.

Ernst Kaltenbrunner was beside himself with rage. Hardly a day passed without a terse summons from Himmler and a relentless catechism on just what was being done about The White Rose.

The Reichsfuehrer-SS was particularly concerned about the effects of the leaflets on public opinion. Kaltenbrunner was instructed quickly to draw up a special report.

The results, collated from eavesdroppings all over the Reich, frightened both men. Early in the war, patriotic Germans did not hesitate to report to the Gestapo examples of what they regarded as sedition. But the days when an anti-Nazi poster glued to the wall would be automatically torn down and sent to the Gestapo were drawing to a close.

Previously reliable informers were now reluctant to come forward. Indeed, there were signs that the leaflets were being passed with increasing boldness from hand to hand.

Hans Scholl had long since joined forces with Dr Hans Huber. Both men worked tirelessly to produce a positive avalanche of leaflets.

But both realised that there was a certain monotony in this form of resistance. What was needed was a major single event to act as a match to tinder.

As it happened, a fatal miscalculation by the SS finally blew the lid from the cauldron.

A posse of SS descended without warning on the University of Munich. Uniformed guards rounded up the entire student body and pushed and shoved it into the assembly hall.

Paul Giesler, Gauleiter of Bavaria and a man loathed above all others by the students, launched into a violent peroration. He declared that there must be an even greater sacrifice by the German people if the war was to be won. Loyalty to the Fuehrer must be unquestioned.

There were, he declared, far too many slackers. Such laggards would be rooted out and sent to fight the Russians. Students were conspicuously guilty; there was special treatment in store for them.

A good many in the audience had already seen some military service, including the Russian front. The implication that they were cowards was insulting enough. At first, Giesler had been listened to in sullen silence. Now there were angry murmurings.

As if conscious that he was scarcely gaining sympathy, Giesler swiftly changed the subject.

At first, he seemed reasonable enough: 'I want to say a word about the very special role of women in this war.' Then his voice rose: 'They have healthy bodies! Let them bear children! That is an automatic process which, once begun, continues without the least attention.

'There is no reason why every girl student should not, for each of her years in the university, present an annual testimonial in the form of a son.'

His words were drowned by a roar of anger and now he was shouting: 'I realise that a certain amount of co-operation is required. If some of the girls lack sufficient charm to find a mate I will assign to each of them one of my adjutants whose antecedents I can vouch for.'

He positively leered: 'I can promise her a thoroughly enjoyable experience!'

The lecture hall erupted. In one single demonstration of rage and disgust, the students rose, shoved and kicked at the SS guards and streamed into the streets.

The mood of rebellion coursed through Bavaria like a running fuse. Anger threw all caution to the wind; rebellion expressed previously through poster and leaflet was now replaced by violence.

Inevitably, hoards of delinquents attached themselves to the students. In Munich, roaming gangs set fire to buildings and sabotaged railway marshalling yards.

But the leaflet war went on just the same. Hans Scholl and Dr Huber realised that, thanks to Giesler, student sympathy had increased a thousandfold.

German students were now urged to 'get out of the party organisations which are used to keep our mouths sealed and hold us in political bondage!'

Both Hans and Sophie reasoned that the driving force of the student revolt was to be found in the university. It was vital for the impetus there to be maintained.

Two days later, Hans and Huber had produced the latest leaflet. Brother and sister set off at dawn from their apartment. It was a day of bright sunshine and they walked eagerly towards the university, their satchels stuffed full with leaflets.

Once inside the building, they moved swiftly along the corridors, leaving packets at the various doors. If they had glanced out of the windows, they would have seen the big black limousines drawing up at one of the entrances.

Building superintendant Jacob Schmidt, on duty at the university, had caught a glimpse of Sophie rummaging in her satchel to scatter a pile of leaflets. Within minutes he had sealed the exits. The round-up was swift. The Scholls were seized, bundled into one of the cars, driven quickly down the Ludwigstrasse and Briennerstrasse to Gestapo headquarters and locked in separate cells.

The questioning of Hans and Sophie began on Friday afternoon and continued without a break until dawn. Both denied all knowledge of The White Rose and of belonging to any of the dissident student organisations. Questions about other suspects were deliberately ignored or greeted with incomprehension. Then the Gestapo was able to produce its findings in the Scholl apartment: brushes, stencils, duplicating equipment.

Hans changed his tack. He tried to persuade his interrogators that the responsibility for distributing leaflets was solely his.

Then Sophie was questioned on her own. Egon Mohr,

who conducted the interview, attempted a rather heavy-handed paternalism.

Sophie sat through a rambling lecture on the glories of National Socialism and the importance of complete loyalty to the Fuehrer.

Mohr said: 'There are brave boys dying for Germany on the Russian front. You have done them no service. If you knew how desperately Germany needed loyalty you would surely have thought twice.'

Sophie listened patiently. Then she shook her head with a slight smile and said softly: 'You are wrong, Herr Mohr. I would do precisely the same thing again.'

That evening, another of the group, Christoph Probst, the son of a Munich academic and father of two small children, was arrested. All were charged with high treason.

The charade of the trial was conducted with pompous legalistic formality. There was a defence lawyer but, like all those practising in Germany, he was a member of the Nazi Lawyers' Association.

A tailor's dummy would have done just as well. Under the powers of Hitler's extraordinary courts, the prosecuting counsel was able to combine his advocacy with the functions of a judge, even determining the sentence. Defence counsel, if he was wise and wanted to keep both job and head, resolutely remained silent.

But there *was* a judge; furthermore, one of the most terrifying figures in the entire macabre gallery of the Third Reich.

Roland Freisler was a vituperative sadist with jug ears and a heart of flint. As a young man he had been a prisoner of the Russians in World War I. Later, as a Communist, he had been chairman of the Workers and Soldiers Council which had taken temporary control of Kassel in 1918. In the early 1920s, when he had shrewdly assessed the way things were going, he switched his allegiance to the Nazis. A state secretary in the Reich Ministry of Justice, he was an ideal choice for President of the so-called People's Court.

But his Communist past bothered him. He knew that he had made a considerable number of enemies, many of whom would be only too pleased to engineer his downfall.

He became almost pathologically devoted to the Nazis, denouncing his former masters whenever he could. His overweening ambition was to be Minister of Justice.

Freisler was not only a nimble-witted lawyer but a consummate actor. His voice could switch from screaming abuse to gentle-toned reasonableness – all calculated to bewilder and intimidate prisoners who were, in almost all cases, condemned from the moment they stood in the dock.

The case against the Scholls and their companions was outlined. With ill-concealed impatience, Freisler asked the defence for its submission. None was given.

Freisler then proceeded to hurl the full force of his abuse at Sophie Scholl. To the judge's fury, she refused to be intimidated and had the temerity to riposte: 'What we said and wrote is what many people are thinking – only they daren't express themselves.'

None of the accused attempted to deny their activities; there was little that remained to do beyond pronouncing sentence.

But Freisler maintained the pretence until the end. A great show was made of whispering deliberation.

Then the scarlet-robed Freisler placed the black cap on his balding head and solemnly intoned the sentences:

'Hans Fritz Scholl . . . Death.'

'Sophie Magdalene Scholl . . . Death.'

'Christoph Hermann Probst . . . Death.'

There was a momentary stir at the back of the court as Frau Scholl collapsed and was helped out of the room. Then Herr Scholl was heard to shout: 'There is a higher court before which we all must stand.'

Freisler swept out. The prisoners were hustled below.

Himmler had ordered death by the guillotine. The condemned were taken swiftly by the Gestapo to the grim Stadelheim prison. The Scholl parents were allowed one brief poignant interview and then were dragged away. Both Hans and Sophie remained calm.

Sophie, in school shirt and blouse, was stretched on to the wooden rack. Her hands were tied behind her back and the heavy blade released. Hans Scholl and Christoph Probst followed.

News of the executions were set in type by the newspapers even before they had been carried out. Himmler personally gave instructions that printing deadlines were not to be missed.

The year 1943 was proving grim for those attempting to wrench Germany from the coils of Hitler and the Gestapo. And it was not just the student movement which was to suffer appalling setbacks.

The writing was also on the wall for the Abwehr.

21

Manfred Roeder, energetic Judge Advocate of the Reich Military Court and scourge of Rote Kapelle, was eager for fresh triumphs. But even a man of his ambition would scarcely have dreamed that the next milestone in his career was to help smash German military intelligence itself.

Indeed, if it had not been for a certain prosperous brewer and part-time Abwehr agent named Wilhelm Schmidhuber the chance of destroying one of the key centres of resistance to Hitler might never have presented itself.

Schmidhuber's role in the opposition dated back to 1940, when he had carried a secret message to Papal circles giving the date of the western offensive – a piece of information which the Vatican had forthwith communicated to the French, British and Belgians. Resistance in the Abwehr employed the highly useful Schmidhuber yet again.

One of the covert activities of the Abwehr had been to help German Jews out of Germany under the guise of employing them as agents. Canaris, who had been known to use his influence to save Jewish victims, not only knew of the scheme but actively approved of it. He turned over its organisation to Hans Oster and to a deputy, former lawyer Dr Johannes (Hans) von Dohnanyi, an anti-Nazi from the early 1930s whom Himmler had discovered unfortunately possessed a 'non-Aryan' grandmother.

The traffic of Jews out of Germany had been highly successful. Then a Jew was picked up by the Gestapo in Czechoslovakia. The man would probably have been shot at once and forgotten – if it had not been for the unusual possession of $400 in American currency.

News of the arrest reached Gestapo headquarters in Munich. Mueller pricked up his ears; this one he would handle himself.

The suspect did not seem as cowed as most of the unfortunates who found themselves before Mueller. In fact, he promptly demanded his rights as an Abwehr agent. Instead, he got a merciless interrogation from Mueller, who learnt among other things that the money had come directly from Herr Wilhelm Schmidhuber.

A Jew in an occupied country with American dollars donated to him by a German businessman working in military intelligence! Mueller could scarcely conceal his triumph at the big fish he had landed. But he was to preen himself considerably more before many hours were up.

It was Schmidhuber's turn to be arrested. Like many, he was no match for hour after hour of relentless Gestapo questioning and threats. The truth eventually came out. And so did the name of Hans von Dohnanyi.

Mueller soon realised how delighted Himmler would be. The Reichsfuehrer-SS, despite a reluctant admiration for Canaris, had long nurtured the dream of smashing the Abwehr machine and replacing it with an all-embracing Nazi secret service. In this, Himmler had been enthusiastically championed by Schellenberg, as hungry for power as ever.

The Abwehr was military territory and jealously guarded. Very well, arrests would have to be carried out by some other body – which is where Manfred Roeder entered the picture.

Early in the morning of 5 April 1943, Roeder, accompanied by a member of the Gestapo in civilian clothes, confronted Canaris himself.

The lawyer said abruptly: 'We have a warrant for the arrest of Sonderfuehrer von Dohnanyi and to search this office.'

The 'little Admiral' thought quickly. There was nothing he could do to prevent the arrest, but surely Oster and the rest would have been sensible enough to keep incriminating documents out of the way.

Canaris sighed: 'Very well, but I must witness both arrest and search.'

Oster, when told of what was happening, bristled with indignation: 'If there are arrests, they can start with me.'

Roeder ignored him; von Dohnanyi was seized. Then the lawyer was demanding the key to a heavy green safe adorned with embossed scrolls. At first von Dohnanyi denied he had the key, then grudgingly handed it over.

Soon Roeder was thumbing through a heavy clutch of files. One seemed to mesmerise the appalled von Dohnanyi. Roeder had removed a file inscribed '*Z grau*' (*Z Grey*) and sticking out of it were three sheets of paper.

Von Dohnanyi made a swift grab and quickly passed the sheets to Oster who concealed them behind the jacket of his civilian suit. The Gestapo official pounced.

Roeder said coldly to Oster: 'I think you had better leave.'

Now Roeder was able to get a closer look at the three sheets, which were covered with typescript. It did not take much reading to decide that they were dynamite. Here was a memorandum which alleged that military groups in Germany and certain elements in the churches were involved in overthrowing National Socialism. Another document outlined in considerable detail the territorial structure of a post-Hitler Germany.

It was enough. Von Dohnanyi's carelessness in not concealing such incriminating documents had cost him his liberty. He was thrown into jail, along with Josef Mueller, the Abwehr's man in Rome, and Pastor Dietrich Bonhoeffer, a Protestant minister also heavily involved in the conspiracy.

Hans Oster was relieved of his duties, cashiered and forbidden by OKW chief of staff Wilhelm Keitel to have any more dealings with the Abwehr. He was finally placed under arrest the following December.

There was as yet insufficient reason for holding the respected Canaris and Himmler was reluctant to move against him.

But, in essence, the Abwehr had been rendered impotent at a single stroke.

Not the least alarmed of the conspirators was Henning von Tresckow. He promptly applied to von Kluge for sick leave, speeding to Berlin to see what could be done to salvage the disaster which had struck at the very heart of the resistance. One of von Tresckow's first acts was to contact Generalleutnant Friedrich Olbricht, the head of the Supply Section of the Reserve Army and another key opposition figure.

Together they began to look for a suitable replacement for Oster.

The need was urgent. On 14 February 1944, a decree ordered the dissolution of the Abwehr and its two subsections, Amtsgruppe Ausland and Abwehr Amt. The former was forcibly merged with Wehrmachts Fuehrungstab (the staff for the Conduct of Operations) of OKW, while RSHA took care of Abwehr Amt under the title of Militarische Amt (Military Office).

Complete power in operations overseas was now vested in Schellenberg's Amt VI. The conspirators were robbed of the protective cover of the Abwehr which previously provided them with fake alibis, false papers and explosives. Heavily compromised conspirators could no longer be smuggled to safety in Switzerland.

Claus Philipp Maria Schenk, Graf von Stauffenberg, was a Swabian aristocrat who could trace his lineage unbroken to 1298. His great-grandfather, Freiherr Franz Ludwig von Stauffenberg, had been hereditary counsellor to the King of Bavaria and had been created Graf by Ludwig II in 1874.

The young Claus grew up in the massive towered Renaissance castle of the Württemburg kings in Stuttgart. The family was proud of its ancient roots, but not complacently so. Von Stauffenberg was taught that wealth and inherited family estates carried heavy responsibilities to the community.

The family was staunchly Roman Catholic and von Stauffenberg clung zealously to his faith even when the Nazis came to power, insisting on going to Mass in full uniform with his family.

As to von Stauffenberg's attitude to Hitler, some witnesses claimed that when the Nazis assumed power on 30 January 1933, Claus, in the uniform of a leutnant, had placed himself at the head of a deliriously happy crowd marching through Bamberg.

Some of his fellow officers were scandalised. Von Stauffenberg pointed out that military leaders in the past had shown sympathy for popular movements. Why should that tendency change now?

If the story was true and not, as has been claimed, invented by the Nazis later, it did not for long represent von Stauffenberg's attitude to Hitler.

The Nazis had been in power for just one year when the young soldier was detailed to represent the Seventh Cavalry Regiment at a Nazi demonstration in Bamberg on a special Party Day.

The main speaker was the notorious Julius Streicher, Gauleiter of Nuremburg, a moral pervert, whom in the end even Hitler had to retire.

On this occasion, Streicher launched into wild invective against the Jews in revoltingly pornographic terms. It was too much for von Stauffenberg, military duties or not. He and a brother officer walked out.

Criticism was to grow rapidly. Von Stauffenberg's deeply felt Christianity and moral conviction fuelled his contempt for Hitler.

Indignation spilled over at the time of the Fuehrer's triumph in France. The fact that Hitler was going personally to Paris to gloat was to von Stauffenberg nothing short of barbarous. He did not conceal his growing belief that Hitler should be removed.

But he was a professional soldier and there was a war to be fought. Von Stauffenberg served on the supply staff of the 6th Panzer Division in Poland and, in June 1940, was transferred to the Army High Command, where he was to remain until February 1943. His job was long-term planning for the army and he travelled widely throughout Europe.

At least there was honour in the profession of arms. Von Stauffenberg applied for transfer to active service and was sent to North Africa.

In Tunisia in April 1943 the position of the German forces was dire. No less than 300,000 Korps troops were caught like rats in a trap, along with forces of the Italian First Army. Von Stauffenberg's Division had previously hurled itself fruitlessly at the US 1st Armored Division. The result had been a rout. Now the Germans were falling back and getting no mercy from waves of American P-40F fighters. In wave after wave, the aircraft swooped down on the strung-out forces of the 10th Panzer Division. The tank crews fired back with light machine guns; few were effective.

Von Stauffenberg and Generalmajor Friedrich von Broich were driving in separate vehicles when the F-40s homed in on the column.

Von Broich saw the .50 calibre bullets strike the thin-skinned trucks. Survival would be out of the question if he stayed where he was. He catapulted out of his car and flung himself into the churning ground. There seemed no end to the American assault, but eventually the aircraft were flying higher and away, their ammunition exhausted.

Von Broich lay still for several minutes, then gingerly got to his feet. He inched forward to look at the extent of the damage.

Von Stauffenberg's Volkswagen lay askew with both doors flung open and its bodywork punctured with holes. There was the cloying stench of raw fuel, but what gripped von Broich's attention was the sight of congealed blood on the front seat, dashboard and windscreen.

Von Stauffenberg's injuries were terrible. When he was rushed to the military hospital he had lost his left eye, his right hand and the third and fourth fingers on his left. The vision in the right eye was affected. The surgeons believed that von Stauffenberg's active military career was at an end.

For days he lay in delirium. When consciousness returned he had to face a series of head and leg operations.

Matters improved with the return of vision to his remaining eye. When he was told the extent of his injuries, he merely shrugged and said: 'Bring me pencil and paper. I've got to learn to write all over again.'

He also practised dressing himself and walking to a bathroom mirror where he shaved with one hand. Deaf to the protestations of his doctors, he would not even permit them to fit him with a glass eye or artificial hand. That would mean months more in hospital. He had never been particularly interested in personal appearance, anyway; on the battlefield, he had frequently worn anonymous combat jackets on which were carelessly pinned his badges of rank.

Above all, he wanted to get into his own private war – which was working for the overthrow of Hitler, whom he saw as needlessly slaughtering men in a cause which was hopelessly lost.

He was in contact with von Tresckow and together they put finishing touches to the military preparation and orders which would follow the assassination and bring about a coup.

The plans were codenamed 'Valkyrie'.

Von Tresckow and von Stauffenberg had embarked on a decidedly perilous course of deceit. Two years before, Olbricht and Canaris had submitted to Hitler a plan to deal with internal unrest within the Reich. Olbricht had pointed out to Hitler that by 1944 there would be something like eight million workers and prisoners of war. These, it was argued, would present a very real threat. There must be a plan available to counter it.

Hitler had given the scheme his blessing. Now it was to be activated. But only the conspirators knew that it was to be used to destroy the Nazi apparatus, not bolster it.

The updated Valkyrie depended upon loyal troops who would have the task of occupying ten SS centres, ten government offices and nine party offices.

Valkyrie also provided for the immediate seizure of broadcasting facilities and telegraphic centres.

With the Wehrmacht in control of the Reich, a new provisional government would be installed with Ludwig Beck designated provisional head of state after Hitler's death.

Then there came a piece of luck for von Stauffenberg. Generalleutnant Fritz Fromm, commander-in-chief of the Reserve Army and sympathetic to the conspirators, managed to secure von Stauffenberg as his chief of staff. Fromm had direct access to Hitler which meant that von Stauffenberg's prospects of getting nearer to the heavily-guarded Fuehrer had been immeasurably enhanced.

The conspirators never gave up the hope of securing what they saw as an honourable peace with the Allies, despite the fact that at Casablanca in 1943 it had been made abundantly clear that nothing but unconditional surrender would be tolerated.

The D-Day invasion of Europe came on 6 June 1944. The Russians had made mincemeat of Army Group Centre and 350,000 Germans went to their deaths. The American Fifth Army was in Rome.

Patently, Hitler could not be allowed to live much longer.

After the failure of the attempt to blow up the Fuehrer at the Berlin War Museum, there had been numerous other assassination plans.

There was an attempt to destroy the Fuehrer's headquarters at Rastenburg by placing under a wooden watch tower two silent explosive fuses obtained from the Abwehr. It failed, along with a plan for a junior officer to shoot Hitler point blank at the conference table. Security at Rastenburg was too stringent: only Hitler's trusted cronies or senior officers were allowed to get anywhere near him or the situation room.

A Rastenburg meeting with the Fuehrer which von Stauffenberg attended on 26 December 1943 was abruptly cancelled.

As Hitler's confidence in the successful outcome of war declined, so his suspicions sharpened and became almost pathological. The Fuehrer was only fifty-five, but looked at least ten years older. The walk which had once been so confident and brisk was now an embarrassing shuffle. Hitler stooped these days and his right hand shook; his complexion was sallow beneath the grey-streaked hair.

The cunning was as sharp as it had ever been. Previously arranged appointments, briefings and travels were altered or cancelled with increasing rapidity.

Despite his obvious anxieties – not least the appalling difficulty of getting anywhere near Hitler – von Stauffenberg seemed almost euphoric in dangerous days when the Gestapo might pounce at any moment.

His enthusiasm was almost schoolboyish, the single eye shining with mischievous delight from the healthy, tanned face. In the presence of more than one conspirator, von Stauffenberg was heard to say with relish: 'I am up to my neck in high treason.'

Parallel with the various attempts on Hitler's life, additional preparation for Valkyrie went ahead. There were a gratifying number of new conspirators. In addition to Arthur Nebe, Berlin police president, Count von Helldorf and his adjutant, Graf Fritz von der Schulenberg, another avowedly repentant Nazi, had come over to the opposition.

Support from the occupied countries looked assured, too. There had been acquiescence from Stuelpnagel in Paris and from von Falkenhausen, the military governor of Belgium. Rommel, commander-in-chief of Army Group B and his chief-of-staff Generalleutnant Hans Spiedel, were particularly glittering prizes.

But ultimate success would all depend on what happened next at the Wolfschanze (Wolf's Lair) at Rastenburg.

The day of action was fixed for 20 July 1944.

Wolfschanze was set up eight kilometres east of Rastenburg (now Ketrzyn in Poland). It was an uninviting location surrounded by lakes, swamp areas and thick forest and had been earmarked for construction by Hitler himself.

A Stuttgart landscaping firm had been hired to install artificial trees, camouflage nets and artificial moss on top of the buildings. Aerial photographs had been taken to make certain that the camouflage was successful.

There were three inner security zones, each complete with checkpoints and guards who were ever vigilant. In 1942, a Polish labourer who attempted to cut his way through on the way home from work had been shot dead. Eventually, thousands of mines covering some fifty metres had been laid.

On this July day, von Stauffenberg stared with scarcely concealed distaste at the sullen array of flak towers, machine-gun nests, slit trenches and thick bunker walls.

It was stiflingly hot. In his concrete cocoon, Hitler was due to discuss plans to launch an offensive in Galicia. There was also to be discussion on the deployment of the Home Army, the special force with the job of repelling the Allies in every town and village.

After breakfast in the Wolfschanze mess and a series of preliminary meetings, von Stauffenberg was ushered into the presence of Generalfeldmarschall Keitel. He was informed that the deposed Mussolini would be arriving at Rastenburg at 14.30 hours, consequently the conference would be held at 12.30 hours.

Keitel stressed: 'The Fuehrer has given orders that reports are to be kept brief.'

The conference was to take place in the usual conference hut which was built of wood and reinforced with concrete walls.

Von Stauffenberg cursed inwardly. He had banked on the meeting being held in the underground chamber; there the effect of the blast would have been much heavier.

Once inside the hut, von Stauffenberg, clutching the briefcase with its burning thin wire within, further noticed that three large windows had been flung open in the heat. That would lessen the blast effect still further.

Well, nothing could be done about that now. What was certain was that the briefcase containing the bomb must be placed as near as possible to the Fuehrer.

Hitler nodded curtly to von Stauffenberg. Generalleutnant Heusinger continued to outline the gloomy situation of Army Group North on the eastern front.

At 12.36, von Stauffenberg placed the light-coloured briefcase on the floor against one of the table's heavy legs. Then he slipped discreetly out of the room on the pretext of telephoning Berlin.

Back inside, Oberst Brandt leant forward to get a better

glimpse of the map. His leg encountered an obstruction; bending down he felt von Stauffenberg's briefcase and moved it aside. Now it was further away from Hitler.

Keitel looked around. Where on earth was von Stauffenberg? His report was due next. This was certainly no time to be telephoning Berlin. Keitel decided to investigate the mystifying conduct of the one-armed Oberst.

And that was becoming odder by the minute. Von Stauffenberg, reported the telephonists, had left the hut altogether.

A mystified Keitel returned, staring for a fleeting moment around the hut as if expecting the reappearance of von Stauffenberg after all.

What Keitel saw was Hitler leaning over a map, propped on his elbow.

What he heard was Heusinger saying:

'West of the Dvina, strong Russian forces are driving northwards. Their spearheads are already southwest of Dvinsk. Unless at long last, the army group is withdrawn from Lake Peipus, a catastrophe will . . .'

And then came the explosion – a flash and a roar likened by more than one person that day to the heaviest artillery shell.

Its force crashed into the conference table, wrecking the supports. One end was blasted to splinters. The greedy flames sped on, snatching at adjacent rooms and tearing down the ceilings.

Hitler was knocked to the left as if by a giant fist. On top of him fell an accumulation of debris. Both eardrums had been burst and there was excruciating pain in legs and elbow. But he had survived.

Gruppenfuehrer Hermann Fegelein and Standartenfuehrer Otto Gunsche had scarcely fared better. They had both been hurled through the windows into unconsciousness, while others had been flung backwards to perish in the flames.

As Hitler, his uniform torn to tatters, stumbled from the conflagration on the arm of Keitel, he left behind four men dead or dying, two most severely wounded and several with minor injuries.

Von Stauffenberg, of course, knew nothing of this. Glowing in the confidence of success, he had bluffed himself through the various checkpoints out of Rastenburg and left for Berlin.

What he discovered on arrival there was like a blow to the solar plexus.

Despite the agreed plan, the conspirators in Berlin had not gone into action. Timidity had won. They wanted to be certain that Hitler was really dead. The proclamation announcing the end of the Fuehrer and the constitution of a new government under Beck and von Witzleben had never been broadcast.

Von Stauffenberg beseeched them: 'Hitler is dead.' He added mendaciously: 'I saw his body being carried out.'

At last the conspirators consented to issue the orders to the garrisons. But by now valuable time had been lost.

22

In Paris, Oberst Eberhard Finckh of Generalfeldmarschall von Kluge's HQ listened on the telephone to the single code word indicating that the attempt on Hitler's life had been carried out.

At 19.30 hours Beck had rung Stuelpnagel confirming that the round-up of SD and Gestapo should go ahead. But by now the entire operation in France was in jeopardy. A question mark had always hung over the dependability of von Kluge, who had succeeded von Rundstedt as commander of the forces in the west. The only promise that the conspirators had been able to extract from the vacillating von Kluge was support if the coup succeeded.

But von Kluge had since heard that Hitler had escaped with wounds; from then on he was lost to the cause.

Nevertheless, the machinery in Paris had been put into motion. It was too late to stop it now.

The Army Commander for Greater Paris, Generalleutnant von Boineburg-Lengsfeld was looking forward to taking on the Gestapo.

For four long years, Oberg's thugs had been the terror of the French capital, arresting and torturing French civilians. The honour of the Wehrmacht had been dragged through the dust. A time of reckoning was at hand.

Von Boineburg-Langsfeld set about mustering units of the first Garrison Regiment poised in the Bois de Boulogne. Here were 2,000 crack troops, just waiting for the word to man the trucks and personnel carriers and start rolling.

Battalion commanders had very clear instructions: at first sign of resistance, their men were to open fire without question or mercy.

The trucks rumbled towards the Avenue Foch. Then with rifles and Schmeisser machine-pistols ready they rushed the building.

It was just 12.00 hours. Some of the Gestapo staff were in bed. The quick-witted managed to grab some clothes and head for the nearest windows. They were either dragged back inside or picked up by the reserves left in the streets.

At the SS Barracks of the Boulevard Lannes, Generaloberst Walther Brehmer led the assault party. In he crashed, yelling '*Hände Hoch!*' and having the thoroughly gratifying experience of seeing bemused SS raise their arms.

But Brehmer was after Oberg. He sent his boot crashing into the door of the Gruppenfuehrer's office. Oberg was talking on the telephone to the ambassador, Otto Abez. Brehmer cut short the other man's bewilderment and indignation. Barely aware of what had happened, Oberg was bundled into a Wehrmacht truck.

The whole operation had been remarkably smooth. Without a single shot being fired, no less than 1,200 SS and Gestapo had been scooped up and put under lock and key either in the jail at Fresnes or the Fort de l'Est. Oberg and other high ranking SS and Gestapo personnel were held at the Hotel Continental.

Only Helmut Knochen, dining with a friend, had missed the initial round-up. He received a telephone call to make forthwith for the Avenue Foch. But Knochen by now was suspicious. He decided instead to call on Oberg – and walked straight into summary arrest.

Plans were then instituted to shoot the prisoners the next morning. Ruthless realism dictated that the executions should have been carried out straight away. But it was already too late. Von Kluge had managed to betray the conspirators and denounce von Stuelpnagel.

The conspirators had made a serious blunder. They were all military men and had reasoned that to secure the co-operation of the army was all that was necessary. No account had been taken of Kriegsmarine (naval forces) in France. Admiral Krancke, commander-in-chief Group West of the Kriegsmarine, had received orders to alert his forces and send an ultimatum to army HQ. He would use force unless Oberg and the SS were immediately let go. The soldiers in Paris were forced to release their prisoners and return their weapons.

Early the next morning, order was restored. Parisians woke completely ignorant that a few hours before there had been a real prospect of release from their Gestapo oppressors.

In Berlin, the wavering Home Army commander Fritz Fromm had learnt on the telephone from Keitel that the attempt on Hitler's life had failed.

Olbricht protested that von Stauffenberg could confirm the Fuehrer's death.

Fromm snapped: 'That's impossible. Keitel had assured me that Hitler is alive.'

Olbricht replied: 'It makes no difference, the orders for Valkyrie have already been sent out.'

Fromm was nonplussed, but only for a moment. If the attempt at assassination had succeeded, he would not have hesitated to come in on the winning side. Whatever happened now nothing could alter the fact that Hitler was still alive.

To von Stauffenberg he said: 'The attempt has failed. You must shoot yourself at once.' Then he swiftly proclaimed the arrest of von Stauffenberg, Olbricht and

Oberst Mertz von Quirnheim, the officer who had issued the Valkyrie order.

Olbricht stood his ground. 'You are mistaken,' he said with contempt, 'It is we who are going to arrest you.'

In the ensuing squabble, the three men leapt on Fromm and swiftly locked him in the room of his adjutant, taking the precaution of cutting the telephone wires.

But von Stauffenberg was far from safe. Orders had come rapidly from Rastenburg that he was to be seized at once. The task had been assigned to one of Himmler's most sinister followers: SS-Oberfuehrer Helmut Piffraeder, whose service with an Einsatzgruppe in the Baltic regions had recently led to the extermination of 20,000 Jews.

His loyalty to the Gestapo was absolute. He turned up with two SD men to arrest von Stauffenberg. The reward for his endeavours was to be pounced on and locked up in an adjoining office to Fromm.

For the moment, the rebels were safe within their own headquarters. But that was far from being the whole of Berlin.

Major Otto Ernst Remer was a man who prided himself on obeying orders without question. For twelve years he had been a serving officer in the German army. He had been wounded several times and had been personally decorated by Hitler with the rare distinction of the Knight's Cross with Oakleaves.

It was unlikely that Remer could have disobeyed an instruction even if he had wanted to, but at this particular time he had begun to develop qualms of conscience. These stirrings were not, of course, prompted by any doubts of the unquestionable justice of Germany's cause. What puzzled him though, was just *who* was ruling the Reich in July 1944.

As commander of the crack Guard Battalion Grossdeutschland, he had received instructions from key conspirator and Berlin commandant von Hase: 'The Fuehrer is dead and there has been an attempted putsch by the SS. Your men are to seal off all the ministries in the Wilhemstrasse and the RSHA in the Anhalt Station quarter.'

The instructions were carried out to the letter in under two hours. But Remer was badly worried. To Oberleutnant Hans Hagen, a liaison officer between the Grossdeutschland Battalion and the Propaganda Ministry of Joseph Goebbels, he confided: 'There's something fishy going on.'

Hagen demanded to know the reasons for the other's suspicions.

Remer explained: 'I was in too much of a hurry to think of it at the time, but these were key orders. Why did I receive them verbally and not in a written despatch?'

Hagen shrugged: 'Why don't I go to Dr Goebbels and find out?'

Remer was aghast. Relatively junior officers in the Wehrmacht were not expected to demand interviews with senior cabinet ministers and ask why they had been given certain instructions. Patently, Hagen was being both impulsive and dangerous.

Hagen pressed: 'If you continue on your present path and there is a putsch, it could mean your head. This is the less dangerous alternative.'

Remer agreed. Hagen was provided with a motor-cycle: he roared away in search of the Propaganda Minister. As for Remer, his behaviour was characteristic. He merely carried on fulfilling the orders he had been given.

Goebbels was the one of the few principal Nazi leaders remaining in Berlin on 20 July. He had only the sketchiest notion of what had been going on. There had evidently been some sort of attempt on the Fuehrer's life and it hadn't come off. Goebbels was a cynic and a realist. He knew perfectly well that the war was lost.

To get through to Rastenburg was impossible; the only thing was to wait.

Goebbels saw no reason to do without his lunch and had left as usual for his official residence on the Hermann Goering Strasse. Then he returned to his office and got on with his work.

Hitler came on the line. Impatiently, he brushed aside the smooth congratulations of his minister.

The hoarse voice said: 'There is a strong rumour of a military putsch in Berlin. I want you to draft for the radio a denial of my death. That will frustrate anything happening in Berlin.'

Meanwhile the various army posts were buzzing. The instructions for Valkyrie had been received and the demand for information was incessant.

Goebbels thrust aside the rest of the papers on his desk and settled down to draft the broadcast. He frowned in annoyance on being told that Hans Hagen was demanding an immediate interview and refusing to go away.

Goebbels listened in open-mouthed astonishment to Hagen's story. He had no idea of the extent of the putsch and was badly rattled.

One thing Hagen did not know was that Hitler had survived the attempt. Goebbels pounced. 'I was talking to the Fuehrer only a short time ago,' he announced crisply. 'Hitler lives. The orders are complete nonsense.'

Hagen didn't answer. Goebbels followed the glance of the other man towards the open window. He limped across and stared down into the street. A company of Grossdeutschland was rumbling past in trucks.

For the first time, Goebbels felt the clutch of fear. Back at his desk, he lifted the phone. A priority call was put through to the commander of the SS Leibstandarte, the Fuehrer's personal bodyguard. Then he said to Hagen: 'I've alerted them, but at all costs I want to avoid an open clash with the SS.

'Get Remer here. If he hasn't arrived in 20 minutes I shall exercise my authority as Berlin Gauleiter and put the Leibstandarte into action. I shall assume that Remer has been captured by the conspirators.'

Goebbels was no stranger to danger. Indeed, he constantly reminded himself that he had been extremely lucky to survive thus far in Hitler's hierarchy. In the old days, he had flirted with Otto Strasser and Ernst Roehm. His total concern now was survival.

And the need was very great. No sooner had Hagen left him than a white-faced aide burst in with the news that three men were outside with instructions for his arrest on the order of the Commandant of Berlin.

Goebbel's hand streaked towards the revolver in his desk

drawer. Then he faced the unhappy Oberleutnant who now stood before him.

Attack was the only possible course. Goebbels screamed: 'The Fuehrer is alive and you are the agents of traitors. Get out of here, collect your men and go back to your posts.'

The verbal onslaught worked and the men withdrew. Hagen meanwhile worked like a man possessed. His motor-cycle screamed through the bomb-scarred streets of Berlin. Everywhere he left the same message. Anyone who obeyed orders not issued by the Fuehrer was a traitor.

Eventually, he ran Remer to earth. The major by now was out to save his own skin. He needed no prompting to make his way to Goebbels.

As for the Propaganda Minister, that formidable character had now recovered his nerve. Hitler had telephoned again, demanding angrily to know why no broadcast had been made. Goebbels rattled out a brief text. Around 18.45 it was broadcast on a wavelength beamed to the whole of Europe.

It said:

'Today an attempt was made on the life of the Fuehrer with explosives. The Fuehrer himself suffered no injuries beyond light burns and bruises. He resumed his work immediately. As scheduled, he received the Duce for a lengthy discussion. Shortly after the attempt on the Fuehrer's life, he was joined by the Reich Marschall.'

Goebbels allowed himself to relax. Soon he would have to deal with Major Remer.

On Remer's arrival, Goebbels asked abruptly: 'Are you a loyal National Socialist?'

Remer replied: 'I am a whole-hearted supporter of the Fuehrer. All I want to know is if he is alive or dead.'

Goebbels, the architect of carefully orchestrated public relations campaigns on behalf of Hitler, had a superb sense of the dramatic.

He lifted the telephone. A priority call was forthwith put through to Hitler. Goebbels spoke briefly and then handed the phone to Remer.

271

For a moment, the Major did not take the receiver. He came swiftly to attention as if his master was physically in the room. Goebbels tutted impatiently. Remer snatched the phone. He had been decorated personally by his Fuehrer. There could be no mistaking that wholly distinctive voice.

Hitler was saying: 'They tried to kill me, but I'm alive! I speak as your supreme commander. You will obey my orders and only my orders!'

Otto Ernst Remer had entered Goebbels's office a Major. He left it with the rank of Oberst. Few promotions in the history of the Third Reich had been earned quite so swiftly.

The fates were gathering to extinguish the brief, fragile triumph of the conspirators.

Badly rattled officers, who a few hours previously had been prepared to go ahead with the putsch, now changed sides rapidly.

Their work was helped by the blundering inefficiency of certain of the conspirators who refused to realise that only the ruthless butchering of captured opponents could possibly save the day.

Generaloberst Fromm had been locked up for four hours and had become restless. Plaintively, he asked to be returned to his private office. He gave his word of honour as an officer that he would not attempt to escape or overthrow the putsch.

With mind-boggling stupidity, his captors agreed. Furthermore, Fromm was supplied with sandwiches and wine. That was bad enough. His captors then proceeded to take leave of the few senses that they still possessed. When three senior officers of Fromm's staff, not members of the conspiracy, turned up they were allowed to join their chief.

Fromm promptly showed just how much his word of honour was worth. He hastily told the men of a convenient rear exit where they could escape. He ordered them: 'Get help. Surround this building and put down the revolt. I'll do the rest.'

Somehow the news that Fromm was regaining the upper hand spread. A group of officers previously loyal to Olbricht, and sensing that their heads would soon be on the block, began to prepare to join the victors. Arms were smuggled into the Bendelstrasse.

In his office, the unsuspecting Olbricht was confronted with a deputation demanding to know precisely what was happening. Von Stauffenberg sensed danger. As he walked into Olbricht's room he was seized. There was a volley of shots. Von Stauffenberg turned and ran. Bullets thudded into his good arm.

All at once, Fromm appeared, brandishing a revolver menacingly at Beck, von Stauffenberg, Olbricht and von Quirnheim. Rounded up also were Generaloberst Erich Hoeppner, who had usurped Fromm's place as Commander, Home Army, and Haeften, von Stauffenberg's aide.

A court martial, Fromm announced, had been convened and four traitors condemned to death: von Stauffenberg, Olbricht, von Quirnheim and Haeften. As for Beck, he had already been given a revolver and told to commit suicide. He bungled the attempt and was forthwith put out of his misery.

Then a firing-squad was detailed to form up in the courtyard of the building. Outside was total darkness. Fromm was impatient at the delay. The longer the conspirators were allowed to remain alive, the greater was his own risk of arrest. In addition, there was talk of an air raid that night.

A Wehrmacht truck edged into the courtyard, which was suddenly thrown into sharp relief by the headlamps.

The condemned men were hustled to the front of a sand embankment which had been intended for use on incendiaries.

Von Stauffenburg, in a grimy and sweat-stained white tunic, stood out from the rest.

The guns of the firing party spoke, but they could not drown the words of Claus von Stauffenberg: 'Long live our sacred Germany.'

Then it was as if an unseen force had lifted him up and

thrown him back bodily against the wall. He slumped forward, his body crashing to earth.

The bodies were left for some hours. And then, along with the corpse of Ludwig Beck, they were thrown into a truck which drove swiftly to the cemetery of Matthaus church.

As in most moments of great crisis, Hitler had hastily sent for the ever-faithful Heinrich Himmler.

In a brief interview, the architect of all the terror in the Third Reich was granted his heart's desire.

He was made commander-in-chief of the Reserve Army and sent to Berlin with absolute power to crush the rump of conspiracy.

A command in the army itself! This had been the lifetime dream of the supremo of the Gestapo and at long last it had come true.

Himmler's eyes shone as he faced Adolf Hitler. The Reichsfuehrer-SS was not a man given to emotion, but he displayed it now. 'My Fuehrer,' he proclaimed, 'you can leave it all to me.'

The rule of the SS and Gestapo had been one long night of barbarism, not just for occupied Europe but for Germany itself. The dawn was not yet.

23

Generaloberst Friedrich Fromm did not feel unduly worried. After all, he had shown his limitless devotion to his Fuehrer by putting down the revolt of von Stauffenberg and his friends. Surely, such zeal would not go unrewarded.

So when he was ushered into the presence of Himmler and Goebbels at the latter's official residence on the Hermann Goering Strasse, he came smartly to attention, positively yelling an enthusiastic 'Heil Hitler!'

But the atmosphere was decidedly frosty. Goebbels looked coldly at the fat red face with the shifty eyes. He snapped sarcastically: 'You seem to have been in a hell of a hurry to get awkward witnesses underground.'

He then went on to berate Fromm for cowardice and indecent haste. Goebbels made no effort to conceal his contempt. Fromm was arrested immediately.

But for all their energy, Goebbels and Himmler were still working to a certain extent in the dark. They had still very little idea of the extent of the conspiracy. It seemed reasonable to suppose that in Germany at least the putsch had failed.

What about the army in the rest of Europe? Could its loyalty be counted on? What if there was another attempt on the Fuehrer's life? The only course was to round up as many suspects as possible and hope for the best.

In Paris, Admiral Krancke's energy had matched that of Goebbels and Himmler. Von Kluge was now in the greatest danger. Admittedly, he had protested his innocence all along, but he was a member of the despised army and he was probably in the conspiracy up to the hilt. The marines were put on the alert. As for von Stuelpnagel, he was forthwith relieved of his command.

On the Russian front, one of the original architects of resistance had vowed to write his own final act in the drama.

Von Tresckow proclaimed: 'Once the Gestapo get hold of me, there's no guarantee that I won't betray my companions. There's only one way to prevent that.'

Von Schlabrendorff was of sterner stuff. He reasoned that there was no clear evidence to involve either him or von Tresckow. If they both kept their nerves, they might still survive.

But Henning von Tresckow was not to be deflected. Hopelessly, von Schlabrendorff watched his friend drive away to the front line. Resolutely, von Tresckow walked straight into the no-man's-land with the Russian forces beyond.

There was a sound like an exchange of shots. The troops were bewildered. Why had von Tresckow walked deliberately into Russian fire?

In fact, he had done no such thing. He had shot his own revolver into the air. Then he had placed a grenade on his head.

Joseph Goebbels had nudged his way briefly into the drama of the conspirators, but the role of nemesis was decidedly not to be his.

Himmler was determined that the SS and Gestapo must solely have the honour of tearing out the canker of betrayal. Himmler reserved special fury for von Stauffenberg and the others who had escaped the Gestapo's own distinctive brand of justice.

He related later:

'They were put underground so quickly that they were buried with their Knight's Crosses. They were disinterred next day, and their identities were confirmed. Then I ordered that the corpses were to be burned and the ashes strewn in the fields. We do not want to leave the slightest trace of these people, nor of those now being executed, in a grave or anywhere else.'

On to the bloodsoaked stage now strode Ernst Kaltenbrunner of the RSHA.

Arrests, interrogations and torture became the sole province of his Gestapo.

Von Stuelpnagel had been summoned to Berlin on the day following the putsch; von Kluge's betrayal had sealed his fate. On the way to the capital, outside Verdun, von Stuelpnagel abruptly ordered a change of route.

The country through which the car was now passing seemed like an old friend. Von Stuelpnagel had fought here in 1916.

On leaving Vacheraucheville, the car turned off to reach the river Meuse.

Casually, von Stuelpnagel said to his chauffeur: 'I feel like stretching my legs. Drive on to the next village and I'll catch you up.'

He watched the car disappear round the corner. Then there was a succession of revolver shots. Von Stuelpnagel's body was found floating face upwards in a nearby canal. One of the eyes had been blown away; a bullet had entered the head at the right temple.

Von Stuelpnagel was rushed to the military hospital at Verdun. After an operation and blood transfusion, it was learnt that he would live. But the optic nerves of both eyes had gone and he would be permanently blind.

But this was not to prevent his arrest by the Gestapo. Blinded and maimed or not, ahead lay the summary court and the ranting of Roland Freisler.

Generalfeldmarschall Walther Model was scrupulously polite. He sat in the office of von Kluge and gave him Hitler's abrupt notice of dismissal.

Von Kluge knew he was finished. And not merely because he had kept his knowledge of the conspiracy to himself. The inexorable advance of the Allies spelt complete failure to defend France for the Reich.

Ahead of the disgraced von Kluge lay Gestapo interrogation. And he knew what that meant.

He too made for Verdun. A halt was called for lunch. Then he took out a small glass vial of cyanide and bit down on it sharply.

Hitler ordered a hasty burial in von Kluge's native village. The official cause of death was given as heart failure.

As operative head of the Gestapo, Heinrich Mueller had always been keen that questioning should be carried out according to a set of rules which were to be scrupulously observed, particularly when it came to what he described with exquisite delicacy as 'sharpened interrogations'.

On 12 June 1942, he had issued a new regulation regarding the interrogation methods of the Gestapo. They were to be employed with brutal strength against the surviving members of the July plot.

The document was issued under the heading 'Secret Reich Matter':

1. The sharpened interrogation may only be applied if, on the strength of the preliminary interrogation, it has been ascertained that the prisoner can give information

about important facts, connections or plans hostile to the state or the legal system, but does not want to reveal his knowledge, and the latter cannot be obtained by way of enquiries.

2. Under this circumstance, the sharpened interrogation may be applied only against Communists, Marxists, members of the Bible-researcher sect, saboteurs, terrorists, members of the resistance movement, parachute agents, asocial persons, Polish or Soviet persons who refuse to work, or idlers. In all other cases, my previous permission is required as a matter of principle.

3. The sharpened interrogation may not be applied in order to induce confessions about a prisoner's own criminal acts. Nor may these means be applied towards persons who have been temporarily delivered by justice for the purpose of further investigation. Once more, exceptions require my previous permission.

4. The sharpening can consist of the following, among other things, according to circumstances:

> simplest rations (bread and water)
> hard bed
> dark cell
> deprivation of sleep
> exhaustion exercises
> but also the resort to blows with a stick (in case of over twenty blows, a doctor must also be present).'

The document was admitted as evidence at the prosecution of the major war criminals at Nuremberg. It was pointed out there that the document, quite deliberately, glossed over some of the worst excesses of the Gestapo. The words 'The sharpening can consist of the following, among other things, according to circumstances' threw the door wide open to the arbitrary sadism of the Gestapo specialists in interrogation.

The deprivation of sleep was connected with incessant questioning, especially at night. Examination lasted hour upon hour. If one Gestapo official became too tired, the interrogations were continued by another.

An interrogator sat, while the prisoner had to stand until he collapsed. After a short pause and a dash of cold water, the questioning went on relentlessly.

Exhaustion exercises consisted, among other things, in the removal of the bed from the cell. Sometimes not even a footstool was left.

A favourite Gestapo torture consisted of a series of knee bends. Beatings were systematically administered if the prisoner remained stubborn. To the deliberately scanty meals, drugs could be added to prostrate nerve and will-power.

The more skilled interrogators knew how to interpret clause 3 to their own advantage. They scrupulously applied the 'sharpened interrogation' towards a prisoner only to inform themselves about the activities of others they were holding.

Not until the interrogated prisoner had reached complete physical exhaustion, was he asked about his own activities. The Gestapo ended up with the information it wanted just the same.

Many of the interrogations following the attempt on Hitler's life made ample use of the vague stricture 'among other things, according to circumstances'.

One leading conspirator has left a searing account of what it was in fact like to fall into Gestapo hands after the failure of the July plot.

Fabian von Schlabrendorff was aroused from his bed at Mackow in Poland near the German Russian front line on 17 August. His first impulse had been to grab his pistol and put an end to it all. An opportunity for escape came when he was taken under military guard to a house in a village only a few kilometres away.

He could have dodged the sentry at the front door by escaping at the back and running for nearby woods, but he reasoned that without shelter or food he was unlikely to get very far. In addition, he had some knowledge of Gestapo interrogation methods. He knew of the lies which would be presented to him as evidence, the forged documents they would try to persuade him to sign. He was a man of considerable resource who believed that, provided he was able to keep his nerve, there was a slim chance of survival.

He also suspected that the Gestapo in fact had very little evidence against him; it was worth staking all on denying all.

On the night of 18 August, he was brought to the cellars of the Prinz Albrechtstrasse. Until then he had been treated with exemplary politeness. Now all that was to change.

First came solitary confinement. But there was a common washroom and there he encountered his fellow prisoners who included Oster, Goerdeler, Fromm and – his luck run out at last – Admiral Canaris.

The initial interrogation was carried out by Kommisar Habecker of the KRIPO. He said briskly: 'You are charged with preparations for the 20 July bomb plot. We know everything and our evidence is corroborated by witnesses.

'Why don't you save time and confess now? All denial is useless.'

But Habecker refused to produce any evidence, real or concocted. Von Schlabrendorff said mildly: 'You cannot expect me to confess if you do not give me your reasons.'

The result was bluster and threats. Von Schlabrendorff knew he had been right: the Gestapo had precious little to go on.

He was not a man to be intimidated by crude threats; the most insulting language left him quite cold.

Beyond manacling him day and night, physical coercion had not yet begun and he was able to marvel at the astonishing crudity of the interrogation methods.

He later wrote:

'The Gestapo agents used a number of different methods in their attempt to play on a prisoner's nerves. One method was to take him out of his cell for questioning, and then let him wait endlessly in an anteroom. If that had no effect, other means of influencing him were employed. Usually, three officials worked together. One would threaten the prisoner and shower him with abuse, the second would talk to him in a soothing manner, urging him to calm down and have a cigarette, the third would then try to appeal to a prisoner's code of honour.

In this way, the Gestapo provided for three different kinds of temperament in the hope that the prisoner would in the end succumb to one of these approaches or to the combination of all three.'

But he persisted in his denials. And then the tortures began.

' . . . First, my hands were chained behind my back, and a device which gripped all the fingers separately was fastened to my hands. The inner side of this mechanism was studded with pins whose points pressed against my fingertips. The turning of a screw caused the instrument to contract, thus forcing the pin points into my fingers.

When that did not achieve the desired confession, the second stage followed. I was strapped face down on a frame resembling a bedstead, and my head was covered with a blanket. Then cylinders resembling stovepipes studded with nails on the inner surface, were shoved over my bare legs. Here, too, a screw mechanism was used to contract these tubes so that nails pierced my legs from ankle to thigh.

For the third stage of torture, the "bedstead" itself was the main instrument. I was strapped down as described above, again with a blanket over my head. With the help of a special mechanism this medieval torture rack was then expanded – either in sudden jerks or gradually – each time stretching my shackled body.

In the fourth and final stage I was tied in a bent position which did not allow me to move even slightly backwards or sideways. Then the Police Commissioner and the police sergeant together fell on me from behind, and beat me with heavy clubs.

Each blow caused me to fall forward, and because my hands were chained behind my back, I crashed with full force on my face.'

After each session, von Schlabrendorff was flung back

into his cell, to lie in his cot in blood-stained underwear. He suffered a heart attack. A doctor was summoned. In a few days, the tortures were resumed.

Then, almost without warning, the ill-treatment ceased. The prisoner was bundled into a car and taken to the concentration camp at Sachsenhausen. There he found himself in an area which showed every sign of having been used as a shooting-range.

The accompanying Gestapo official gestured with a sneer: 'Now, you know what is going to happen to you. But first we have other plans for you.'

They were more horrible than von Schlabrendorff could have conceived possible.

He was taken into a room in a part of the camp crematorium. Before him stood the coffin of the mutilated but recognisable Generalmajor von Tresckow, seized by the Gestapo from the grave at Brandenburg.

Before Schlabrendorff's eyes, it was opened. But now it was the turn of the Gestapo to be disconcerted. They plainly expected that the body would not be that of von Tresckow.

During investigation into the conspiracy, it had been found that the Generalmajor had been secretly disregarding Hitler's orders. The Fuehrer's most oft-repeated command was 'No retreat'; the only exception allowed was to make small tactical adjustments known as 'straightening out the front'. Von Tresckow, in a feverish bid to save as many lives as he could, had taken full advantage of that permission, pulling the line back the prescribed maximum of ten kilometres. His unit had straightened out the front every single day.

By the end of the month, the line was 300 kilometres away from its proper position. The troops had sworn volubly at having to dig freshly every twenty-four hours, but the stratagem had saved countless lives.

Such a man, the Gestapo reasoned, was the sort to fake his own suicide. After all, the death had taken place in no-man's-land without the presence of witnesses. What would have been easier than for von Tresckow to desert to the Russians, leaving a dead Russian soldier behind?

Von Schlabrendorff smiled grimly. The Gestapo had hoped to uncover yet another conspiracy. It had conspicuously failed.

Another plea was made to persuade von Schlabrendorff to confess but he told his captors nothing.

Then the Gestapo took the coffin containing von Tresckow's body and, still in front of von Schlabrendorff, set it alight.

Von Schlabrendorff's end was not to be before a firing squad at Sachsenhausen. He was taken back to the Prinz Albrechtstrasse to await the People's Court.

Ever since he had stumbled singed and deafened but otherwise unhurt from the Wolfschanze at Rastenburg, Hitler had screamed for bloody vengeance, vowing that the sins of the fathers should be visited not only on their children but on their entire families.

Himmler responded to the orders of his Fuehrer with unstinted enthusiasm. He went further. As a terrifyingly over-credulous reader of the myths and legends of a land too far lost in the mists of time even to be called Germany, he resurrected and swiftly activated an ancient law of abysmal barbarity.

On 3 August 1944, Himmler told the Gauleiters (district officers) at conference at Posen: 'All you have to do is to read up on the old Germanic sagas. When they proscribed a family and declared them outlaws, or when they had a vendetta, they went all the way. They had no mercy. They outlawed the entire family and proclaimed, *This man is a traitor, there is bad blood in that family, the blood of traitors, the whole lot must be exterminated*.

'In the case of vendettas, that is exactly what they did down to the last member of the clan.'

As was characteristic of so much of the more outrageous activities of the SS and the Gestapo, Himmler's actual intentions were wrapped up in circumlocution. He went on to talk about 'a system of absolute liability on the grounds of kinship'.

A new word was coined: 'Sippenhaft'. It meant literally 'tribe liability'.

The law of Sippenhaft was, in fact, not instituted as thoroughly as Himmler would have liked. The sheer size of the undertaking made it impractical; also Hitler was shrewd enough to realise that with the loyalty of Germany already at breaking point, such a move would scarcely help his regime.

But the Gestapo went into action nonetheless. Von Stauffenberg's wife and newborn child were arrested; his other four children were dragged from their mother and sent to foster homes. Other relatives of the conspirators suffered the same fate, many of them hauled bewildered and terrified from their homes, sometimes totally unaware that there had been involvement in a conspiracy at all.

Kaltenbrunner was proving a worthy successor to Reinhard Heydrich. He worked ceaselessly day and night. Some four hundred Gestapo officials were involved in the arrest of some seven thousand people.

Roland Freisler had presided over the first trial in the dreaded Volksgerichthof (People's Court) on 7 and 8 August. In the dock were Generalfeldmarschall von Witzleben and assorted Generals who had been involved directly with von Stauffenberg.

All had been beaten and starved in the Gestapo cellars. To these privations had been added another: deliberate humiliation. The accused were made to look as shabby as possible.

Von Witzleben's false teeth had been taken away from him. He had not been allowed to shave. The once proud Generalfeldmarschall was decked out in the old clothes of a tramp. Like a toothless scarecrow, he summoned what dignity he could under the sneering, ranting tirade of Freisler.

The entire proceedings were filmed and recorded; Freisler's rantings sent the recording-level needle bouncing to the end of the scale.

Freisler seized on a conversation von Witzleben held with Beck the previous year. Both men had deplored Hitler's tendency to pick senior commanders for their political reliability rather than their military prowess.

Freisler, playing up gleefully to the lenses of the hidden

cameras, bellowed: 'Did you think on that occasion who could do it better?'

Von Witzleben did not flinch and replied, 'Yes!'

'Who, then, could have done it better?'

'Both of us,' replied the Generalfeldmarschall.

Freisler's voice rose beyond the pitch of hysteria:

'Both, both of you! That is an outrage that has never before been perpetrated here. A Generalfeldmarschall and a Generaloberst declare that they could do things better than he who is the Fuehrer of all of us, who has made the borders of the Reich the borders of Europe ... You profess to having said this?'

Von Witzleben riposted resoundingly: 'Yes!'

The attitude of the defence was every bit as derisory as it had been during the trial of the Scholls. Dr Weissmann, who represented von Witzleben, said: 'You might ask, "Why conduct a defence at all?" It is stipulated by the letter of the law, and moreover, at a time like this in our view it is part of the task of the Defence to help the court find a verdict. Undoubtedly in some of the trials it will prove impossible even for the best counsel to find anything to say in defence or mitigation of the accused ...'

All in the dock were condemned to death by hanging. A request to face a firing squad was sneeringly rejected. Hitler had previously ordered: 'They are to be hung like cattle.'

And they were. To this day, the execution chamber inside Plotzensee prison in Berlin is a permanent memorial to those who opposed Hitler in the July plot.

When the second day of the trial had ended in the foreseen 'guilty' verdict, the eight men were hanged in circumstances of revolting barbarity.

Hans Hoffman, warder in charge of von Witzleben at the Plotzensee, whose account was supported by the testimony of another warder and of the cameramen in charge of the film unit, described the scene:

'Imagine a room with a low ceiling and white-washed walls. Below the ceiling a rail was fixed. From it hung six big hooks, like those butchers use to hang their meat. In one corner stood a movie camera. Reflectors cast a dazzling, blinding light, like that of a studio. In this strange, small room were the Attorney General of the Reich, the hangman with his two assistants, two camera technicians, and I myself with a second prison warden. At the wall there was a small table with a bottle of cognac and glasses for all the witnesses of the execution.

The convicted men were led in. They were all wearing their prison garb, and they were handcuffed. They were placed in a single row. Leering and making jokes, the hangman got busy. He was known in his circles for his "humour". No statement, no clergyman, no journalists.

One after another, all faced their turn. All showed the same courage. It took in all, twenty-five minutes. The hangman wore a permanent leer, and made jokes unceasingly. The camera worked uninterruptedly, for Hitler wanted to see and hear how his enemies had died. He was able to watch the proceedings that same evening in the Reich Chancellery ...

The defendant went to the end of the room with his head high, although urged by the hangman to walk faster. Arrived there, he had to make an about-face. Then a hempen loop was placed around his neck. Next he was attached to the hook in the ceiling. The prisoner was then dropped with great force, so that the noose tightened around his neck instantly. In my opinion, death came very quickly.

After the first sentence was carried out, a narrow black curtain was drawn in front of the hanged man, so that the next man to be executed would not be aware of the first one ... The executions were carried out in very rapid succession. Each doomed man took his last walk erect and manly, without a word of complaint.'

The People's Court sat in session until well into 1945. The sightless von Stuelpnagel had been led by the hand to the gallows, while his aide, Oberst von Hofacker, had, in the throes of torture by the Gestapo, admitted that Generalfeldmarschall Rommel had undertaken to end the war in the west once Hitler was dead.

Rommel was the undisputed hero not only of the German people but of Hitler himself. When Rommel had indulged in defeatist talk about the conduct of the war, Hitler had ignored his temerity. Indeed, he had been anxiously awaiting the day when Rommel should have recovered sufficiently once again to take up command.

Hitler was anxious above all to avoid dragging the military paladin of the Third Reich before Freisler.

On 12 October, Generalleutnant Wilhelm Burgdorff, the Head of the Personnel Department of OKW, was entrusted with a top secret mission.

The Generalleutnant was to go to Rommel's house and present him with a letter containing von Hofacker's admission. If the statement was false, then Rommel would plainly have nothing to fear from an investigation. If it were true, then Rommel, as an officer and a gentleman, would know what to do.

Burgdorff was given a box of poison ampoules and told to assure Rommel that, should he choose to use them, the Fuehrer would guarantee a state funeral and no reprisals against his family.

Burgdorff took his deputy, Generalleutnant Ernst Maisel, with him, leaving Berlin by car that afternoon.

Rommel's house was surrounded by SS. Rommel made his choice quickly. Within an hour of arrival of the two men, Rommel with his Afrika Korps uniform and his Generalfeldmarschall's baton made a final farewell to his wife and son and entered a waiting car.

He was driven a couple of kilometres. Maisel and the SS driver got out, leaving Rommel in the car with Burgdorff. When the two men returned, Rommel's body was slumped in the back.

Before he left home, Rommel had told his wife: 'It's all been prepared to the last detail. In a quarter of an hour, you will receive a call from the hospital in Ulm to say that I've had a seizure on the way to a conference.'

Hitler kept his promise; he could scarcely afford to do otherwise. Rommel received his state funeral and the family was left unmolested.

*

Hans von Dohnanyi had the supreme gift of cunning. He knew he would be unable to withstand Gestapo torture for very long. His only hope, he calculated, was to play for time. Inside Berlin's Tegel prison, he toyed with his inquisitors, teasing them with a succession of wildly misleading statements and false leads.

Calculatingly, he made sure that what he told the Gestapo would take time to prove. His inquisitors were reluctant to be rid of him or bring him to trial so long as there remained the prospect that he would betray his friends.

Von Dohnanyi next infected himself with dysentery bacilli smuggled into the prison. When that failed to work, his wife managed to get him a supply of diphtheria cultures which severely weakened him. Then by an ironic stroke of fortune, Allied bombs fell on the Abwehr offices of the Tirpitsufer. All the incriminating files were destroyed. But it was too late to undo the work of his initial carelessness in letting so many highly incriminating documents fall into the hands of the Gestapo.

Soon after the failure of the July plot, von Dohnanyi was taken from the Gestapo cells to Sachsenhausen concentration camp. Not only was he weakened by the drugs with which he had injected himself, but he had been badly mauled by the Gestapo.

Max Geissler, a medical orderly in the sick ward of the camp, was ordered to prepare a room. Von Dohnanyi was brought in on a stretcher by SS and Gestapo men.

Geissler received strict instructions that under no account was he to speak to the patient. Geissler later stated: 'As a result of ill-treatment von Dohnanyi was so weakened and paralysed that he was unable to wash or feed himself or even turn over in bed.' Von Donanyi in great pain stated that his spine had been damaged by the Gestapo beatings. The interrogations later continued within Geissler's hearing.

'These uneducated boors tore into him unspeakably, in their frustrated rage. It can be said without any doubt that von Dohnanyi proved both the better and the stronger party in this unequal contest.'

At the end of January, von Dohnanyi was taken to the Gestapo prison in Berlin where he was incarcerated along with Pastor Bonhoeffer and von Schlabrendorff.

The latter had reasoned that to admit his involvement in the plot with von Tresckow could scarcely do anyone any harm now. This simple admission at least had the virtue of putting a stop to the Gestapo's torture.

Von Schlabrendorff's turn to appear before the People's Court came on 21 December. He and five others were ushered before the ranting Freisler. Schlabrendorff watched his comrades, one after the other, be condemned to the gallows. Mentally, he began to prepare himself for the ordeal which now he felt sure he could no longer escape.

He was held until the following February and then it was back to court to hear Freisler pronounce the death sentence on yet another conspirator.

On the morning of 3 February 1945, he stood listening to Freisler's shower of abuse. But there was a dramatic interruption. With their sinister wail of warning, the sirens of Berlin opened up.

The skies turned black with American B-17 bombers. They arrowed in on the already battered capital of the Reich. The courtroom emptied fast and there was a rush towards the basement cellars.

At first it seemed as if the bombs were far away, then the sound of explosions grew progressively louder. Von Schlabrendorff remembered that even before the raid, he had been praying.

There was shifting and rumbling of the ground beneath him as the room was wrenched apart. He later recalled an awful greyness as the dust billowed upwards, muting the screams and groans of the dying.

The uninjured scratched and clawed at bricks and debris. As for Freisler, a heavy beam had sliced his skull. In one hand, he clutched von Schlabrendorff's file. Justice had come literally from the heavens.

But still Hitler's remorseless revenge against the conspirators dragged on. Von Schlabrendorff was hauled before yet another court. But this time he felt a sort of exhilaration: an unerring certainty that, come what may, he would survive.

Freisler's successor was Wilhelm Krohne who, much to the prisoner's surprise, actually allowed him to speak in his own defence.

Von Schlabrendorff took full advantage of the opportunity. He argued that such confessions as he had made had been extracted under torture – a practice which had been abandoned by Frederick the Great two centuries before.

Krohne dismissed the charges. But von Schlabrendorff was not free yet. He was forthwith despatched to the concentration camp at Flossenburg near the Czech border. The Gestapo was in control there too.

Ernst Kaltenbrunner, as head of the RSHA, had been given a free hand to snuff out the lives of the conspirators, in particular the faction controlled by Canaris and Oster. No one would have objected particularly if Kaltenbrunner had merely ordered wholesale liquidations, but there was enough of the policeman in him to insist that a spurious cloak of semi-legality should characterise the investigations.

He conferred with Mueller, who was all for carrying out the killings as fast as possible. A compromise was agreed to. An SS court of summary conviction was to be set up. Over it would preside judges and prosecuting counsel. The executions could only be carried out once the death sentences had been announced.

Von Dohnanyi, Kaltenbrunner had stipulated, was to be sentenced at a summary court to be convened at Sachsenhausen on 6 April 1945.

A hastily prepared indictment was read to von Dohnanyi, who was carried into court on a stretcher. No defence counsel was permitted and von Dohnanyi was scarcely in a fit state to make any plea of defence. The charges of high treason and treason in the field were found proved. Some three days later he went to the gallows.

Mueller next ordered his Gestapo subordinates to proceed at once to Flossenburg and deal with the prisoners there.

One of the headquarters buildings was converted into a make-shift courthouse. The lawyers who took part in the 'trial' were perfectly conscious that, even under the laws of the Third Reich, their activities were illegal. Canaris and the other accused were members of the armed forces and should have been tried by a military court.

The choice of a concentration camp for the trial was illegal also, but the absence of a defence counsel itself made such infringements of the law decidedly academic.

Oster was sentenced to death on the same day as the proceedings. Then came the turn of Canaris. The charges against both men were broadly similar: that since 1938 they had been aware of plans for a coup d'etat, that everything possible had been done to conceal the existence of a subversive group inside the Abwehr.

Canaris put up a brave fight. He argued that he had only played along with the conspirators because it seemed judicious to do so. He had fully intended to expose the conspiracy at the last moment.

It all proved useless. The outcome would only be the death sentence.

Canaris was the first to enter the death yard. Under its roof were supporting beams with hooks and nooses. Beneath each stood a small stepladder.

All the prisoners went naked to the gallows. Canaris, according to witnesses, submitted meekly to the noose.

Although the SS physician, Fischer, stated 'Admiral Canaris died a staunch and manly death,' it could not have been anything else but an agonising end. An SS witness put it more graphically and accurately: 'The little Admiral took a very long time – he was jerked up and down once or twice.'

The bodies were hastily flung on a pyre and burnt. Josef Mueller, a lawyer and a leader in the 'Catholic wing' of the conspiracy who was also a prisoner at Flossenburg but survived to be liberated by the Allies, later spoke of 'a definite smell of burning bodies'.

He had rushed to his cell window and looked out: 'Specks were eddying through the air – eddying through the bars and into my cell. I had the impression that they were fragments of human skin.'

As the Allied armies advanced further into the Reich, the SS fled the various concentration camps, often herding their prisoners with them. Executions continued right to the end, but there were lucky survivors, von Schlabren-dorff among them.

On 4 May, he and many others were south of the Brenner Pass in the village of Niedernhausen. Here the SS guards at last abandoned their prisoners. Von Schlabrendorff and some of his companions fell in with an advance party of Americans.

Upwards of 10,000 had been arrested by the Gestapo, following the July plot. Very few of the ringleaders escaped. Carl Goerdeler, who had been nominated to be Chancellor of the new regime, had gone into hiding three days before 20 July. A warning had reached him that the Gestapo was on his track.

For three days he wandered between Berlin, Potsdam and East Prussia. He depended for his survival on friends and relatives who sheltered him.

He steadfastly refused to stay in one place for very long, knowing what fate the Gestapo would have in store for anyone who helped him. Hitler had put a price of one million marks on his head.

On 12 August, desperately exhausted and hungry, he decided to risk an appearance at an inn in a village near Marienwerder.

It was a fatal move. He had scarcely taken his seat at a table when he noticed he was being watched closely by a woman in Luftwaffe uniform. Hastily, he slipped out.

But Helene Schwaerzel had been an acquaintance of the Goerdeler family. He was swiftly arrested, hauled before the People's Court in September 1944. He went to the gallows the following February.

Herbert Kosney walked the streets of Berlin with fear as his companion that dawn of 23 April 1945.

He was a young Potsdam lawyer who had been con-demned by the People's Court. All his fellow prisoners had been told they were being removed from Moabit Prison for Potsdam.

By the side of the column of prisoners marched the sinister escort of SS, their machine-guns unslung.

Beneath his feet, Kosney could feel the rubble and broken glass of this shattered city. The destination appeared to be the bomb-cratered park which lay ahead.

Then came the one-word command from an SS Sturmfuehrer: *Halt!*

The gun-muzzles spoke. A bullet ripped through Herbert Kosney's neck and he pitched forward. He stared at his own blood spilling on the pavement, telling himself constantly: 'Appear to be dead. They won't hang around to find out.'

In a few moments, he was scrambling over the bodies of his fellow prisoners, struggling away like an animal to die. But eventually he found a doctor and survived to testify to yet one more hideous SS crime,

Guns blazed many times in the cellars of the Gestapo at Plotzensee. Then the killers discarded SS and SD uniforms, their one fear the prospect of falling into Russian hands.

For the war had at last come home to Germany.

25

Danish resistance worker Ove Kaupmann darted a quick glance towards the large clock hanging in the Gestapo interrogation centre at Shellhus.

The hands pointed to 8.00 a.m. Kaupmann had only to hold out for another couple of hours. Then he could quite safely tell Heinz Hoffman's men where the latest cell of the resistance was meeting. By 10 o'clock Kaupmann's colleagues would be well clear of the rendezvous.

Kaupmann had been grabbed by the Gestapo in a surprise raid on the Copenhagen telephone exchange that February 1945. The Gestapo had known that Danes were tapping German telephones and warning members of the resistance when their lines were being spied on.

Kaupmann was a key figure in the resistance network and attended its meetings regularly. Now the fate of his colleagues was up to him.

With agonising slowness the hands of the clock crept towards the all-important hour. Fortunately, the Gestapo had ceased beating Kaupmann and were contenting themselves with relentless questioning. He kept silent.

He waited until the clock registered five past ten and suddenly announced: 'You'll find them all in the Technical High School.'

His interrogator shot out: 'All of who?'

Kaupmann assumed an air of depression: 'The leaders of the resistance, the whole lot. I can't give you names but that's where they meet each morning.'

He felt desperately tired. If it had not been for the clock on the wall he would have had no idea of time. Only the hint of wintery sun peering through the blinds told him it was morning.

The two Gestapo officials were now glancing at each other and smiling broadly. With elaborate politeness, one of them looked at Kaupmann and said: 'Thank you very much.'

He rose languidly, strode across to the wall, opened the glass cover on the clock – and moved the hands back to the right time. The clock now read 8.00 a.m.

The raid that followed was a rich haul. It netted not only key members of the resistance, but also those who masterminded the underground army awaiting Allied orders to battle with the Germans in the streets.

But the Gestapo, busy with arrests like these and countless others, overlooked the most important resistance centre of all.

And that was inside Shellhus itself.

*

Much had changed inside that sinister building since the Gestapo had moved in over a year before. It was bursting with prisoners. The Danes had become particularly adept at learning and reporting to England on every Nazi move: Hoffmann was determined to get as many resistance workers off the streets as possible.

Workmen were ordered swiftly to set up flimsy concrete-block partitions so that the attic could be turned into a jail of its own. Twenty-two small makeshift cells were constructed in this way. Five were along the west side of the building which faced a large lake, on the left arm of the U shape. The other cells were situated on both sides of a corridor along the front at the base of the U. The plywood doors each had five small ventilation holes drilled into top and bottom. Judas windows were covered with a wooden flap. Each cell was bare save for a cot and a small stool. There were six other cells which had no cots and were used for prisoners awaiting interrogation.

Prisoners made use of three toilets and a washroom and there was a small kitchen.

Hoffman warned all captives that they would be shot instantly if they made any contact with one another. But small holes had been left for electric wiring between the cells and a whispering grapevine was soon buzzing.

The lavatories became glorified post-boxes. Endless notes were left behind bathroom mirrors. They set out what questions had already been asked by the Gestapo and, equally important, what answers had been given.

The prisoners had a useful ally in the Danish char-woman, Emma, who smuggled letters past the guards; vital contact was maintained with the resistance outside. But the day came when the Germans caught Emma. Even when she had been taken away, prisoners were able to keep abreast of the progress of the war.

The Allied push was steady and remorseless. Such knowledge was a considerable comfort, but it did nothing to stop the flow of Gestapo arrests, the long interrogations, the inevitable tortures.

Surveillance of the prisoners within their chilly cells was

stepped up. Every ten minutes, the guards pulled back their flaps on the Judas windows and stared in. But the prisoners had their own way of watching the guards. They learned to stand on tip-toe on their stools, squinting through the ventilation holes to see what was happening in the corridors. They even learned how to push aside the flaps of the Judas windows.

The arrests swelling Shellhus were bad enough, but what really worried the chiefs of Danish resistance was the valuable records on their activities being compiled by the Gestapo. As the Germans sifted and cross-checked documents, they were able to round up still more groups.

Soon urgent messages from the various cells of Danish resistance was reaching England: destroy Shellhus, not to release the prisoners, but to destroy the records which were bleeding the life out of the resistance.

The blunt truth had to be faced that any raid would almost certainly lead to the death of some of those housed in the makeshift attic prison.

Britain's Air Ministry initially regarded the suggestion with horror. In no way would bomber crews be asked to carry out what would amount to the slaughter of Allies.

The Danes persisted. Every member of the resistance, both outside and inside Shellhus, was given his tasks. Detailed drawings and plans were to be made of every centimetre of Gestapo headquarters. The complete architect's plans were sent to London together with available photographs.

Maps were made of the surrounding area. The positions of other office buildings were indicated. Even tourist postcards were forwarded to London.

The locations of German anti-aircraft and direction-finding ironmongery were also included.

Still, the Air Ministry was adamant. The general attitude was that, since the invasion of western Europe was in full tide, all available resources must be concentrated on that. Any attack on Shellhus would need precision bombing; there were neither aircraft nor crews available.

The Danes wasted no time in pious exhortations. Its

leaders reasoned that their best course was to minimise the risk of unnecessary loss of life. They must bombard the Allies with enough data to prove conclusively that the raid could be carried out with every chance of success.

In London, Major Svend Truelson, ardent champion for the raid among the exiled Danes and attached to the headquarters of Air Vice-Marshal Basil Embry, faced a frankly pessimistic Squadron Leader Ted Sismore of the RAF.

Sismore, sifting through the latest material submitted by the resistance, sighed: 'It's hopeless. Look at these photographs of the Copenhagen streets. Every damn house looks alike. Are you seriously suggesting that we should wipe out the lot?'

Truelsen smiled: 'Certainly not. But, as it happens, the Germans themselves are helping us out over that one.'

The Dane then went on to produce some more intelligence reports. The latest news was that the Germans had recently camouflaged Shellhus.

Truelsen went on: 'The Gestapo is so keen on protecting its precious headquarters, it hasn't realised what a sitting target it has made of the place.

'In the whole of Copenhagen, there's only one building painted with bold brown and green stripes – and that's Shellhus.'

Air Vice-Marshal Embry was still reluctant to act. Later, he confessed that the awful knowledge that innocent lives in surrounding buildings must surely be sacrificed had made him almost morally powerless to act.

He was able to plead with a certain amount of justification that the weather reports currently being submitted to him by the Air Ministry were so bad as to make the very idea of the raid impractical, anyway.

Sismore continued to find himself submerged under the mountain of intelligence reports. Slowly, he became certain that the chance could not be passed up.

He was finally convinced when he said casually to Truelsen: 'It would help me a lot if you were able to get a photograph of the target from the bridge over St Jorgen's Lake.'

Two weeks later, the Dane strode into Sismore's office and dropped something on his desk and said: 'Will that do?'

It was a photograph taken from the precise angle asked for.

At a rush of meetings held in the Air Ministry, plans went ahead in earnest for Operation Carthage.

The plans, photographs and written information were collated. Embry instructed his staff to build a model showing an area of approximately one square kilometre centred on Shellhus.

Sismore got together with Group Captain Bob Bateson to map out the route. Soon they were immersed in the logistics: flying speeds, formations, strength of the attacking force.

This was all part of the trade of air war and by no means the toughest problem facing the planners of the raid. The greatest anxiety was that they were being asked to do something entirely new: a low-level attack on a building whose interior was of solid concrete and steel. Nothing quite like it had been attempted before in terms of a low-level attack.

There was another consideration. When it came to destroying cities, bombers could always return for a second crack. In this case, no such opportunity would present itself. The raid must be a success on the one and only attempt. A repeat performance would be out of the question.

The whole thing could only be executed with first rate talent. Bateson thought he knew where it could be found – among crack crews of 140 Wing. He reasoned that an attacking echelon of six aircraft stood the best chance of crossing Jutland and Zeeland undetected. That would be good news for succeeding waves: they would be unlikely to get such a hot reception, once the first lot had been allowed over Copenhagen relatively unchallenged.

And the aircraft for the job? There was no doubt about that. Swiftly earmarked was the Mark IV Mosquito, armed with four Browning machine guns and four 20-mm cannon.

Bateson grinned confidently at Truelsen and said: 'You

could say this baby is highly capable of looking after herself.'

Nevertheless, everyone was talking of a raid deep inside enemy territory, and those Mosquitoes would need a fighter escort to deal with German fighter and anti-aircraft guns clustered in the fighting area.

The Mosquitoes would be flying across the North Sea at wave height and at no higher than sixty metres across South Jutland and Zeeland. Three waves would be flying in echelon formation. They would make a left-handed turn over the target, returning to base via north Zeeland and the southernmost point of Samso. Speeds would be 400kph over the North Sea, increasing to 440 overland. Of course, the Mosquitoes could go a lot faster, but here was a sharp necessity to conserve fuel.

Equally there was a need to get Carthage off the ground at the earliest possible moment.

News from the Danish resistance was unremittingly grim. The number of arrests and interrogations continued. If they were allowed to go on at their present rate, opposition to the Nazis in Denmark would be reduced to little more than a rump.

Embry refused to be hurried. He needed an absolute guarantee of favourable weather forty-eight hours ahead. On 19 March it came.

At Fersfield Aerodrome, Norfolk, Group Captain Bob Bateson addressed seventy eager-faced airmen. He was flanked by Sismore, Truelsen and a certain 'Wing-Commander Smith'.

The latter wore the uniform bearing pilot's wings but lacking decoration. 'Smith' had previously flown a Mosquito in an attack on the Gestapo headquarters at Aarhus. Now he would be in the first wave to hit Shellhus. 'Smith' was Air Vice-Marshal Basil Embry.

Bateson came straight to the point. Because of the men in the building, it was vital for the bombs to hit the base of Shellhus or the pavement in front of it.

The over-riding purpose was to explode the files and records. The two main staircases in the Gestapo head-

299

quarters were at either corner in front, at the base of the U. On these, the Nazis and Danish traitors must take their chance; there was no way in which the stairs could be saved.

But there were others at the back of the building from which, it was hoped, the prisoners would be able to escape.

Truelson had volunteered to fly in the first aircraft, since he was familiar with Copenhagen. The offer was vetoed out of hand: it would never do to risk the capture of an intelligence officer. Sismore, who had never visited Denmark, was to find his way as Bateson's navigator.

In the clear of the early morning, a solitary Mosquito scythed through the sharp wind and circled the Norfolk airfield.

'Wing-Commander Smith' gave the order for the mission to start. Two by two, eighteen Mosquito bombers took off first, then twenty-eight of the faster P.51 Mustangs.

On 21 March 1945, Operation Carthage had unleashed its tools of death. At Shellhus, a new day had begun.

Gale force winds whipped at the aerial formations. The angry water of the North Sea boiled and spat. Sismore kept his eyes peeled for the south Jutland coast.

With one accord, the aircraft climbed to 45 metres. Now there was the grey finger of water of the Little Belt and, beyond, the green of South Zeeland.

In the fields below, Danes had spotted the RAF roundels and waved cheerfully.

There was a lifting of spirits too among pilots and navigators who knew they were on course. Sismore indicated to Bateson St Jorgen's Lake and the camouflaged building which lay beyond it.

The scream of the sirens sliced into the Copenhagen morning. They had been heard so often that few Danes paid much attention. As often as not, the sounding was only practice; the Germans were getting increasingly jittery.

Sismore was roaring above the Roskildevej highway and the road to Frederiksberg. The eighteen Mosquitoes had already divided into three ranks of six each, looking from the ground like a three-spoked wheel.

The target was coming up now. Machine-gun fire and tracer opened from the German roof-top emplacements.

Bateson pointed the aircraft down as if aiming direct for the pavements.

Bateson felt sure the aircraft would hit the building and be annihilated. Then all at once he had released the bomb; his hand darted lightning-fast to the stick. A quick pull back and the aircraft banked above Shellhus.

At 11.14 precisely, the bombs tore at the first and second storeys.

Minutes before, Captain Poul Borking of the Danish Army had been marched from his cell in the attic prison for interrogation by Gestapo officer Weise.

The questioning was interrupted and Weise called away. Borking, closely guarded, sat waiting patiently, idly staring out of the window at the broad lake and the silhouettes of apartment blocks.

Borking's next action was gingerly to move his hands outwards under the edge of the desk. The guards did not notice. Thankfully, he found a strut of wood and gripped it firmly. He was careful to keep his face expressionless, but his eyes never left the window.

For above the lake and the buildings he had spotted a row of dots which were getting larger by the minute.

The steady hum of the aircraft became a mighty roar. At precisely the moment that the bombs fell, Borking rose. He sent the desk toppling straight into the laps of the guards. Then he was out in the hall, pursued by yells. He ran along the fifth floor hall to the staircase at the building's right hand side. He had reached the third floor when the first bomb erupted.

Five other aircraft had tipped their high explosives at the base of Shellhus. The building trembled. German anti-aircraft fire orchestrated the noise of the explosions.

Two more prisoners were being questioned and had been ordered by the Gestapo to surrender their identity cards. The next act of the Germans was to quit the room in terror and run towards the basement. The two men also ran – after pausing long enough to snatch back the identity cards.

On the pavement outside, they almost fell over the dead bodies of the German guards littering the ground.

Across the road, a car park used by the Germans had been reduced to a tangle of metal and rubble.

In the attic, prisoners snatched up tools and beat frantically with them on the plywood doors.

Then had come disaster for the raiders. In the second wave, the leading Mosquito had come in fatally low. Too late, pilot Pete Kleboe saw the tall railway pylon ahead. Desperately, he tried to wrench the aircraft up and away. The Mosquito clipped the pylons and ploughed into a building; Kleboe died as petrol blazed and a ton of bombs tore the aircraft asunder. He was nine seconds flying time from the target.

The German guardroom in the south west corner of Shellhus was no more. All the Danish Nazi translators had perished in the cellar. The courtyard awaited the explosion of bombs with long-delay fuses.

In the attic, keys had been secured from dazed guards and the prisoners ran from cell to cell releasing their comrades.

Mogens Fog had thought that the approaching aircraft were German fighters. But at the first sound of the machine-guns he had climbed on to his upper bunk to squint out of the small window. A series of loud thuds sent him scuttling under the lower bunk. Then came the overwhelming fear of being trapped in his cell and burnt alive. Soon, along with the rest, he was banging desperately on the cell door until he too was released.

On the stairs was a tableau of horror. The second wave had caught a number of Gestapo and German soldiers in full flight. Now their bodies cascaded over the steps. One young German had a severed leg; Fog found it hard to tear his eyes away from the stream of blood gushing from the wound. It dripped remorselessly on to the other bodies of the dead and dying.

The escaping prisoners put as much distance as they could between themselves and the destroyed Gestapo headquarters. Many made contact with their former resistance cells. Borking managed to be smuggled to England, but he immediately prepared for a return to Denmark.

As the third wave roared overhead, the last of the Danes

managed to quit the attic. But it was then that there came senseless appalling tragedy.

A pilot spotted the billowing smoke from Pete Kleboe's Mosquito. This, he thought, was plainly the target, so bombs streaked down on adjacent buildings.

In the direct line of fire was the Jeanne d'Arc School. Of 482 children between the ages of seven and seventeen, eighty-six were killed. Seventeen adults died, many of them teachers who insisted on returning time and again to the blazing building to rescue those they could.

If there were tears that day, there was also bitterness – bitterness against the fiendishly good luck of Karl Heinz Hoffmann. He and a number of senior Gestapo had, at the time of the raid, been at the funeral of a colleague who had shot himself. Carthage had failed to trap them. But several hundred other Germans had died in Shellhus.

The raid itself was an undeniable coup. By dusk, Shellhus was no more. And along with it, the hated Gestapo records had also perished. A number of heavy safes did, however, survive. When they were blown open, they were found to contain names of Gestapo members and collaborators. These were to prove invaluable when it came to gathering evidence for war trials. Of the attic prisoners, only six were dead. Twenty-seven had escaped.

But for some the ordeal did not end with the bombing of Shellhus and their release.

Paul Sorensen, Secretary-General of the Danish Conservative Party, was vaguely aware that he was no longer in his attic cell. He rememberered the strange, not unpleasant sensation of falling and now here he was on his back on the fifth floor of Gestapo headquarters, staring at the sky. The Mosquitoes he saw flying above seemed to him to be breathtakingly beautiful; he was later to describe them as being 'like silver grey pearls in the sun'.

But the feeling of being agreeably detached from it all did not last. It was shattered by the terrible screams of men burning to death as flames licked greedily at their clothes.

Sorensen staggered to his feet as he was joined by two of

his comrades, Mogens Prior and Karl Wedell-Wedellsborg. All three suddenly realised that they would be able to make their way down to the fourth floor but from there on their would be no way out beyond jumping. Ahead of them another prisoner, Poul Brunn, stood half-conscious staring down at the street with its bare stone pavement.

They watched mesmerised as Brunn, for all the world as if he faced nothing more daunting than a diving-board in a swimming pool, strode forward to the edge and leapt. A strange, overwhelming compulsion to survive and beat the Germans gripped Sorensen, Prior and Wedell-Wedellsborg.

For a few seconds they stared at the gathering crowds below. Then they too jumped.

The four bodies lay like broken dolls on the streets below. They were eventually gathered up and taken to lie with the other injured and dying from Shellhus.

Morphine was found and shot into them. But by then contingents of the Gestapo had arrived. An order was barked: 'Stand up.' The bruised and shattered bodies were dragged unceremoniously into a car. Mogens Prior was taken to the orthopaedic hospital and left to die.

Brunn was conscious of being transferred to an ambulance. Frantically, he whispered his name and address over and over again to the driver, but the man was too scared to pay any attention.

At the infirmary, Brunn, Sorensen and Wedell-Wedellsborg were treated with indifference rather than active cruelty. A doctor, realising that Sorensen's lungs were filled with blood, pressed his chest. Black fluid gushed from his mouth. The action probably saved his life. But when a German doctor was summoned, he merely asked: 'Do you want to write your wills?'

Desperately, Sorensen assented. There might just be a faint opportunity to make some sort of contact with the outside world.

Wedell-Wedellsborg's last words were: 'I would give my entire fortune just to be able to turn over on my left side.' In a little while the Germans carried his body away.

Poul Brunn was more fortunate. His life was saved by surgery. He had managed to get a letter out to his wife. Eventually, the couple were able to read it in freedom together.

The RAF could be excused self-congratulation. Under the intense heat from its incendiaries, the steel portions of Shellhus had buckled. The walls had thus been drawn inwards until they collapsed. And then the files and records, together with the cheap wooden furniture, added to the fury of the blaze. The largest store of Gestapo records in Denmark was no more.

There remained at Odense yet another Gestapo centre. Into the skies again went Ted Sismore and Basil Embry. This time there were no civilian casualties.

The Gestapo's hold on Denmark was at last cut free.

The survivors of the Jeanne d'Arc School in Copenhagen were among those who greeted the liberating Allies. There was no bitterness.

One of the school's pupils, Merete Jensen, twelve years old at the time of the raid, probably best summed up the general feeling when she wrote later:

> 'We were all so jubilant because at last here were our friends flying in from the sea. Then there was a terrible crash and everything went dark and it seemed as if after that there was just a long silence. I thought, maybe I am dead. So I sat waiting. And then I heard children crying and praying and crying.
>
> Then suddenly there was the smell again of Spring. It had been such a marvellous day, you know. The first day of spring ...'

Elsewhere in Europe, the situation was of unrelieved chaos. American troops under General George S. Patton had thrust into Czechoslovakia. Russian troops were penetrating Berlin. Northern Holland had been liberated. Resistance in the area of Hamburg was crumbling.

As the war drew to a close, the white buses and ambulances of Count Folke Bernadotte, head of the Swedish Red Cross, had made forays into Germany. They moved

305

among the concentration camps to rescue surviving Danish and Norwegian prisoners.

At the end of April, Bernadotte met Heinrich Himmler who, unknown to Hitler, had been trying to negotiate surrender terms for all German troops on the western front. Bernadotte had managed to secure promises of the safe removal from Nazi hands of Danes and Norwegians.

By mid-April, the vehicles were making almost daily trips. Scandinavian women from Ravensbruck concentration camp danced in the aisles with delirious joy. Manpower was short, however, and Gestapo prisoners were detailed along with Swedish attendants to look after the women. Fearful of the future, most of the former guards handed out sympathy and food supplies with fevered eagerness.

But retribution, in different ways, was to be meted out to many of them.

26

At the corner table in the Le Chapiteau nightclub, some of the leading resistance workers in Paris waited anxiously.

The rendezvous in the summer of 1943 constituted a dangerous gamble: failure could lead to the annihilation of them all.

The ferocious Henri Lafont had dealt a series of terrible blows to the networks of the underground movements; arrests had reached terrifying proportions. Several assassination attempts had been planned against Lafont. But the hated master of the French Gestapo was too well guarded for the bids to be successful.

With the reverses in Russia it had become unlikely that Germany would gain total victory in the war. Resistance chiefs reasoned that Lafont must be aware of this.

A bid was made to appeal to his overwhelming sense of self-preservation, even though the very idea of making overtures to the butcher and traitor of the rue Lauriston stuck in the craw of those who sanctioned a desperate attempt to take the heat off France.

It was only the desperate plight of the resistance which led its members to gather that day in Le Chapiteau. They tensed as a familiar figure, flanked by bodyguards, was suddenly framed in the half-lit entrance.

Lafont, completely confident of his own safety, advanced to the corner table, sat down and began to talk business.

One of the Frenchmen tersely outlined the proposal: 'It's quite obvious that Germany is going to come badly out of this war. Where would that put you? We're giving you a chance to extricate yourself and your friends and work for us. We could use your talents.'

Lafont pondered the question. A short time before he had been watching the pick of his stable of racehorses doing miraculously at a meeting at Longchamps. The animals had been bought at the behest of his latest mistress, a red-headed aristocrat and expert horsewoman. Life was undeniably sweet just now.

Lafont replied coolly: 'What are you offering me? An opportunity to be a good patriot? Gentlemen, I will be frank. You can never give me as much money, as many women or as much power as I have now. These things are important to me. I will never give them up.'

With that Lafont rose, summoned his acolytes, bowed in mock politeness and swept out of Le Chapiteau.

The attempt to turn round Lafont had been an ignominious failure. Yet the scourge of the resistance fully realised that the writing was on the wall. His address and that of Pierre Bonny had been sent long ago to London. The BBC had broadcast them, together with a promise of retribution.

As the months wore on, Lafont's organisation began to indulge in an orgy of oppression born of fear. In the summer of 1944 came the invasion of Europe.

Between mid-June and mid-August 1944, there were 110 murders and 400 deportations of Jews and resistance workers. Less than half of those sent to Germany were to survive the war.

Loyal French patriots began to prepare for the insurrection that was to free their capital. In circumstances of violence and betrayal, the desperate scramble for arms was on.

In one incident, three resistance groups from the Paris suburbs rendezvoused at a garage with a likely supplier of weapons. But the man was a traitor; the Gestapo and collaborating French were waiting.

After 'process' and interrogation at the rue des Saussaies, the end was swift and brutal. The prisoners were driven to a remote corner of the Bois de Boulogne.

Their fellow Frenchmen then ordered them to leap out of the trucks. Bullets thundered into the bodies. Some of the victims, barely out of their teens, crouched in the back of the vehicles, too terrified to move. Guns were emptied into them on the spot; the corpses were flung in a heap and left.

While other Frenchmen attempted desperately to destroy evidence of their treachery or fled in the direction of Germany in search of illusory protection, Henri Lafont set about destroying his files and paying off former members of his French Gestapo. Then he scuttled into retirement with Bonny at a farm at Bazoches, east of Paris.

Bonny was in a blue funk. Fear made him talkative. He let drop the name of the farm. Betrayal was inevitable. Police surrounded the hideout, Lafont and Bonny surrendered meekly enough.

Twelve men, all members of Lafont's Gestapo organisation of the rue Lauriston, stood in the dock of a special tribunal which opened in Paris on 1 December 1944. Lafont flinched at nothing. He admitted responsibility not only for his own crimes, but for those of his colleagues. To spectators, he seemed oddly detached, as if the proceedings bored him.

All this was in sharp contrast to the craven Bonny who attempted to convince the court of his penitence. Lafont, he protested, had been solely responsible. He then proceeded to give the names of more French traitors.

It availed him nothing. On the day after Christmas, he and Lafont were driven to the firing squad at the dour Fort de Montrouge.

Lafont remained stoical as he was tied to the post. The broken Bonny screamed his innocence above the noise of fire.

Pushed eastwards by the advance of the Allies, Himmler's two lieutenants, Oberg and Knochen, established themselves in a general headquarters at Vittel.

It was there that they received a series of shocks.

The first came in a letter from Himmler. Its tone was positively arctic. Both men, Himmler proclaimed, had betrayed the Reich shamefully by allowing themselves to be arrested without resistance at the time of the bomb plot. Where was their sworn loyalty to the Fueherer?

This ominous communication was swiftly followed by another, this time from Kaltenbrunner. For Knochen in particular it spelt deadly peril. He was to present himself in Berlin forthwith.

The interview with Kaltenbrunner was brisk. The head of the RSHA snapped: 'You'd have been luckier dancing on the end of a noose like so many of those damned generals. As it happens, I've something far worse for you.'

Knochen was promptly stripped of his rank and posted as a private soldier to the Leibstandarte SS Adolf Hitler, the most ferociously disciplined of the Waffen-SS regiments. He was sent to a training camp for a course in tank warfare.

But luck was with him. Normally, Hitler would not have dreamt of interfering with the excesses of Kaltenbrunner, but he considered Knochen too valuable to be wasted as mere cannon fodder. The Fueherer had him rehabilitated and given the job of building up those sections of the SD which had replaced the disgraced Abwehr. Knochen was to hold on to the job until the end.

While negotiating on one hand with the Allies, Himmler still held on grimly to the tattered vestiges of his empire. Eventually, only a small part of France remained in German hands, but that did not stop the Reichsfuehrer-SS from attempting to bring a new security organisation into being there.

The plan was to infiltrate agents recruited from French collaborators who had scurried into Germany.

Most of the attempts were total failures, as was Himmler's assumption of military command. The days of the Reich were drawing to a close; its malign architect, his reason all but unseated, lurked balefully below ground in a concrete bunker.

Oberg's last action as Gestapo chief in France was fully in the tradition of the SS.

The inhabitants of the town of St-Dié in Plainfaing crowded around the notice board in the town hall. An immediate evacuation was announced. It was explained: 'It is the intention of the Wehrmacht to remove the population as far as possible from the combat zone, in order to spare them unnecessary losses and suffering.'

The evacuation complete, Oberg and his men threw themselves upon the town and pillaged it ruthlessly. The contents of factories — stock, tools and machinery — were dismantled and sent to a Reich scarcely in a position to make use of the booty, anyway. Then the Germans set about the houses. Those who risked returning to retrieve their property were either mown down by firing-squads of deported to Germany.

After this gratuitous orgy of spite, the surviving members of the Gestapo continued their progress east. Back in Germany, Oberg was given the job of commander-in-chief of the army groups of the Upper Rhine, responsible directly to Heinrich Himmler.

With the arrival of 1945 and its message of doom for Hitler's Germany, the identity of Karl Oberg disappeared. It was replaced by that of Albrecht Heintze, who was found by the Americans hiding out in a Tyrolean village near Kitzbuehel. Oberg was soon unmasked and handed over to the French.

Helmuth Knochen managed to escape detection for seven months. But he too was eventually picked up by the Americans. It was not until October 1954 that retribution finally came to the two men who had held Paris in the grip of terror for four long years. Both Oberg and Knochen were brought to trial and condemned to death.

Walter Schellenberg continued to be one of life's most dedicated survivors. His unique position as a leading figure in foreign intelligence made him only too well aware of the way the war had been going. His elaborate network of agents in the neutral countries left him in no doubt of what the future held for leading figures in the SS, SD and Gestapo. He became solely interested in saving his own skin.

The RSHA, he realised, must be disowned utterly. To be associated with an appalling individual like Kaltenbrunner was but a short cut to the noose. He became convinced that he must do his own small bit by attempting to negotiate a peace of sorts with Germany's victors. He decided to go to work on the ultimately pliable Heinrich Himmler. Subtly, he dropped a hint that only by seeming willing to end the war would the Reichsfuehrer-SS have any sort of future at all.

At first, the very suggestion threw Himmler into a rage, then he confessed gloomily: 'Schellenberg, I dread the future.' The wily intelligence professional kept on nagging at his worried superior.

Himmler, increasingly at the mercy of the stomach cramps which had always plagued him, said wearily: 'We must admit to defeat by the western powers. I beg you to transmit this to General Eisenhower through the Swedish Government.

'We must negotiate a separate peace. The war against Bolshevism, of course, goes on.'

Schellenberg felt easier in his mind now that he had the instructions and therefore the protection of the Reichsfuehrer-SS. But the scheme, needless to say, came to nothing. The US government ignored the proposal.

Schellenberg tried anew. In the bizarre setting of the candle-lit cellar of the bombed city of Lübeck, Himmler confronted Count Bernadotte with his proposals. They were transmitted direct to President Truman. The idea of partial capitulation in any form was rejected out of hand. All hope had gone.

On 29 April, the newly wed Hitler and Eva Braun had killed themselves. On 6 May, Himmler received a short courteous letter of dismissal from the new head of the Third Reich, Grossadmiral Doenitz. Clean-shaven, in an ill-fitting private's jacket and with an incongruous black patch over one eye, Himmler was caught by the British, announced his identity, then panicked and crushed the Zynkali capsule of potassium cyanide wedged in his mouth.

Ernst Kaltenbrunner was brought to trial before the International Military Tribunal at Nuremberg.

On one hand, the head of the RSHA had attempted to curry favour with General Patton by handing over the notorious Mauthausen camp to the Americans. But there was no way in which Kaltenbrunner could dodge the formidable charges. After 1943 he had been the head of the RSHA, the Reich Security Main Office, with the rank of SS Obergruppenfuehrer and General of the Police.

Under the RSHA had been the entire secret police operation of the Reich with the full authority of the concentration and extermination camps behind them. Organisations had included the Security Police (SIPO); the Gestapo; the Criminal Police (KRIPO) and the SD.

Kaltenbrunner had been directly responsible to Himmler, who was Reichsfuehrer SS, and as Eichmann's superior was in charge of all 'actions' against the Jews – in short, their total extermination.

To his Allied interrogators and later to Gustave Gilbert, the prison psychologist at Nuremberg, Kaltenbrunner protested that he had nothing to do with the mass murders, that he neither gave orders nor executed them.

He told Gilbert: 'You cannot conceive how secret these things were kept, even from me.'

Gilbert riposted: 'Frankly, I doubt if many people are going to believe that you, as chief of the RSHA, knew nothing about the mass murder programme.'

In the witness box, Kaltenbrunner found himself bombarded with documents and evidence of his own inconsistent statements, even denial of his own signature.

Kaltenbrunner went to the gallows at Nuremberg on 16 October 1946, after a trial which had started on 20 November 1945 and dragged on through 403 public sessions.

Goering, due to die at the same time, had managed to lay hands on cyanide. Like Himmler eighteen months before, he took his own life.

At the time of Germany's collapse, Schellenberg had found shelter with Count Bernadotte in Sweden. Forthwith, the Gestapo's most tireless bureaucrat busied himself with a report on the negotiations in which he had been involved during the war's final months.

But his extradition was soon requested by the Allied powers. He returned to Germany in June 1945 to stand trial. At the proceedings against the major war criminals, Goering, von Ribbentrop and the other Nazi leaders, he appeared merely as a witness.

In January 1948, it was Schellenberg's turn to face indictments. These ranged from planning an aggressive war and crimes against humanity to membership of the SS and SD which the International Military Tribunal had declared to be criminal organisations. He was acquitted on all but two charges.

Amt VI, of which he had been head, was declared guilty of complicity in the execution without trial of a number of prisoners recruited for Operation Zeppelin. This scheme had employed captive Russians who were sent to spy on their own people and to infiltrate partisan bands as German agents.

It was considered that Schellenberg, whatever his motives, had lessened his guilt by efforts to aid prisoners in the concentration camps at the close of the war. He received six years' imprisonment – a remarkably light sentence for one of Himmler's chief technicians of dictatorship. But his health broke down and in 1951 he was released as an act of clemency. He died in March the following year.

With the eventual tracking down and execution of Adolf Eichmann on 1 June 1962 in Israel's Ramleh prison, justice had at last caught up with the remaining heads of the Gestapo.

Or had it?

Heinrich Mueller, who had hauled himself sensationally from the drudgery of a policeman's beat to one of the most awesome positions of power within the Third Reich, never stood in the dock of any war crimes trial.

Walter Schellenberg felt he knew why.

In his memoirs, Schellenberg recalled a remarkable string of indiscretions uttered by Mueller one spring evening in 1943.

Hardly able to believe his ears, Schellenberg had heard one of Hitler's supreme architects of terror roundly condemn the spiritual anarchy of Western culture – the Third Reich included.

Mueller had held forth: 'National Socialism is nothing more than a sort of dung on this spiritual desert. In Russia there's an uncompromising and unified spiritual and biological force.'

Mueller had rambled on in the same sort of vein, punctuating his remarks with countless swigs from balloons of brandy.

Doubts and fears had gripped Schellenberg. Was Mueller merely drunk? Was this a not very subtle attempt to get Schellenberg to betray disloyalty?

Mueller had then gone on roundly to condemn Nazism and some of its leaders.

The amazed Schellenberg heard the other man proclaim: 'Stalin does these things better. Just think what his organisation has stood up to during the last two years. He's immeasurably superior to any leader in the west. If I'd had any say in the matter, we'd have reached agreement with him at once.'

Schellenberg had attempted rather clumsily to lighten the conversation, saying: 'All right, Comrade Mueller, let's all start saying "Heil Stalin!" right now – and our little father Mueller will become head of the NKVD.'

Mueller had looked daggers and snapped: 'That would be fine. You'd be ready for the high jump, you and your diehard bourgeois friends.'

Mueller had been praised by Hitler for deliberately basing a number of Gestapo methods on those favoured by the Russians. Indeed, Mueller had visited the Soviet Union to carry out just such a study.

Supposing, Schellenberg postulated, that Mueller had been a long-time undercover agent – furthermore, had been a paid-up Communist as far back as 1928 when the Communist Party in Germany had been at its peak of membership of a quarter of a million? True, Mueller had done sterling work to break up the Rote Kapelle network, but since the broadcasts to Russia continued long afterwards, might not the sacrifice of the Schulze-Boysens and the Harnacks have been considered well worthwhile by his Russian masters?

Schellenberg was to remember his strange evening when, seven years later, a German officer who had been a prisoner of war in Russia had insisted he had seen Mueller in Moscow in 1948.

Hans Bernd Gisevius had also escaped retribution from the Allies but for different reasons. The burly Prussian had joined the Gestapo when it was still under Goering, but he had gradually become a convinced anti-Nazi and thrown in his lot with the Abwehr. As early as 1939, he had made overtures to British intelligence in Switzerland.

But the British regarded him as just another young man on the make – quite capable of selling out to his own advantage. England was still smarting under Schellenberg's coup at Venlo; intelligence chiefs did not wish to be caught napping again.

Gisevius next tried the Americans. He made contact with Allen Dulles of OSS (Office of Strategic Services). He informed Dulles of the existence of a genuine resistance movement to Hitler, and as earnest of good faith produced a number of secret telegrams sent by the American Embassy in Berne, but intercepted and broken by the Germans. He convinced Dulles be could be trusted and continued to brief him on the progress of the conspiracy.

Five months after the unsuccessful bomb plot, Gisevius

315

was still at large in Berlin. But the Gestapo was after him and he lived like a hunted animal. Dulles was determined to get him out of Germany and approached the British.

This time, intelligence circles in London had not hesitated. A plan had been concocted to deliver to Gisevius in Berlin the papers of a Gestapo official which would include orders for him to proceed to Switzerland. The papers would carry full Gestapo authority.

The first step had been to unearth a photograph of Gisevius but only a group shot could be found. It was smuggled into Switzerland. A photographer had got to work. The picture was enlarged so that a passport-size print could be cut from it. This and some stolen Gestapo stationery was smuggled to London.

Counterfeiters had next produced a Reich passport and a set of orders from Gestapo headquarters informing government officials that all necessary assistance must be given to 'Dr Hoffman' in whose name the documents were made out. For good measure, a fake covering letter bearing Himmler's 'signature' had also been produced.

There had been particular difficulty in manufacturing the Silver Warrant identity disc of the Gestapo. This was a grey medallion of a special alloy known to contain a deliberate flaw to trap forgers.

It was an essential item for Dr Hoffman; the disc gave its holder absolute right of access and power of arrest.

The Americans had found it impossible to reproduce the medallion plus its serial number. The job was turned over successfully to the British.

In January 1945, Gisevius had gone to ground in a girl-friend's Berlin apartment. His nerves were in tatters. When one morning the door-bell rang it was some time before he could dredge up sufficient courage to answer it.

He had heard a car driving off. Cautiously, the door was opened. On the doorstep was a package containing the precious medallion, orders and a passport made out to Dr Hoffman.

He had known that he would have to act fast. All civilian trains were gradually being cancelled and even officials moving outside the Reich had to have special police permits.

The subway journey to the station was nightmarish. Every passenger, he felt sure, was Gestapo.

Buying a ticket for Stuttgart was a further agony. Each traveller was surveyed with infuriating slowness. On the platform all was chaos. The SS shoved civilians aside unceremoniously. Gisevius learnt why. Kaltenbrunner, on his way to his native Austria, was due to board the Vienna express.

Gisevius had fought his way on to the crowded Stuttgart train. Everyone had been desperate to leave Berlin. There had been struggles and slanging matches with train staff.

Gisevius had taken his courage in both hands. He had whipped out the medallion and yelled: 'Gestapo! What the hell is going on here?' To an official he had demanded: 'Let me aboard. I'll help you clear the luggage van.'

Then he had literally kicked himself aboard, thrusting himself into the van. Next to him had been a couple with two children. Gisevius had snatched the children and planted them firmly on his knee, briefly hiding his face from possible prying eyes on the platform. He had then heard the officials pleading with him to make more room by throwing out the luggage.

The train began moving and passengers fell back on the platform. From the guard came grateful thanks. The officials told him deferentially: 'We can make room up the front for you, sir. There's an official reserved compartment.'

Gisevius had smiled quietly: 'No thanks, I'll stay where I am.'

The Dr Hoffman who two days later found himself at the tiny border crossing of Kreuzlingen presented a battered figure. Gisevius had been clad in the same summer suit he had worn on the fateful 20 July.

Luckily, the tired German border officials – including, ironically, one Gestapo – had been unable to summon the will to examine his papers properly.

Gisevius had given a tired Nazi salute and staggered into friendly Switzerland.

317

In the blazing inferno that was Berlin, Gestapo headquarters were surrounded by the Russian 5th Army of General Berzarin. Smoke poured out of makeshift chimneys let into bricked-up windows. The Gestapo cellars had been converted into quarters for the SS themselves. Soviet troops came across a jumbled but otherwise complete card index of all 'suspect Berliners'. Many of the records were destroyed by the invaders.

All over the Reich and the occupied countries, Allied bombing ripped into offices, camps and block houses. No longer did interrogation rooms reek of sweat and terror and fear. Corridors that had resounded to the screams of agony of victims were silent at last.

Equally as terrifying as the obscene instruments of torture had been the bulky dossiers which housed the intimate secrets of millions. Many of these had perished in the final annihilation.

But not quite all. Enough of the meticulously collated files and the precisely phrased memoranda survived to confront criminals brought to justice in a shattered but liberated world.

Because of its passion for bureaucratic detail and documentation, Nazi Germany – and with it the Gestapo – literally condemned itself. And, incidentally, delivered a warning to future generations which remains shrill and potent after more than thirty years.

TABLE OF SS RANKS AND THEIR
APPROXIMATE EQUIVALENTS

SS	British Army	US Army
Reichsfuehrer-SS	Field Marshal	General of the Army
SS-Oberstgruppenfuehrer	General	General
SS-Obergruppenfuehrer	Lieutenant-General	Lieutenant-General
SS-Gruppenfuehrer	Major-General	Major-General
SS-Brigadefuehrer	Brigadier	Brigadier-General
SS-Oberfuehrer		
SS-Standartenfuehrer	Colonel	Colonel
SS-Obersturmbannfuehrer	Lieutenant-Colonel	Lieutenant-Colonel
SS-Sturmbannfuehrer	Major	Major
SS-Hauptsturmfuehrer	Captain	Captain